Malcolm Parry's love of history has inspired him to write this interesting and fascinating book, a subject of much research, verification of accepted facts, of many details not usually included in such works e.g. the formation and development of army regiments, the Royal Navy and the Royal Air Force, and the early organizing of sports.

Born just two months before the outbreak of World War II in 1939, Malcolm now lives in the re-generated centre of Bristol within its ancient boundaries. An accountant by training; a retailer by profession, having been a company director; involved in politics since his teens; and a student of history and Russian literature.

The people who have influenced him include: Sir Winston Churchill, whom he saw in the House of Commons in 1959, former Prime Minister Harold Macmillan, Trade Union Leader and Foreign Secretary Ernest Bevin, the 1st and 35th Presidents of the United States of America, George Washington and John F. Kennedy, and the respected historian writer A.L. Rowse.

Malcolm's passion for England and her history has been aroused by the great importance and successful progression brought about by William the Conqueror, who laid the foundation of England with the Norman feudal system; King Henry VIII for breaking the power of the Roman Catholic Church in England; and the wonderful accomplishments of the Victorian age.

ENGLAND

William I to Elizabeth II

Dedicated to my late Mother
Vera May Parry (née Attwood)
1912 to 2005

Malcolm Parry

ENGLAND

William I to Elizabeth II

Vanguard Press

A CIP catalogue record for this title is
available from the British Library.

ISBN 978 1 843866 58 9

Vanguard Press is an imprint of
Pegasus Elliot MacKenzie Publishers Ltd.
www.pegasuspublishers.com

First Published in 2011

Vanguard Press
Sheraton House Castle Park
Cambridge England

Printed & Bound in Great Britain

Author's Note

Each reign of a monarch is a chapter, identifying his or her influence and contribution to society. The events of each reign are told, mainly in chronological sequence of power struggles, wars, the development of parliament and democracy, the judiciary, exploration, culture and sport.

To complete this work, but very much part of it, are the appendices which details the development and decline of the Empire, Poet Laureates, United Kingdom winners of the Nobel Prize, and very much more...

Contents

INTRODUCTION

What is the Magna Carta?

Queen Anne? Who?

When did England enlarge to become Great Britain, then the United Kingdom?

Where is Trafalgar?

Did John Macadam really develop a road surface in 1811?

Questions, questions...

Here is a book to easily find the answers. It's easy to read, informative and gives you concisely, in most instances in date order, of how England developed, with its ups and downs, from the period of petty kingdoms to today, as part of the European Union.

Each chapter of the book covers a monarch's reign, including the Commonwealth 1649 to 1660, giving biographical details. The 'Persons of Note' in the early reigns identifies important persons; in the later reigns of people who have made their mark and helped develop the culture of the country, whether in the arts, industry, exploration or sport.

The eight appendices, a must, include the Poet Laureates, the United Kingdom Nobel Prize winners for Physics, Chemistry, Medicine, Literature and Peace, and of the countries/territories once ruled by the United Kingdom.

England's history is fascinating, always dominated by the strengths and weaknesses of individuals, whether it be monarchs, popes and archbishops, political leaders, explorers and industrialists.

The early history was dominated for survival to remain free and independent against the threats from neighbouring countries and the Roman Catholic Church; barons and, later, politicians fought and exerted pressure to control the power of the monarchy.

It is a history of a small country, whose navigators explored the World and whose people migrated to 'far-off' lands settling in every continent making it the largest and greatest empire in World history.

INTRODUCTION

Its language is one of the most widely used throughout the World; its judicial system, Parliamentary system and democracy are a basis for many countries. Although most former countries of the Empire are independent states; nearly all are members of the Commonwealth of Nations. England's role in the World, as the United Kingdom, has changed dramatically since the end of World War II. It does not have the military strength to dominate, but remains influential in the 'Halls of Power'.

The next chapter in its long history is its membership of the European Union. Where this road leads will be told in future centuries.

THE NORMANS

Monarch	Reigned	Family
William I	1066 to 1087	William the Conqueror, Duke of Normandy
William II	1087 to 1100	Third son of William I
Henry I	1100 to 1135	Youngest son of William I
Stephen	1135 to 1154	Son of Adela, fifth daughter of William I

NORMAN

KING WILLIAM I

Born	1027
Accession	1066
Age at Accession	39
Death	1087 September 9
Age at Death	60
Reigned	21 years

William I (the Conqueror) was the illegitimate son of Robert II, 6th Duke of Normandy. He became 7th Duke of Normandy on his father's death in 1035, his father having chosen him his heir, this being then the custom.

He married Matilda, daughter of Baldwin V, Count of Flanders. They had 4 sons and 6 daughters.

The eldest son became 8th Duke of Normandy in 1087, having been chosen by his father.

The second son died in 1081.

The third son, William Rufus, having been chosen by his father, became King William II of England in 1087.

The fourth son became King Henry I of England in 1100.

The fifth daughter's son became King Stephen of England in 1135.

THE NORMANS: KING WILLIAM I

Person of note:

Archbishop of Canterbury, Lanfranc (b.c.1010, d.1089), Italian. He was Archbishop from 1070 until his death. He reorganized the English church as a mainstay of Norman rule. He rebuilt Canterbury Cathedral after the fire of 1067.

The Roman invasion of England in AD 43 created a united country under their rule until 410, by which time their governance had diminished. The country fragmented into tribal and petty kingdoms until Canute (whose father Sweyn Forkbeard had invaded England in 1013) became king in 1016. In 1020 he ascended to the Danish throne; in 1030 to the Norwegian throne; so becoming joint monarch of England, Denmark and Norway simultaneously until his death in 1035. His sons, Harold I and Hardicanute, successively succeeded him, until the latter's death in 1042. The Witan council, an assembly of ealdomen of the shires, some nobles and important men, whose duty it was to choose a leader, elected Edward the Confessor, as King of England.

Edward, whose mother was from Normandy in France, had spent his boyhood living with monks, and was very religious. He spoke French, which became the official language of the Court of England for many years.

After the Romans left, its successive invaders influenced the country. Edward the Confessor introduced some Norman customs and placed Normans into official positions in both the church and state.

In 1051, Duke William of Normandy (later known as William the Conqueror) visited Edward, his cousin. Edward had neither son nor obvious heir at this time: it is believed he promised that William would be his successor to the English throne, but, Harold (Earl of Wessex, born 1022) a powerful person in England, intended to be the next king. On a sea voyage Harold was shipwrecked off the Normandy coast and was detained by Duke William: he was released by agreeing to recognize the Duke's claim to the English throne.

To confuse the situation, Edward, who died in January 1066, had named Harold as his successor, although Edward the Atheling, a twelve-year-old boy, Edward's nephew, had a claim to the crown. The Witan council chose Harold as king, probably for fear of an invasion should a minor ascend the throne.

During the autumn of 1066 the King of Norway led an attack on England: in September at Stamford Bridge, Yorkshire, Harold defeated the invaders. Within days Duke William of Normandy landed at Pevensey and Hasting in Sussex, with a force of about 7,000. Harold's exhausted and depleted army immediately had to travel south to confront William, but were outfought and defeated at the Battle of Hastings. Harold was killed, at a location later to be known as Battle, believed by an arrow piercing an eye.

THE NORMANS: KING WILLIAM I

Christmas Day in 1066, William the Conqueror was crowned at Westminster as King of England, with support and approval of the Pope.

By 1068 William had subjugated southern England; in the north from the River Humber to the River Tees the land was depopulated by a most brutal and wholesale massacre of the rebellious inhabitants; by 1071 the whole of England had been conquered. For the next twenty years military encampments were constructed and manned to keep the population under control.

In those days of small European feudal states, Normandy, although part of France and under the supremacy of the French monarchy, was considered a great power. William, a statesman experienced in the intricacies of foreign politics, was able to exert his independence and authority.

The French system of strict feudalism was imposed throughout England using the already established shires (counties) as the structure. Simplistically, at the top of the feudal system was the King; under him a baron for each shire; under each baron a number of knights; and under them the peasantry of which there were different categories.

The manorial feudal system was based on land tenure: cultivation of land was on the 'open-field' structure; the lord owning the estate; the tenant held land in return for obligatory service to the lord. People in the manor included freemen, villeins (villagers) and some slaves. Disputes between parties, e.g. lord and villein, were adjudicated in the manorial courts.

In addition to the feudal customs he introduced, William accepted some Old Saxon laws, and it was from these two systems the course of laws and liberties evolved in England.

Christianity had been introduced into England by Saint Augustine, the first Archbishop of Canterbury, in 597. In due course parishes developed to be administered by parish priests who were not necessarily monks.

William's great ecclesiastical reform was the separation of the state into secular and spiritual: previously, the bishops and sheriffs presided together at the Shire Courts dealing with all matters and cases. This separation eventually resulted in the development of English Common Law for the secular, and Canon Law for the Church. The king nominated the clergy, i.e. the bishops and abbots, with the Pope confirming appointments.

At this period the Pope was increasing the character of the Roman Catholic Church. The doctrine of transubstantiation (the theology that the bread and wine of the Eucharist are transformed into the body and blood of Christ, although their appearances remain the same) became accepted theology; importance was attached to the worship of the Virgin Mary; and the compulsory celibacy of all priests. The latter was resisted during the reigns of the Norman kings and transubstantiation caused ecclesiastical schisms during the following centuries. Latin became the language of the church.

William began to bring all the forests under the private jurisdiction of the monarchy: during the following century this area amounted to one third of the acreage of England. The newly founded Forest Court administered the forests, and subjected poachers and thieves to harsh punishments. Deer, boars, hares, etc. were protected for the monarch's hunting; poaching was punishable by mutilation or even death.

A survey, much later referred to as the 'Domesday Survey', of 1086 was taken by commissioners from sworn juries, which consisted of the priest, the reeve (a local steward) and six villeins (free villagers) of each community. Every detail and aspect of land (including ownership), livestock and property was recorded for the purpose of fiscal, judicial, military and policing purposes. A book was compiled of the survey setting-out details of each manor's resources within each shire throughout the whole of England.

England's population was about 1.5 million at this time.

Periodically, rebellions in England and Normandy had to be resisted and defeated: William being the ruler of both spent much of his time in Normandy defending his boundaries. He allowed the governance of England to be administered by the bishops, trusting especially his friend the Archbishop of Canterbury, Lanfranc.

In 1087 he was at war with King Philip of France, when during the fighting at the town of Mantes, Normandy, his horse stumbled and threw William against the pommel of the saddle. From his head injury he never recovered, dying a few weeks later at Rouen. He was buried at the Church of St Stephen at Caen, Normandy.

Finally, the Bayeux Tapestry is an embroidered strip of linen cloth about 230 feet in length and 19 inches in depth which depicts the events leading to and including the Norman Conquest of England. It is thought to be 11th century and is on display in the town of Bayeux, Normandy, France.

NORMAN

KING WILLIAM II

Born	**1056**
Accession	**1087 September 9**
Age at Accession	**31**
Death	**1100 August 2**
Age at Death	**44**
Reigned	**12 years**

William II (Rufus) was the third son of William I and designated by his father to be his successor as King of England.

He died unmarried.

He was mortally wounded by an arrow whilst hunting in the New Forest, Hampshire.

Persons of note:

Archbishop of Canterbury, Lanfranc (b.c.1010, d.1089), Italian. He was Archbishop from 1070 until his death.

Archbishop of Canterbury, Anselm (b.1033, d.1109). Archbishop from 1093 until his death, although in fear of William II he fled to Rome from 1097 for six years.

Ranulf Flambard (b.c.1060, d.1128). Justiciar (chief-justice); Bishop of Durham in 1099.

THE NORMANS: KING WILLIAM II

William I decided that England and Normandy should be governed separately by his successors.

The eldest son, Robert, became the Duke of Normandy and his third son, Rufus, the King of England. The second son died in 1081.

This situation created problems of loyalty for many barons who possessed properties in both England and Normandy. Robert, now 8th Duke of Normandy, encouraged a rebellion by the barons in 1088. William fought against Robert in Normandy for seven years.

Rufus, now William II, continued with his father's policies by ruling strictly throughout the country; he defeated a Welsh invasion and strengthened defences at the Scottish border.

Ranulf Flambard, his Justiciar (chief-justice) used many means to provide the King with much needed revenue, e.g. when Archbishop of Canterbury, Lanfranc, died in 1089, the See of Canterbury remained vacant for over four years, during which time its income went to William instead of the Church. Another lucrative taxation for the King, which caused outrage, was in the form of inheritance tax: when an estate was inherited by a minor or heiress the profit from the estate went to the King until the minor reached adulthood or the heiress married.

After a failed invasion of England in 1091, King Malcolm III of Scotland was forced to accept William as his overlord, but when Malcolm invaded again in 1093, he was killed in the battle.

In 1095 a further baronial rebellion was ended when the leaders were brutally executed.

Robert, Duke of Normandy, joined the First Crusade to the Holy Land, Palestine, in 1096, a military expedition undertaken by European Christians in an attempt to recover the Holy Land from the Muslim invaders. Robert sold Normandy to William in order to finance his expedition, so re-uniting England and Normandy under one ruler.

Four years after Archbishop Lanfranc's death, Anselm (later sainted) became Archbishop of Canterbury, but William undermined the Church authority, forcing Anselm to flee to Rome, in 1097. William seized the lands of Canterbury Cathedral.

In 1097 Wales was subjugated.

Whilst hunting in the New Forest, Hampshire, William was mortally wounded by an arrow, either accidentally or murder, on August 2, 1100. His body was taken to Winchester Cathedral, Hampshire.

NORMAN

KING HENRY I

Born	**1068**
Accession	**1100 August 2**
Age at Accession	32
Death	**1135 December 1**
Age at Death	67
Reigned	**35 years**

Henry I was the youngest son of William I and brother of William II.

He married, firstly, Matilda (b.1079, d.1118), daughter of King Malcolm III of Scotland.

They had 2 sons and 1 daughter. The eldest son, William (b.1100) became the 10th Duke of Normandy but drowned when the Royal Yacht 'White Ship' sank off the Channel Islands in 1119, the year he married Isabella, daughter of Fulk of Jerusalem. They had a son, Clito, who was murdered 1128.

The second son, Richard, also drowned in the 'White Ship'.

The daughter, Matilda also known as Maud (b.1103, d.1167), was prevented from being crowned monarch of England.

He married, secondly, Adela, daughter of Godfrey, Duke of Lower Lorraine. They had no children.

THE NORMANS: KING HENRY I

Persons of note:

Archbishop of Canterbury, Anselm (b.1033, d.1109), Italian. Archbishop from 1093 until his death.

Ranulf Flambard (b.c.1060, d.1128). Justiciar (chief-justice); Bishop of Durham in 1099.

Henry I (known as Beauclerc) ascended the throne at the death of his brother, King William II. Their eldest brother, Robert (8th Duke of Normandy), was in the Holy Land, Palestine, fighting in the First Crusade. On returning from Palestine, Robert with some supporting barons attempted to depose Henry in 1101. Peace was reached: Robert relinquished his claim to the throne; Normandy was returned to him together with a pension for life, but the agreement was not kept.

In 1106, fighting between the two brothers ended in Robert being captured at the Battle of Tinchebrai, south-western Normandy, and to be imprisoned for the rest of his life, dying in 1134. The two states of England and Normandy were reunited again, under one rule.

Henry issued the Charter of Liberties, decreeing the end of abuses that occurred during the reign of King William II, commencing with changes to the onerous taxes. Ranulf Flambard, now Bishop of Durham, was dismissed as Justiciar (chief-justice) and imprisoned for a short duration.

Henry promised fairness in the collection of taxes. The post of Exchequer was created for financial purposes of keeping records of important documents in order to give the King a tighter control of the finances.

Furthermore, to bring stability the King pronounced that he would keep and obey laws created since the time of Edward the Confessor.

The royal power against the barons was strengthened: the power of the feudal lords was diminished, and the manorial courts were curtailed in favour of the shire and hundred courts, both of which were to be administered by a body of free-tenants. Differing feudal justice throughout England began to be replaced by royal justice in a standardized form.

Henry instituted an advisory body: the King's Council (called Magnum Consilium or Curia Regis) as a first step in delegating responsibility. In due course the Council would be divided into specialist councils, e.g. justice, revenue, each to be administered by people holding specific offices.

Henry and Archbishop Anselm differed over responsibilities of the Church. The Archbishop and bishops were large landowners, which Henry considered dangerous in allowing owners of a large part of England to owe allegiance to foreigners, i.e. the Pope in Rome. Henry considered it imperative that he should have control over the Church. Furthermore, the Archbishop promoted new claims of the papacy: the dispute whether Crown or Pope appoint prelates. A compromise was reached. The bishops were to be chosen by the cathedral chapters (of clergy) and the abbots by their monks. All were to receive investiture from the Church, but to do homage for their lands to the monarch.

In November 1119, Henry's son and heir and his other son drowned when the royal yacht 'White Ship' was wrecked off the Channel Islands.

On the deaths of Henry's two sons, his daughter, Matilda, was recognized as heir presumptive. Her first husband having died, in 1127 she married the 16-year-old Geoffrey Plantagenet, the Count of Anjou, who became the Duke of Normandy on marrying, then the custom of a husband taking his wife's titles and some of her responsibilities.

Henry died on December 1, 1135 at Saint-Denis-en-Lyons, Normandy. He was buried at Reading Abbey, Berkshire.

Matilda, a woman, was heir. Problems ahead.

NORMAN

KING STEPHEN

Born	**1096**
Accession	**1135 December 1**
Age at Accession	**39**
Death	**1154 October 25**
Age at Death	**58**
Reigned	**18 years**

Stephen was the son of Adela, the fifth daughter of William I, and nephew of William II and Henry I.

He married Matilda, Countess of Mortain and Boulogne in 1123. They had 3 sons and 2 daughters, none of whom had children.

Person of note:

Archbishop of Canterbury, Theobald (b.c.1090, d.1161). Archbishop from 1139 until his death. He appointed Thomas Becket (Thomas à Becket) as Archdeacon of Canterbury.

King Henry I's only living child at his death was Matilda (sometimes referred to as Maud) who in 1119 was recognized as heir presumptive.

The barons, uncertain of having a woman monarch arranged a Great Council, which elected Stephen, Count of Blois, a grandson of William the Conqueror, cousin to Matilda, to be King of England. His support from the Pope resulted in an increase of papal influence in his kingdom.

This divisive decision caused anarchy in the country throughout his whole reign. Stephen and Matilda raised armies; fought against each other regularly; the barons battled to gain personal advantages to enlarge their estates and influence, and in doing so people were cruelly affected as well as much property being destroyed.

The Church and others regularly changed sides of support for gain and protection.

Early in 1141 at the Battle of Lincoln, Matilda captured and imprisoned Stephen, but in the November he was exchanged for Robert, Earl of Gloucester, Matilda's half-brother, the illegitimate son of King Henry I, who had been captured by Stephen's forces. For a time Matilda was considered monarch, but having quarrelled with the Church, they removed her, uncrowned. Eventually, she left England in 1148.

In 1153, Archbishop of Canterbury, Theobald, managed to bring the two sides together. Under the terms of the Treaty of Wallingford, Oxfordshire, Matilda recognized Stephen as King on the condition that her eldest son and heir, Henry, would be crowned King at Stephen's death.

The Church took advantage of the anarchy to increase its power, steadily working towards greater independence of monarchical control. The Roman Catholic order of Cistercian, founded in 1098, commenced building abbeys in England.

In 1154, the year following the signing of the Treaty of Wallingford, Stephen, the last Norman king, died at Dover, Kent, at the age of 58. He was buried in the monastery at Faversham, Kent.

THE PLANTAGENETS

Monarch	Reigned	Family
Henry II	1154 to 1189	Grandson of Henry I
Richard I	1189 to 1199	Third son of Henry II
John	1199 to 1216	Fifth son of Henry II
Henry III	1216 to 1272	Son of John
Edward I	1272 to 1307	Son of Henry III
Edward II	1307 to 1327	Son of Edward I
Edward III	1327 to 1377	Son of Edward II
Richard II	1377 to 1399	Grandson of Edward III
Henry IV	1399 to 1413	Grandson of Edward III
Henry V	1413 to 1422	Son of Henry IV
Henry VI	1422 to 1461 and 1470 to 1471	Son of Henry V
Edward IV	1461 to 1470 and 1471 to 1483	Great-great-grandson of Edward III
Edward V	1483	Son of Edward IV
Richard III	1483 to 1485	Great-great-grandson of Edward III, younger brother of Edward IV

PLANTAGENET

KING HENRY II

Born	**1133 March 5**
Accession	**1154 October 25**
Age at Accession	21
Death	**1189 July 6**
Age at Death	56
Reigned	**34 years**

Henry II succeeded to the English throne from Stephen, his mother's cousin: he succeeded as the Duke of Normandy by cession from his father in 1149. He was the son of Matilda (sometimes referred to as Maud) and her second husband Geoffrey Plantagenet, Count of Anjou.

In 1152 he married Eleanor (b.1132, d.1204), the divorced wife of Louis VII, King of France. They had 5 sons and 3 daughters.

The eldest son died in childhood (b.1152, d.1156).

The second son, Prince Henry (b.1155, d.1183), was crowned King of England in 1170 during his father's reign; married in 1173 Margaret, daughter of Louis VII, a daughter of the King of France's second marriage. They had no children. He died 6 years before his father's death, and although crowned King, he was never monarch.

The third son became King Richard I, Coeur de Lion (The Lionheart).

The fifth son became King John.

THE PLANTAGENETS: KING HENRY II

Persons of note:

Thomas Becket (b.1118, d.1170), also known as Thomas à Becket. Appointed Chancellor and Archdeacon of Canterbury in 1154; Archbishop of Canterbury 1162 until his death, although in fear of Henry II, he fled to France in 1164 until his return in 1170.

Nicholas Breakspeare became Pope Adrian IV from 1154 to 1159, the only Englishman ever to become a Pope. He was born near St Albans, Hertfordshire.

Prince Henry, son of Matilda, grandson of King Henry I, became King Henry II.

Earlier in 1149 his father, Geoffrey Plantagenet, had ceded to him the Dukedom of Normandy. In 1152 he married Eleanor, the divorced wife of the French king, Louis VII: as was then the custom he inherited her titles and domains so giving Henry control over France, west of the River Rhône and south to the Pyrenees.

Much in England had to be rectified after King Stephen's reign: Henry accomplished this quickly, including the restoration of the royal revenues; control of the barons; and recovery of the northern shires from the invading Scots.

Henry used the foundations laid down successively by the Saxons, William the Conqueror and King Henry I to extend and develop laws throughout England. He increased the power and jurisdiction of the King's Court (Curia Regis), which replaced the various provincial customs administered in the shire and hundred courts, developing a law common to the whole country, Common Law. The King's Court began to expand the scope of King Henry I's specialist councils, to be regulated by standard laws.

In 1155 Henry was given permission by Pope Adrian IV to invade Ireland subject to certain conditions, but owing to domestic opposition his expedition was postponed.

The disputes and power struggles between state and Church was a feature of Henry's reign that continued after his Chancellor, Thomas Becket, was appointed Archbishop of Canterbury. Thomas Becket put Church matters ahead of state: was determined to retain the powers that the Church had gained during the anarchical reign of Stephen, but which Henry wanted returned to the monarchy. The King wanted to change the legal procedure of certain offences and circumstances, e.g. when a cleric was charged with a crime, in future to have the accused tried under the jurisdiction of the King's Court rather than the Church. Thomas Becket refused the proposed changes.

The Grand Council of barons and prelates summoned to define the boundaries of state and church, issued the Constitution of Clarendon in 1164.

Thomas Becket was persuaded to sign the Constitution, but, subsequently refused its sealing, so it remained invalid. As a consequence, he was summoned to the King's Court to answer charges of contempt together with an investigation into his control of the finances during his Chancellorship. Fearful, he fled to France where he remained for 6 years.

A dispute amongst feuding Irish kings in 1169 gave Henry the opportunity to exert authority in Ireland, although it extended only to the area of Dublin and Wexford, called the 'English pale'. Henry gave himself a new title, Lord of Ireland.

In 1170 the King's eldest son, Prince Henry, was crowned King of England at the age of 15, the ceremony being performed by the Archbishop of York and the Bishop of London, to be co-regent with his father, but, in fact, he was never granted any power.

Shortly afterwards a truce was reached with Thomas Becket who returned to England, but, he invalidated the crowning of Prince Henry and excommunicated the prelates involved in the ceremony.

King Henry, in Normandy, on hearing the news is said to have cried out, "Are there none of the dastards eating my bread who will rid me of this turbulent priest?" Soon afterwards, four knights left for Canterbury where they murdered Thomas Becket on the altar steps of the Cathedral.

Henry felt guilty of the murder: by the Concordant of Arranches in 1172 he made his peace with the Pope. Eventually, the Church accepted the main principles of the Constitution of Clarendon of 1164.

In 1174 the Scots crossed the border into England, supported by rebel English barons and aided by the King of France. At the Battle of Fornham, in Suffolk, the Earl of Leicester and the Earl of Norfolk were defeated and killed. The Scottish king, William the Lion, was captured: by the Treaty of Falaise (1174) he secured his release by agreeing that he and every succeeding Scottish monarch would regularly pay homage to the English monarch.

The beginning of the jury system commenced. The Assizes of Clarendon (1166) and Northampton (1176) and the Possessory Assizes, which Henry introduced, instituted the process where twelve sworn men representing each Hundred were to attend court as witnesses to the committed crime which was being heard before the justices. Justices travelled around the country to administer the King's law: also, it was their duty to collect the King's taxes.

A change to the feudal system related to hereditary ownership of land: under new primogeniture laws the estates had to pass on inheritance to the eldest son only. Therefore, the wealth of families remained with one member, and, consequently, having greater assets this led to improved methods of agriculture, and further investments assisted in the early development of commerce, manufacturing and trade.

The feudal system obligated a knight to give forty days a year to the monarch for military duties: by now it had become impractical, and Henry preferred experienced militia mercenaries, both English and foreign, who were paid. The income raised to pay for the mercenaries, known as 'scutage' begun by King Henry I, came from barons and prelates who paid a fee based on their land holdings in *lieu* of the military service of their knights.

The Assize of Arms (1181) decreed in detail that all freemen were to possess certain weapons and armour, to be kept in good order and to be inspected periodically, for use when freemen could be summoned for the King's service.

In 1183 Henry's son and heir, Prince Henry who had been crowned in 1170, died.

The Second Crusade to the Holy Land, Palestine, in 1147 led by the King of France and the German Emperor ended in defeat, in 1187. A Third Crusade, summoned by Pope Gregory VIII, was being prepared with Henry's involvement in 1188. To pay for the expedition, Henry imposed the Saladin Tithe, named after the Muslim leader in Jerusalem: it was the first instance in England of a tax based on personal possessions, i.e. on goods as distinct from property.

Before the preparations for the crusade were completed, on July 6, 1189, Henry died at Chinnon, France. He was buried in the abbey church at Fontevrault, west of Tours, France.

During his reign of 34 years, Henry collectively spent no more than 14 years in England. The population of England had risen to at least 3.25 millions, maybe as many as 4 million people.

PLANTAGENET

KING RICHARD I

Born	**1157 September 8**
Accession	**1189 July 6**
Age at Accession	**31**
Death	**1199 April 6**
Age at Death	**41**
Reigned	**9 years**

Richard I was the third son of Henry II. (The first son died aged 4, the second son died without an heir in 1183.)

In 1191 he married Berengaria (b.1163, d.1230), daughter of Sancho VI, King of Navarre, Spain. They had no children.

Persons of note:

William FitzRobert, 2nd Earl of Gloucester (b.1116, d.1183). His father was the illegitimate son of King Henry I who was exchanged for King Stephen in 1141, after the Battle of Lincoln.

William Longchamp (d.1197), Bishop of Ely 1189 until his death; a Justiciar (chief-justice) 1189 to 1191; Chancellor 1189 to 1197.

Hugh de Puiset (b.c.1125, d.1195), nephew of King Stephen; Bishop of Durham 1153 until his death; a Justiciar (chief-justice) 1189 to 1190.

Hubert Walter (b.c.1160, d.1205), Archbishop of Canterbury 1193 until his death; a Justiciar (chief-justice) 1193 to 1198. (Lord Chancellor to King John)

THE PLANTAGENETS: KING RICHARD I

Richard I succeeded his father King Henry II, but became an absent monarch spending only about ten months in England during his reign of almost 10 years. He was known as Richard the Lionheart (Coeur de Lion) because of his bravery.

In alliance with other Christian European rulers, Richard joined the Third Crusade, in another attempt to defeat and remove the Muslims, under Saladin's leadership, from the Holy Land, Palestine. He appointed two justiciars (chief-justices), William Longchamp (the Bishop of Ely) and Hugh de Puiset (the Bishop of Durham) to govern the country under the supervision of Queen Eleanor of Aquitaine, Richard's mother, during his absence.

To finance the expedition, Richard used many sources including his father's innovation of the Saladin Tithe, a tax based on personal possessions; 'scutage', a fee paid by barons and prelates based on their land holdings in *lieu* of military service of their knights; and by forcing the King of Scotland to buy back the homage to the English monarch by the revocation of the 1174 Treaty of Falaise.

Richard left England in 1189.

His younger brother, Prince John, was considered a threat to the throne so Richard appointed him to the lordship of Ireland. Within a year, Prince John returned to England, quarrelled with William Longchamp and began to rule over the vast estates which he had acquired by his marriage to Isabel, the daughter of William FitzRobert, 2nd Earl of Gloucester.

Further, Prince John's association with the French provoked Richard to return to England. During the Crusade, Richard had quarrelled with most of his allies, which made him very unpopular. On his voyage to England in 1192, he was shipwrecked off the Adriatic coast, and resuming the journey overland, was captured and imprisoned by one of his adversaries, Leopold of Austria, who in turn, sold him to another adversary, the Emperor Henry VI of the Holy Roman Empire (now mainly Germany).

The news of Richard's captivity tempted Prince John to act as monarch; he defied the justiciars, and gathered together a group of supporters.

Richard was released from captivity in 1194 on the payment of a very large ransom and the acceptance that the Holy Roman Empire be the feudal overlord of England. On his return to England, Richard was re-crowned King. Prince John on swearing allegiance to Richard was pardoned but he forfeited his entire vast estates.

In 1194 Richard left England to secure his French possessions, which were under threat from the French King. Hubert Walter, the Archbishop of Canterbury, was appointed Justiciar.

Hubert Walter was an excellent, reforming and constructive chief-minister. He brought peace; trusted those with responsibilities; granted charters to various towns; and gave Londoners the right of electing a mayor. A new procedure for law and order was instituted; the office of Coroner emerged for the first time; new assessments of land were begun; and weights and measures were standardized.

Richard was injured by an arrow whilst fighting at the Castle of Chaluz (south of Limoges, France). In preparing for death caused by gangrene, he declared his brother, Prince John, to be heir to the throne.

The fourth son of King Henry II was Prince Geoffrey who died in 1186, and his son Prince Arthur was recognized as heir presumptive from 1190. Prince John was King Henry II's fifth and youngest son.

Richard died on April 6, 1199. His brain was buried at the Abbey of Charroux in Poitou; his heart was buried at Rouen in Normandy, and his body at his father's burial site at Fontevrault, west of Tours, France.

PLANTAGENET

KING JOHN

Born	**1166 December 24**
Accession	**1199 April 6**
Age at Accession	**32**
Death	**1216 October 19**
Age at Death	**49**
Reigned	**17 years**

John succeeded his brother Richard I, being the fifth and youngest son of Henry II.

In 1189 he married, firstly, Isabel (Avice), daughter of William FitzRobert, 2nd Earl of Gloucester. They were divorced in 1200. They had no children.

In 1200 he married, secondly, Isabella, daughter and heir of Aymer de Valence, Count of Angoulene. They had 2 sons and 3 daughters. Isabella was previously married to the Count of La Marla (part of Aquitaine, France).

King Henry II's fourth son, Prince Geoffrey (b.1158, d.1186) had married Constance, daughter and heir of Conan IV, Duke of Brittany and Earl of Richmond. They had 1 son and 1 daughter. The son, Prince Arthur, born posthumously in 1187, was next in line to Richard I, and had been recognized as heir presumptive in October 1190. He was killed in 1203. The daughter (b.1184, d.1241) did not marry.

Persons of note:

Pope Innocent III (b.c.1160, d.1216). Pope 1198 until his death.

Stephen Langton (b.1151, d.1228), Archbishop of Canterbury, 1206 until his death. Advisor to the insurgent barons who forced John to sign the Magna Carta.

Hubert Walter (b.c.1160, d.1205). Archbishop of Canterbury from 1193, and Lord Chancellor from 1199 until his death.

King Richard I decreed that Prince John should be his successor, although King Henry II's fourth son, Prince Geoffrey, who died in 1186, had a posthumously born son, Prince Arthur, who in October 1190 had been recognized as heir presumptive to King Richard I. Prince Arthur's mother was French, and King Philip II of France had been involved in his education, a situation that caused some concerns.

The Archbishop of Canterbury, the justiciar and the important barons declared John to be the rightful King. Shortly after King Richard's death, John was invested as the Duke of Normandy. Normandy, Maine and Anjou acknowledged John as Duke; his mother secured for him Poitou and Guienne, but Philip II of France supported Prince Arthur's right to Anjou, Maine and Brittany (Prince Arthur was Duke of Brittany).

The dispute was resolved, seemingly, when John and Philip II signed the Treaty of Le Goulet in 1200.

By divorcing his first wife, John upset his powerful and influential father-in-law the 2nd Earl of Gloucester; by marrying his second wife, he annoyed the French.

In 1202, Philip II summoned John to France to answer charges made against him by the barons of Poitou: when John declined to attend, Philip II reminded him that in France John was a subject. In absentia, John was sentenced to forfeit all of his French possessions excepting Normandy and Guienne. Later that year Philip II together with Prince Arthur invaded Normandy. In the ensuing battle, the 15-year-old Prince Arthur was taken prisoner at Mirebeau-en-Poitou on August 1, 1202, and by April 13, 1203, had been murdered. In 1204 after a long period of fighting the French gained Normandy and by 1206 Anjou, Maine and parts of Poitou had fallen to Philip II.

During this time, two of John's most important and influential advisors, his mother Queen Eleanor and Hubert Walter (Archbishop of Canterbury and Lord Chancellor) died in 1204 and 1205, respectively.

The appointment of the next Archbishop caused a fractious dispute between the monks of Canterbury, the King and the Pope. Pope Innocent III, who had the responsibility, rejected two separate nominees. John asserted that it was the monarch who should supervise the election, not the Pope. Eventually, the monks accepted the Pope's choice of an Englishman, Stephen Langton, although for most of his clerical life he had been abroad.

John refused the choice: the Pope replied by issuing an interdict (a prohibition decree) in 1208, which suspended all church activities, including Christian burials and marriages in England. In retaliation John seized church lands and confiscated their income. The impasse lasted for more than six years.

Pope Innocent III threatened to depose John as King of England. In 1213 John, fearful of an invasion and without the support of the population and barons, capitulated. John was obliged to swear allegiance and pay an annual pension to the Pope; forced to transform England into a papal fiefdom, i.e. a subject state to the Catholic Church in Rome. This permitted the papacy to interfere in England's affairs, including the levying of taxes.

The following year, 1214, John joined a continental alliance to invade France at La Rochelle. It was a failure and John's forces were defeated at Bouvines, in Poitou.

By now the barons were completely disgruntled by the actions of their King. Under the leadership of the Archbishop of Canterbury, Stephen Langton, a document was presented to John, the Magna Carta. It consisted of sixty-three clauses dealing with feudal administration and customs; details of how to enforce its measures; and the methods of solving abuses in the feudal system. John, now so impotent, sealed the parchment document at Runnymede, Surrey, on June 15, 1215.

One of England's most precious documents, the Magna Carta is held at the British Museum in London.

For the first time the monarchy became subject to the law: the power of the English Crown was no longer absolute, but the Pope, now overlord of England, annulled the Magna Carta and forbade its observance under the threat of excommunication from the Church.

The barons were exasperated with the situation and turned to France for leadership: they offered the Crown to the 28-year-old Prince Louis, son of King Philip II. Prince Louis landed a force, which led to a civil war for about a year, until, quite suddenly John became ill and died at Newark, Nottinghamshire in 1216.

He was buried at Worcester Cathedral, where his effigy survives.

PLANTAGENET

KING HENRY III

Born	**1207 October 1**
Accession	**1216 October 19**
Age at Accession	**9**
Death	**1272 November 16**
Age at Death	**65**
Reigned	**56 years**

Henry III succeeded his father John.

In 1236 he married Eleanor (b.1223, d.1291), daughter of Raymond Berenger IV, Count of Provence. It is thought they had 6 sons and 2 daughters.

Persons of note:

Roger Bacon (b.c.1219, d.1294). Studied at Oxford and Paris. Considered to be the founder of English philosophy.

John Balliol (d.1268). Founded Balliol College, Oxford. (Thought to have been an English family – not connected with John Balliol who became King of Scotland 1292.)

Hubert de Burgh, 1st Earl of Kent (b.c.1175, d.1243), Justiciar (chief-justice) 1215 until dismissed in 1232, considered the last of the great justiciars.

Stephen Langton (b.1151, d.1228), Archbishop of Canterbury, 1206 until his death.

William Marshall, 1st Earl of Pembroke (b.c.1146, d.1219), Regent of England, 1216 to 1219.

THE PLANTAGENETS: KING HENRY III

Simon de Montfort, Earl of Leicester (b.1208, d.1265). Married to Eleanor, youngest sister of Henry III, as her second husband. Killed at the Battle of Evesham, 1265.

Peter des Roches (d.1238), Bishop of Winchester, 1205 until his death.

Popes: Gregory IX, 1227 to 1241. Celestine IV, 1241. Innocent IV, 1243 to 1254.

King John had lost the diadem (a crown) when crossing The Wash, off the east coast of England, so at Henry III's coronation at Gloucester Cathedral on October 28, 1216, he was crowned by the placing of a plain gold circlet on his head.

At the commencement of the 9-year-old Henry's reign, three outstanding men governed England. They were the Regent, William Marshall (1st Earl of Pembroke), the Justiciar (chief-justice), Hubert de Burgh, and the Archbishop of Canterbury, Stephen Langton.

The sudden death of King John altered the monarchical position of the barons. They withdrew their offer of the English throne to Prince Louis, son of King Philip II of France, to support their new king, Henry.

Prince Louis was determined to continue the struggle of the previous year with his forces, but defeat by William Marshall at the Battle of Lincoln, and with Hubert de Burgh destroying the French reinforcements at Dover, in Kent, peace was signed, and Prince Louis left England.

Hubert de Burgh successfully opposed rebellions against Henry, and Stephen Langton, although Archbishop of Canterbury, defended the rights of the English against outside influences, including Rome. The Magna Carta was re-issued indicating that those in power would adhere to its provisions.

On reaching his age of majority Henry began to exert authority. Hubert de Burgh advised for a continuation of his policies, but, under the influence of Peter des Roches (the Bishop of Winchester), Henry dismissed Hubert de Burgh in 1232 and seized his estates. Peter des Roches, a Poitevin (France) filled every office that became vacant with his own relatives and foreign friends. Within two years the barons rebelled, forcing the King to dismiss the Poitevin officials and other foreigners, and to restore the land and possessions to Hubert de Burgh.

In 1236 Henry married the young Eleanor of Provence (France), and influenced by his wife, a new influx of foreigners filled official positions in England. Pope Gregory IX exacerbated the problem in 1240, by demanding exorbitant taxes and rents from the clergy, and also declared that Italian clergy should fill the next three hundred vacancies in church benefices. In 1243 the new Pope, Innocent IV, renewed these demands. Although accepting the authority of the papacy, the English clergy resisted.

THE PLANTAGENETS: KING HENRY III

Henry's request for money to finance papal wars in Sicily was refused by the barons unless their demands were met, these being that the Justiciar, Chancellor, Treasurer and certain judges should be elected by the Grand Council, on which the barons were well represented, and that the Great Council, predecessor of Parliament, should elect four members to the King's Council. Henry objected to these demands.

Reform was needed: commissions were summoned; and in 1258 proposals were embodied in the Provisions of Oxford, supplemented and extended in 1259 by the Provisions of Westminster. The Magna Carta was mainly concerned to define various points of law, whereas the Provisions of Oxford dealt with whose advice and through which officials the royal government should operate. Many of the clauses in the Provisions of Westminster indicated more a limitation of baronial powers than of royal jurisdiction; although it stated that the monarch should govern with a Council of Fifteen.

Henry's declaration in accepting these Provisions was a sham: he persuaded the Pope to free him from his declaration: on the matter of whether he was bound by the Provisions of Oxford and Westminster, it was referred to King Louis IX of France to adjudicate. By the Mise of Amiens of 1264 it was decided that Henry might do as he wished.

The consequences of this caused the Civil War, the Barons War, led by Simon de Montfort (the Earl of Leicester) who was the husband of Henry's sister, Princess Eleanor. Simon de Montfort defeated and captured both Henry and his son Prince Edward (the heir) at the Battle of Lewes, Sussex, in 1264. The detained King was forced to accept the Provisions of Oxford required by the barons.

Simon de Montfort is credited with founding the Parliament of England: in fact it was a further stage in the development of England's government because representatives from the shires and boroughs had long attended the King's Court to transact business and advise the monarch. Early in 1265 Simon de Montfort summoned two knights from each shire; representatives from certain boroughs and cities; and twenty-three of the fifty important barons, those who would most likely support him, to London for a parliament. This can be considered to have been a starting point in representative government, a body of people with differing interests, background, and influence.

The 26-year-old Prince Edward, whilst out hunting, escaped from his loosely controlled imprisonment. He promised the young Earl of Gloucester, and with the support of the majority of barons, to overthrow Simon de Montfort; expel all foreigners from England; and, eventually, when King, to rule according to the laws of the country.

The Civil War continued. Prince Edward's royalist forces attacked Simon de Montfort's forces at Kenilworth (Warwickshire) in the July; achieved victory at the Battle of Evesham (Worcestershire) where Simon de Montfort was killed in August 1265.

THE PLANTAGENETS: KING HENRY III

At the conclusion of the Civil War, the 1267 Statute of Marlborough re-enacted the Provisions of Westminster, making Henry's resumed rule acceptable to the barons. The King enjoyed comparative peace for the remaining years of his long reign.

The development of universities in England commenced during Henry's reign. Students had been at the University of Paris, but following troubles between the English and French, many students moved to Oxford, where in due course the University of Oxford was founded. University College was founded in 1249, Balliol in 1263, and Merton in 1264. Cambridge soon followed.

A typical student would have been a clever boy of lower-middle class origin, having gone to university at 14 years of age and studying until 21 or more.

Henry died, weak and senile, on November 16, 1272, and was buried at the largely rebuilt Westminster Abbey, London.

PLANTAGENET

KING EDWARD I

Born	**1239 June 17**
Accession	**1272 November 16**
Age at Accession	**33**
Death	**1307 July 7**
Age at Death	**68**
Reigned	**34 years**

Edward I succeeded his father Henry III.

In 1254 he married, firstly, Eleanor (b.1241, d.1290), daughter of Ferdinand III, King of Castille. They had 4 sons and 5 daughters.

The first 3 sons died in childhood. Their youngest son became the first Prince of Wales, and later King Edward II.

In 1299 he married, secondly, Margaret (b.1282, d.1317), the young daughter of Philip III, King of France. They had 2 sons and 1 daughter.

Persons of note:

John Balliol (b.1250, d.1313). King of Scotland 1292 to 1296.

Robert Burnell (d.1292). Lord Chancellor from 1274, and Bishop of Bath and Wells from 1275, both until his death.

Walter Langton (d.1321). Treasurer 1295 to 1307; Bishop of Litchfield 1296 until his death.

THE PLANTAGENETS: KING EDWARD I

John Peckham (b.c.1230, d.1292). Archbishop of Canterbury 1279 until his death.

Edward I was recognized as King to succeed his father. He was in Sicily, Italy, at the time of his father's death, and it would be almost two years before he returned to be crowned King, at Westminster Abbey, London.

His reign of thirty-four years was full and eventful, but England was only part of his responsibilities. Parliament continued its development under his leadership; Wales was subjugated; problems occurred in Scotland; complications arose with the Church and Popes; complexities in Gascony; and always a need for money to finance wars, but in England there was relative peace.

Edward received advice from his Lord Chancellor, Robert Burnell, and after his death from Walter Langton, the Treasurer.

His first Parliament in 1275 was instrumental for the introduction of Statute Law, i.e. a law established for legislation by Parliament. The initial statutes are considered important in the continuing development of the government of England from the time of William the Conqueror's feudal society to the emerging stages of a parliamentary democracy. The first Statute of Westminster in 1275 dealt with administrative abuses; the Statute of Gloucester in 1278 (Quo Warranto) of the rights of feudal lords to administer the law; the Statute of Mortmain in 1279 (De Religiosis) forbade gifts of land to the Church; the second Statute of Westminster in 1285 (De Donis Conditionalibus) structured the system of inheritance of estates; the third Statute of Westminster (Quia Emptores) dealt with land in fee simple, i.e. unconditional inheritance.

Edward used Parliament as a means of easing differences, solving problems, receiving petitions, and levying revenues for his requirements, usually to fight wars and rebellions.

The King, barons and representatives of the church attended the first parliaments; in addition knights and burgesses from the shires and towns were summoned to attend, but only participated when invited by the King for their opinions, etc. In due course the knights and burgesses would discuss these matters in a separate chamber to prepare their replies, and one person would be selected to speak on their behalf. This *modus operandi* developed into the House of Commons and the Speaker. The original body would become the House of Lords.

Edward wanted to rule not only England, but also a united Britain.

John Peckham, a Franciscan friar, and Archbishop of Canterbury from 1279 until his death in 1292, defended what he regarded as the rights of the Church and its independence from the Crown. On his appointment he issued a number of pronouncements, which angered Edward; then in 1281 declared that divine authority was supreme. Edward ignored this challenge to his authority, but ordered his justices to act circumspectly in ecclesiastical matters.

THE PLANTAGENETS: KING EDWARD I

In 1277 a leader of the Welsh, Llewellyn ap Gruffydd, rebelled against Edward's rule. Although victorious, Edward initially allowed Wales to retain certain powers, but five years later decided to divide Wales into shires, copying the English system. Llewellyn ap Gruffydd led another rebellion, but in defeat was killed and his brother, David, was executed for treason. The Statute of Rhuddham of 1284 declared Wales to be annexed to England; to be divided into shires; justiciars (chief-justices) appointed; Welsh laws to be kept and administered in the courts; and Welsh customs and language be retained.

In education the first University of Cambridge College, Peterhouse, was founded in 1284.

An issue confronting Edward was the growing strength of the Jewish community, which started to arrive in England at the end of the 11th century. They thrived by lending money with interest payments, a practice forbidden by the Church, and they had acquired considerable acreage of land by the default of mortgage and loan repayments. By 1290 the great antagonism towards the Jews compelled Edward to expel them from England. It did not affect Edward because his borrowings were from Italian bankers.

The legal system was developing and during this reign lawyers founded the first Inns of Court. The famous Year Book commenced, this being the unofficial verbatim reports of legal proceedings.

King Alexander III of Scotland died in a horse-riding accident in 1286. His three children had died by this time, leaving a young granddaughter, Margaret, as heir. Her late mother, Alexander's daughter, had married the King of Norway. In 1290 it was arranged that the 7-year-old Margaret, known as the Maid of Norway, should marry Edward's 6-year-old son, Prince Edward. Tragedy occurred on the journey from Norway when she became ill on the voyage and after disembarking at Orkney, northern Scotland, she died. Edward had planned to take control of Scotland by this marriage, but now Scotland was left without a successor to their throne.

Edward agreed to adjudicate the selection of a new King of Scotland with a court of eighty Scots and twenty-four English. In 1292 John Balliol was selected, having previously agreed that he would be subordinate to the King of England.

Since the Treaty of Paris of 1259, nearly thirty-five years of peace existed between England and France, but in 1293 the Parlement de Paris declared that England should forfeit Gascony. Edward agreed to a token forfeiture but soon realised that he had been misled, so, in 1294, the English Parliament decided to go to war against France, but the necessary increases in taxes caused some problems, e.g. the clergy were ordered to contribute one-half of their revenue.

By the winter the Welsh were in revolt, although it was quickly repulsed. The following year the Scots expelled the English and seized their Scottish estates; John Balliol, their King, made an alliance with the French, and as Edward was at war with France, this was tantamount to open defiance. In 1296 Pope Boniface VIII attempted to stop the war by issuing a Papal Bull, Clericus Laicos, forbidding the clergy of England and France paying taxes towards the war. By

1297 the Pope withdrew many of his extreme demands for ending the war, but by then the fighting had subsided.

Having ceased fighting in France, Edward moved to concentrate on subduing the Scots. Various battles were won and lost until the Battle of Stirling of 1297, where the Scots lost fifteen thousand men, but their leader Sir William Wallace escaped from defeat. In 1296 Edward removed the Stone of Scone, the Coronation Stone, from Edinburgh to Westminster Abbey, London. (Seven hundred years later in 1996, it was returned to Edinburgh.)

The Regency Council ruled the country when Edward was away fighting: they supported the barons' complaints against the King's demands for war service and certain aspects of his rule. Reform was agreed for Parliament to increase its control over the monarchy and taxation. Edward in Ghent, modern day Belgium, accepted the changes. In February 1301, the King formally agreed to the Charter of Articles, confirming all the rights enacted since the Magna Carta of 1215.

In 1301 Edward's surviving son, Prince Edward, was appointed the Prince of Wales at the age of 17, the first creation of this title.

The war with France was concluded with the Treaty of Paris in 1303.

Edward still wanting Scotland to be under his authority and control, in battle captured Stirling in 1304; the next year the Scots leader, Sir William Wallace, was betrayed, captured, found guilty of treason and hanged. In 1306, Robert Bruce (also known as Robert the Bruce), who commanded the English artillery at the Battle of Stirling in 1297, became the leader of the Scots and was crowned King of Scotland.

Edward was pursuing Robert Bruce, when he died at Burgh-on-Sands (Hadrian's Wall), north-west of Carlisle, Cumbria in July 1307. He was buried at Westminster Abbey, London.

PLANTAGENET

KING EDWARD II

Born	1284 April 25
Accession	1307 July 7
Age at Accession	23
Deposed	1327 January 7
Reigned	19 years
Death	1327 September 21
Age at Death	43

Edward II succeeded his father Edward I.

In 1301 he was created the first Prince of Wales on February 7.

In 1308 he married Isabella (d.1358), daughter of Philip IV, King of France. They had 2 sons and 2 daughters.

In 1327 having been deposed on January 7, he was murdered at Berkeley Castle, Gloucestershire on September 21.

Persons of note:

Robert (the) Bruce (b.1274, d.1329), son of Robert Bruce, Earl of Carrick. He was Robert I, King of Scotland 1306 until his death.

Piers Gaveston (b.c.1284, d.1312). Married Margaret, daughter of Earl of Gloucester; conferred Earl of Cornwall 1307.

THE PLANTAGENETS: KING EDWARD II

Roger (de) Mortimer (b.1287, d.1330). Conferred Earl of March 1321.

Hugh Le Despenser (father) (b.1262, d.1326). Conferred Earl of Winchester c.1322.

Hugh Le Despenser, the Younger (son) (d.1326). In 1306 he married Eleanor, daughter of Earl of Gloucester.

Prince Edward, the first Prince of Wales, became Edward II on his father's death.

Robert Bruce (also known as Robert the Bruce) had been crowned King of Scotland in 1306, and Edward continued his father's campaign to compel the Scots to recognize that Scotland was subjugated to England.

Concerned by Edward's behaviour and general incompetence, the King's Council (Curia Regis) in 1310 appointed a committee, named Lords Ordained, which represented baronial and ecclesiastical interests. Their reforms, called Ordinances, included changes to the system of appointing Court officials and the procedure of summoning Parliament. Further, the Lord Ordinars had serious concerns regarding Edward's close friend Piers Gaveston, originally from Gascony, France, who had been expelled from England during the reign of King Edward I. Piers Gaveston returned from exile in 1307; conferred Earl of Cornwall; banished a second time; but illegally returned in 1312 in defiance of the Lord Ordinars. He was arrested and taken to Blacklow Hill, near Warwick, where he was executed by beheading.

Edward's weak leadership caused discontent and discord in the country. His attempt to assert control over Scotland ended in a terrible defeat: on June 24, 1314, his army of fifteen thousand men was completely and thoroughly routed at Bannock Burn, just south of Stirling, by Robert Bruce's smaller army of eight thousand men.

Thomas (Earl of Lancaster), with the support of Roger Mortimer, led an opposition against Edward, his cousin. It is believed that Thomas held supreme power in England for a couple of years until Edward attempted to replace him with the Despensers, a father and son, from the Welsh Marches. In 1321 Thomas's banishment of the Despensers led to battles between the antagonists, ending with the Battle of Bouroughbridge, Yorkshire, in 1322. At nearby Pontefract, Thomas was captured and beheaded; a number of his supporters were either hanged or imprisoned; amongst the prisoners was Roger Mortimer, who eventually escaped to France.

The King with the support of the Despensers repealed the Ordinances, and declared that the affairs of state were matters for Parliament, not the Lord Ordinars, although Parliament had continued to meet regularly during the disruptions.

Edward's breakdown of his marriage to Isabella and his close relationship with Hugh Le Despenser (the son) created further problems. The French born Queen with their son Prince Edward had left England for France, where she and Roger Mortimer became lovers.

In 1326 Queen Isabella and Roger Mortimer organized an invasion to depose the King: Edward attempted to escape to Ireland but was captured at Neath Abbey, in south Wales, on November 16. He was forced to surrender the Great Seal of England by the Bishop of Hereford, before being imprisoned at Kenilworth Castle, Warwickshire, in the custody of Henry (Earl of Lancaster), brother of the late Thomas. The Despensers were captured and hanged.

Edward refused to abdicate but was deposed as King on January 7, 1327. Gradually sympathy and support for him grew, and it was considered prudent to move him to Berkeley Castle, Gloucestershire, at the beginning of April 1327. There in the September he was brutally murdered. As "his bowels were burnt out by red-hot irons passing into his body", it is said his screams "were heard outside the Castle walls".

As soon as Parliament received the news of his death, a sumptuous funeral was arranged at Gloucester Abbey, now the Cathedral.

PLANTAGENET

KING EDWARD III

Born	**1312 November 13**
Accession	**1327 January 7**
Age at Accession	**14**
Death	**1377 June 21**
Age at Death	**64**
Reigned	**50 years**

Edward III succeeded his father Edward II.

In 1329 he married Philippa (d.1369), daughter of William II, Count of Holland and Hainault. They had 6 sons and 5 daughters.

The eldest son, Edward, Prince of Wales (known as the Black Prince) (b.1330, d.1376), died the year before his father's death. In 1361 he married Joan, 'The Fair Maid of Kent', daughter of his step great-uncle Edmund, Earl of Kent. They had 2 sons. The eldest died in 1372 aged 8; the second son became King Richard II.

The fourth son of Edward III, John of Gaunt (b.1340, d.1399), conferred Duke of Lancaster in 1362, married three times. His first wife, Blanche (d.1369), daughter and heir of Henry, 1ˢᵗ Duke of Lancaster, was the great-granddaughter of King Henry III. Their eldest son became King Henry IV.

Person of note:

John Wyclif (also spelt as Wycliffe) (b.c.1329, d.1384) was an English religious reformer. His itinerant preachers spread his philosophy; his followers, the Lollards, often were imprisoned, although John Wyclif remained free.

THE PLANTAGENETS: KING EDWARD III

Edward III succeeded to the throne at 14 years of age: this gave the real power of ruling the country to his mother, Queen Isabella, her lover Roger Mortimer, the Council of Barons and Henry, 3rd Earl of Lancaster, his guardian. Not surprisingly disputes arose over policy and influence.

A treaty with France in 1327 committed England to pay a war indemnity and restricted the English possessions in France, being Guienne, Gascony and Pontieu.

Parliament continued to develop. The presentations of petitions from the shires and boroughs became an integral part of the procedures for consideration by the knights and burgesses. In 1327 the knights and burgesses asked of the King that such petitions should become parliamentary statutes, and also, for the first time their own clerks were permitted to draft the petitions for the King's attention.

In 1327 a charter was granted to the Goldsmith Company, nowadays the official assayers of gold and silver.

Roger Mortimer summoned Parliament to meet in Salisbury, Wiltshire (at this time there were no fixed meeting-places for Parliament). He was conferred with the title Earl of March in addition to holding the office of Justice of Wales.

By the 1328 Treaty of Northampton, Robert Bruce was recognized as king of the country north of the River Tweed: considered as 'shameful' it caused widespread anger. At the death of Robert Bruce in 1329, his 5-year-old son, David Bruce became King of Scotland.

Roger Mortimer's position of power was resented by the barons who then conspired to have him arrested at a parliamentary sitting in Nottingham in 1330. He was taken to London, tried for murder of King Edward II, found guilty and hanged. Queen Isabella was placed under supervised house arrest for the remainder of her life, almost thirty years.

Edward Balliol, son of the former King of Scotland, John Balliol, led a successful revolt against the young David Bruce's supporters in battle at Dupplin Moor, near Perth, in 1332, but his reign lasted only a few months. Edward Balliol had previously agreed to recognize Edward III as his overlord, and promised to return the town and shire of Berwick to England, the area north of the River Tweed.

The following year Edward's forces overran Berwickshire and the whole of south-eastern Scotland, forcing David Bruce (King David II of Scotland) and his supporters to flee to France for refuge. Edward Balliol only established a temporary rule of southern Scotland with English support until 1336.

England, at this period, had developed a successful trade in Flanders (part of modern day Belgium and France) and its possessions of Gascony, in south-west France. Wool was exported from England to Flanders and wine from Gascony to England. Both areas were under threat from the French; in fact France invaded Gascony in 1332. In Flanders, the Flemish towns had become very prosperous and looked to England as their ally and benefactor, whereas their overlord, the

Count of Flanders, was a subject of the King of France. This situation created tensions

English kings had paid homage to French kings for the English possessions in France from the time of William the Conqueror, although most had been lost by the time of this reign. Charles IV of France, the last of the Capetian Dynasty, died in 1328 without a natural successor. Edward, angry at the French interference in Scottish affairs, their threatening manoeuvrings in Flanders and the invasion of Gascony gave Edward the pretext to claim the French throne for himself: his mother was the daughter of King Philip IV of France.

Ducal titles in England were introduced in 1337 when Edward created his heir and son the Duke of Cornwall. Initially, dukedoms were created only for royalty of the male line.

Edward declared war on France in 1338, the start of the Hundred Years' War, although it was not a continuous war and throughout it ebbed and flowed, and lasted for more than one hundred years. The King assembled an army and navy: Parliament raised taxes to support a paid force instead of a feudal levy, as was the custom in the past. Command of the English Channel was decided by the naval Battle of Sluys, adjacent to Flanders, in 1340, when the French fleet was decisively beaten so giving England uninterrupted passage of the Channel. Small land battles were fought. Eventually, the income from taxes was exhausted, but as the wool trade with Flanders was very important, the wool merchants loaned money and paid extra custom revenues.

In 1343, the barons and prelates met for a parliament in the White Chamber at Westminster, and the knights and burgesses met in the Painted Chamber. The role of Speaker had gradually evolved, but Edward wanted the right to select the person. The King agreed to accept formal drafts of petitions as a parliamentary basis for future statutes, and for Parliament to have a greater part in the setting of taxes. By the spring of 1346 Parliament accepted more taxation was necessary to finance a new invasion of France.

The Battle of Crecy, about one hundred miles north-east of Paris, is one of the most famous battles in the history of England: eight thousand French were killed and only about one hundred English died. At Crecy, with the death of the blind King of Bohemia, the Prince of Wales (also known as the Black Prince) took his crest of 'three feathers' and motto "Ich Dien" (meaning "I Serve"), which are retained for every Prince of Wales, continuing to this day. Calais capitulated to Edward after a siege lasting about a year.

At this time, with the support of the French, the King of Scotland invaded northern England: the English captured the King and he was imprisoned for the next eleven years until an enormous ransom was paid for his release.

The first Order of Chivalry was introduced in 1348: the Most Noble Order of the Garter was bestowed by Edward. Its motto is "Honi soit qui mal y pense", meaning "Shame on him who thinks evil of it". Its recipients are Knights of the Garter.

THE PLANTAGENETS: KING EDWARD III

Disaster struck England in this year when the Black Death (so-called because it caused dark splotches on the skin) killed one-third of the population, reducing it from four millions to two and a half millions. The plague had a devastating effect on the domestic and social history of the country. Labour became scarce; harvests could not be gathered, corn rotted in the ground; and prices soared. Parliament made efforts to remedy the situation by passing legislation to control prices and wages, initially by the 1349 Proclamation, then the Statutes of Labourers of 1351, repeated Statutes in 1357 and 1360, but the economic realities of need meant that these measures mainly failed, as demonstrated by the time-scale.

The crisis caused by the Black Death was the end of feudalism as established by William the Conqueror. There were many fewer people to work on the land: a large part of the country was no longer being cultivated; some of it was being enclosed for the grazing of livestock, mainly sheep, which eventually brought great wealth to England from the wool trade. Now villeins (villagers) and freemen were able to demand their own terms of employment and could change landlords, which previously had not been permitted.

In 1351, Parliament passed the Statute of Provisions, which stopped a priest from accepting an appointment made by the Pope to an occupied benefice, until the incumbent priest had died.

The first 'non-royal dukedom' was conferred in 1351 to Henry, Earl of Lancaster (his other titles being earls of Derby, Lincoln and Leicester) as the Duke of Lancaster. He was a great-grandson of King Henry III. His daughter Blanche became his heir, and on her marriage to Prince John of Gaunt (Earl of Richmond), he took her title (then the custom) as Duke of Lancaster.

The Statute of Praemunire of 1353 prohibited appeals of jurisdiction within the King's Court to be made to the papal court.

In 1355 the Hundred Years' War flared up again. The following year at the Battle of Poitiers, in Aquitaine, King John II of France and his son Philip were captured, remained imprisoned in the Tower of London until the Treaty of Bretigny was concluded in 1360. This treaty gave England the whole Duchy of Aquitaine including Gascony, the county of Ponthieu (where Crecy is situated) and Calais, all in full sovereignty, plus a large ransom for the release of the French King and his son. In return, Edward relinquished all claims including that of the French throne.

Peace, however uncertain or short of duration, allowed the wool trade to continue and expand. Wool from the great flocks of Yorkshire and the Cotswolds (mainly Gloucestershire) were exported all over Europe. The right to export wool was placed under the control of 'The Merchants of Staple', and from this trade the King received taxes amounting to £68,000 per year. To expand and enlarge the woollen industry Flemish weavers were brought to England. The trade grew to be one of the chief sources and foundation of the wealth of England.

The system of Justices of the Peace derived from the 1361 Statute, appointed responsible laymen, unpaid, to carry out certain duties within their community.

Further, a Statute of 1362 declared that the "French tongue was now unknown in the Realm" and that English must be used in the law courts, although the records continued to be written in Latin. English was being spoken in schools.

The Hundred Years' War resumed in 1369, with a victory at Limoges (south of Poitiers) in 1370, and a devastating defeat at the Battle of La Rochelle, Aquitaine, in 1372. It became impossible to fight and defend Aquitaine resulting in a 1375 truce in which England forfeited all its conquests except Calais, in the north, Bordeaux and Bayonne in Aquitaine.

After these latest battles, the Church claimed exemption from taxation, despite their obvious wealth. This raised resentment at Oxford University against the Pope leading to demands for reform by an Oxford don, John Wyclif. His 'Theory of Dominion'; opposition to annate (a tax on a new incumbent's first year's income); the holding of more than one benefice by one clergy; absent clergy; and doubting the bases of transubstantiation (the theory that the bread and wine of the Eucharist are transformed into the body and blood of Christ, although their appearances remain the same), all received support. John of Gaunt, Edward's fourth son, initially became a supporter of John Wyclif, particularly when the latter was arraigned on charges of heresy.

Prince Edward (the Prince of Wales, the Duke of Cornwall, the Black Prince) was exhausted by his war exertions, and died in June 1376.

By now Edward had become senile and he died the following June 1377, leaving the late Prince of Wales's young son, Richard, the successor to the throne. Edward was buried at Westminster Abbey, London.

PLANTAGENET

KING RICHARD II

Born	**1367 January 6**
Accession	**1377 June 21**
Age at Accession	**10**
Deposed	**1399 September 30**
Reigned	**22 years**
Death	**1400 February 14**
Age at Death	**33**

Richard II, son of Prince Edward (the Black Prince) who died June 1376, succeeded his grandfather Edward III.

In 1382 he married, firstly, Anne (b.1366, d.1394), daughter of Charles IV, the Holy Roman Emperor. They had no children.

In 1396 he married, secondly, Isabella (b.1389, d.1409), the 7-year-old daughter of Charles VI, King of France. They had no children.

Persons of note:

Henry Bolingbroke (b.1366, d.1413), the son of John of Gaunt (Duke of Lancaster), who was the grandson of King Edward III and usurped the throne from his cousin Richard II. He became King Henry IV.

John of Gaunt (b.1340, d.1399), 4th son of King Edward III, brother of the Black Prince, uncle of Richard II. Became Earl of Lancaster by his marriage to Blanche, daughter and heir of Henry, Earl of Lancaster and subsequently Duke of Lancaster.

THE PLANTAGENETS: KING RICHARD II

Duke of Gloucester (b.c.1355, d.1397), 6th son of King Edward III. Had children.

John Ball (d.1381). English priest and a leader of the Peasants' Revolt; was executed.

Geoffrey Chaucer (b.c.1342, d.1400). English poet, considered the father of English poetry. Also a diplomat and customs official, travelled extensively in Europe.

William Courtenay (b.c.1342, d.1396). Archbishop of Canterbury 1381 until his death. A great-grandson of King Edward I.

Sir Robert Hales (b.c.1325, d.1381). Lord High Chancellor.

Thomas Mowbray (1st Duke of Norfolk – first creation) (b.1366, d.1399). Earl Marshall of England, 1386.

Simon Sudbury (b.c.1316, d.1381). Archbishop of Canterbury 1375 until his death, and Lord Chancellor.

Wat Tyler (d.1381). An English leader of the Peasants' Revolt who was killed whilst protesting.

John Wyclif (also spelt as Wycliffe) (b.c.1329, d.1384), was an English religious reformer. His itinerant preachers spread his philosophy but his followers, the Lollards, often were imprisoned, although John Wyclif remained free.

The 10-year-old Richard II's reign was troubled almost from its start. England was ruled by a Council of Regency headed and dominated by his uncle John of Gaunt (Duke of Lancaster), his father's brother.

Parliament was eager for war, but expected the Regency Council to raise its own revenue. In 1377, the French landed an invasion force in Sussex, but quickly withdrew. This was the only disturbance between England and France during Richard's reign of twenty-two years.

The Roman Catholic Church was in turmoil. From 1378 there were two Popes: one in Rome and the other in Avignon, France. Each named the other "anti-Christ". Taxation on the church was increased to support both Popes. This situation continued for seventy years until 1448.

The repercussions of the Black Death continued to adversely affect England.

Villeins (villagers) and freemen were angry because various Parliamentary Statutes, introduced from 1349, attempted to control their employment and lives.

A poll tax, based on graduated levels was introduced, followed three years later in 1380 by another poll tax, which had less distinction in the levels of payment between the rich and poor. The next year a spontaneous revolt arose in many parts of the country, and led by John Ball, protesters converged on London. Violence erupted, arson and murder, including the beheadings of the Archbishop of Canterbury (Simon Sudbury) and the Lord High Treasurer (Sir Robert Hales).

John of Gaunt (Duke of Lancaster) was in the north of England at the time, so the young King went to meet the protesters. In a skirmish, Wat Tyler, one of the leaders of the Peasants' Revolt was killed, but Richard pacified the rebels by promising to accede to their demands for the repeal of the Statutes; the abolition of villeinage; and end to slavery. In January 1382 a general amnesty was proclaimed, but all the concessions promised by Richard to the rebels were annulled.

In 1380, John Wyclif, the reformist Oxford don, became the first person to translate the Holy Bible into English. His supporters, called the Lollards, preached his philosophy, but the country was not prepared to accept the Lollards' demands for further church reform. The new Archbishop of Canterbury, William Courtenay, an adversary of John Wyclif, held a convocation at Oxford in 1382 demanding that the Lollards retract their dogma, which they did. Even John of Gaunt, once a supporter of John Wyclif, deserted him. Isolated, John Wyclif left Oxford and returned to his parish church at Lutterworth, Leicestershire, and died in 1384.

Richard began to rebel against his uncle, John of Gaunt: by 1386 John of Gaunt had become very unpopular throughout the country and left England for a few years, leaving the King in a defenceless position, but John of Gaunt's 20-year-old son, Henry Bolingbroke, entered politics to oppose Richard, as part of the Lords Appellants group. The Lords Appellants were a number of barons who wished to seize control of power from the King.

The Duke of Gloucester, brother of John of Gaunt and uncle to the King, as a Lords Appellants member attempted to control Richard and his assertive friends.

The Chief Justice, Sir Robert Tresilian, at the 'Merciless Parliament' at Nottingham in 1387, emphatically declared that the doctrine of Royal Supremacy to be superior to the principle of Parliamentary authority. The parliamentarians considered this to be tantamount to treason.

In 1389 the Lords Appellants, created an eleven-man commission to oversee the King. When Richard declared this to be treasonous they retaliated by arresting the Chief Justice, Sir Robert Tresilian, and many of Richard's supporters, sending them for trial: those found guilty were imprisoned or hanged at Tyburn, London.

The return of John of Gaunt later in the year brought stability in organizing Richard and the Lords Appellants, and with him worked in harmony to rule the country successfully for a few years.

THE PLANTAGENETS: KING RICHARD II

Richard's wife Anne died in 1394, and in 1396 he married Isabella, the 7-year-old daughter of the French King, Charles VI, as part of a truce of non-aggression, and for the French to supply Richard with military support if required. There was much opposition to this agreement in England.

By January 1397 Richard believing himself to be in a position of strength declared his opponents, the Lords Appellants, to be traitors: the Earl of Arundel was beheaded; his uncle the Duke of Gloucester, and the Earl of Warwick, were both expelled to Calais, where his uncle was murdered.

Parliament, meeting in Shrewsbury, was packed with Richard's supporters and it suspended almost every constitutional right and privilege it had gained for itself and the people during the preceding century. A committee of eighteen members was appointed to supervise any parliamentary business. Richard became arbitrary and violent; he taxed ruthlessly; raised illegal forced loans and imposed heavy fines; causing sufferance to his subjects who now began to object to this absolute rule. His cousin, Henry Bolingbroke and Thomas Mowbray (the Duke of Norfolk) were expelled from England in 1398 after a fearsome quarrel in the King's presence.

The following year John of Gaunt died and Richard confiscated all of his vast Lancastrian estates and possessions. This action caused concern and fear amongst the nobles for the safety of their own estates; as a consequence they decided to take action. Whilst Richard was in Ireland, Henry Bolingbroke took the opportunity to return to England, and arriving in Yorkshire in July 1399 he began to organize his supporters. When Richard returned he discovered his subjects and soldiers had deserted him in favour of Henry Bolingbroke, to whom he surrendered peacefully at Conway, north Wales.

Richard was forced to abdicate: the abdication document was read to Parliament, which they accepted.

Henry Bolingbroke, the son of John of Gaunt and cousin to Richard, was declared King of England.

A few months later Richard was moved to Pontefract Castle, Yorkshire, and died, as officially suggested, by starving himself to death. William Shakespeare's play indicated that he died by murder of which there is no reliable evidence.
Richard was buried at Westminster Abbey, London.

In the accepted opinion, the heir to Richard was Edmund Mortimer, who was descended from the second son of King Edward III. Roger Mortimer had been recognized by Richard as his heir, but was killed in an Irish battle in 1398, and the claims of his 7-year-old son Edmund, were disregarded by Henry Bolingbroke, who became King Henry IV.

Henry Bolingbroke was descended from King Edward III's third son.

PLANTAGENET (LANCASTRIAN)

KING HENRY IV

Born	1366 April 3
Accession	1399 September 30
Age at Accession	33
Death	1413 March 21
Age at Death	46
Reigned	13 years

Henry IV was the son of John of Gaunt, Duke of Lancaster, and grandson of Edward III. Known as Henry Bolingbroke, he usurped the throne from his cousin Richard II.

In 1380 he married, firstly, Lady Mary de Bohun (b.c.1370, d.1394), daughter of Humphrey, Earl of Hereford. They had 4 sons and 2 daughters.

In 1403 he married, secondly, Joanne (b.1370, d.1437), widow of the Duke of Brittany, Count of Monfort, and daughter of King Charles of Navarre. They had no children.

Persons of note:

4th Earl of Douglas (b.c.1369, d.1424). He was captured at the Battle of Homildon Hill, near Berwick-upon-Tweed in September 1402 by the Percys.

Owen Glendower (b.c.1359, d.1416). He led a revolt against the English in 1400; by 1404 he controlled most of Wales. In 1405 he summoned a Welsh Parliament, but two military defeats marked the end of his rebellion. The rest of his life was in hiding.

THE PLANTAGENETS: KING HENRY IV

Edmund Mortimer, 5ᵗʰ Earl of March (b.1391, d.1425). His father was killed in Ireland 1398; his father's brother, also named Edmund, was the younger Edmund's promoter in claiming the throne.

Henry Percy, 1ˢᵗ Earl of Northumberland (b.1341, d.1408). Marshal of England 1377; Father of Sir Henry Percy (see below).

Sir Henry Percy, called Hotspur (b.1364, d.1403). English soldier. He plotted with his father, the Earl of Northumberland, to overthrow Henry IV; killed at the Battle of Shrewsbury.

Thomas Percy, 1ˢᵗ Earl of Worcester (b.1343, d.1403), supported his nephew, Sir Henry Percy (Hotspur). Beheaded at Shrewsbury.

Richard Scrope (b.c.1350, d.1405). Archbishop of York 1398 until his death by execution.

Henry Bolingbroke was chosen by Parliament to succeed his cousin King Richard II as King of England. Although a member of the Plantagenet family line, Henry was considered the first member of the Lancastrian branch as monarch.

There was much hostility towards Henry from the outset of his reign: the Earl of Kent and the Earl of Huntingdon planned to capture Henry during Christmas 1399 whilst he was at Windsor Castle. The scheme became known and immediately Henry left for London to avoid capture. The two earls were arrested, and without trials, they were beheaded.

Because many doubted that King Richard II had died, it was arranged for his body to be taken to London for proof, and for his burial at Westminster Abbey. This instigated Edmund Mortimer (the uncle) to lead a campaign for his nephew, the 5ᵗʰ Earl of March, as the rightful heir to King Richard II, being descended from the second son of King Edward III, whereas Henry Bolingbroke was descended from the third son.

In 1400 Owen Glendower of north Wales became an ally of the Mortimers and led a rebellion, which Henry failed to defeat.

Parliamentary procedures continued to be developed and the powers it had forfeited during the previous reign were restored. Parliament now began to prepare and present their own petitions, in addition to those presented for consideration by outside groups and bodies. Later these would be known as Parliamentary Bills. The King accepted these changes in order that he would receive the taxes to pay for the various military campaigns, all of them in Britain. Now Parliament required Henry's records of expenditure: nothing like this had been tolerated by previous monarchs.

In 1401, Parliament passed the infamous statute *De Haeratico Comburendo*: anyone convicted by the Church of heresy was to be executed by being burnt alive, the first such act for religious beliefs in England. It was aimed at John

Wyclif's sect, the Lollards, and many who did not retract their beliefs lost their lives in this way.

Parliament approved Henry's proposal that in future the eldest son of the King and to his male issue should inherit the Crown thereafter.

A very powerful and influential northern family were the Percys (the Earls of Northumberland, the Earls of Warwick, amongst their titles). An attack against the Scots by Henry failed, and, in revenge the Scots invaded England in 1402. In defeat many of the Scots were taken prisoner: the custom was for the victor to demand a ransom for the prisoners, but Henry refused to give his sanction on this occasion, and in doing so offended the Percys, who would have financially benefited.

Subsequently, an alliance against Henry comprising the Earl of Northumberland (Henry Percy), his son Harry Hotspur, the Earl of Douglas (a Scottish noble prisoner from the invasion of 1402), the Mortimers and Owen Glendower, culminated in the Battle of Shrewsbury in 1403. Seven thousand were killed, including Harry Hotspur, in probably the fiercest battle on English soil since the Battle of Hastings in 1066. Henry was victorious: in revenge the Earl of Worcester (Thomas Percy) was beheaded, but the Earl of Northumberland was reprieved.

In 1405 the Earl of Northumberland assembled an army of eight thousand men in Yorkshire to oppose the king; the battle was abandoned: a series of serious accusations were made against Henry. After the rebels dispersed two of the leaders, the Earl of Nottingham and the Archbishop of York (Richard Scrope), were arrested and beheaded.

At about this time the French planned to assist Owen Glendower against Henry, with some assistance from the Scots. The heir to the Scottish throne, the future James I of Scotland, was sailing to France when his ship was intercepted by the English; he was taken to London where he remained a prisoner for nearly twenty years. As a consequence the Scots ceased to cause problems.

In 1408 the Earl of Northumberland once again organized rebellion, and once again lost, but this time with his life. He was killed at the Battle of Bramham Moor, south of Harrogate, Yorkshire. This was the last rebellion against Henry.

Later in the year, Henry developed an illness after which he became an invalid for the rest of his life.

Parliament took advantage of Henry's failing health to exert its powers. It decided that foreigners should be expelled; the King's Council should include parliamentary leaders; and the royal household to be reorganized. The King's Council, now expanded with parliamentary leaders, demanded further powers and the King agreed to govern by their advice.

As the King's health declined, his son Prince Henry, the Prince of Wales, became involved in matters of State, but when he wanted more influence, even for his father to abdicate, Henry refused and in 1411 Prince Henry withdrew from all his official posts.

In the spring of 1413, Henry died in London at the age of 46. He was buried at Canterbury Cathedral, Kent.

PLANTAGENET (LANCASTRIAN)

KING HENRY V

Born	**1387 September 16**
Accession	**1413 March 21**
Age at Accession	**25**
Death	**1422 August 31**
Age at Death	**35**
Reigned	**9 years**

Henry V succeeded his father Henry IV.

In 1420 he married Catherine (b.1401, d.1437), daughter of Charles VI, King of France. They had 1 son.

Catherine married, secondly, Owen ap Meredith Tudor in 1428, and was grandmother of King Henry VII.

Persons of note:

Sir John Oldcastle (d.1317). A leader of the Lollards.

Richard of York, Earl of Cambridge (b.c.1374, d.1415).

Henry V had been involved in governing England for some five years until the quarrel with his father in 1411. He accepted the strengthened powers of Parliament and declared that no laws should be instituted without its assent. Lawyers now regarded Parliament as the High Court of all the law courts, and, they too assisted in its further development.

Henry attempted to reconcile the various factions in England by declaring a general pardon to all those who had been involved in rebellion and dissent. For those who continued to threaten him execution was likely.

John Wyclif's followers, the Lollards were continuing to cause problems with their religious activities by an uprising in 1414. Sir John Oldcastle, their leader, was arrested, escaped from the Tower of London, but recaptured in St Giles's Fields, London. In 1417 he was executed in accordance with the 1401 Statute *De Haeratico Comburendo*, that anyone convicted of heresy be executed by being burnt alive at the stake.

Henry learnt of a conspiracy, the Southampton Plot of 1415, led by Richard of York (who had married Anne, daughter of Roger Mortimer), Lord Scrope (a relative of the late Archbishop of York beheaded in 1405), and Sir Thomas Grey. All were arrested and executed.

During this period, the papacy did not consider England of great importance. At the 1414 Council of Constance, whereas each country had a vote, England was grouped as one with the German states.

Meanwhile, divisions between the Orleanists and the Burgundians split France. The King was weak: France was drifting without leadership and being vulnerable to outside influence; Henry revived the English claims to the French throne. Although they were tenuous, Parliament supported the King and voted taxes to promote his claims.

In a resumption of the Hundred Years' War, Henry maintained naval supremacy in the English Channel, and the invasion of France in 1415 culminated in the famous Battle of Agincourt (about thirty miles south of Calais) on October 25. In England's history to that date, it was their greatest of all land battles in continental Europe: seven thousand English defeating at least twenty thousand French forces. Five months after leaving England, Henry returned triumphantly: he was now considered the supreme military figure in Europe.

The next year Henry returned to France, for a successful campaign lasting three years, eventually reaching Paris, the capital. The Treaty of Troyes (south-east of Paris) of 1420 acknowledged that Henry would succeed to the monarchy of France on the death of King Charles VI, even though Charles had a son, the Dauphin; Charles VI's daughter, Catherine, would marry Henry; that Henry would govern France in consultation with a council composed of Frenchmen; and he would preserve all of their ancient customs.

While the French acknowledged Henry as heir to the French throne, the English Parliament began to have serious concerns of the constitutional position of the monarch, who could become monarch of a foreign country as well as England. Henry was requested to return to England for discussions. The Statute of 1340 guaranteed the freedom of the English from subjugation of a king, particularly, if he was king of a foreign country, which Henry could be in the future.

Shortly, Henry became ill and died whilst besieging Meaux, just east of

Paris, in 1422 at the age of 35. He was buried at Westminster Abbey, London.

Two months later the King of France, Charles VI, died at the age of 53.

The terms of the Treaty of Troyes of 1420 meant that the heir to both the English and French thrones was the nine-month-old Prince Henry, the child of Henry V and Queen Catherine.

PLANTAGENET (LANCASTRIAN)

KING HENRY VI

Born	1421 December 6
Accession	1422 August 31
Age at Accession	9 months old
Deposed – 1st time	1461 March 4
Reigned – 1st time	38 years
Restored	1470 October 30
Deposed – 2nd time	1471 April 11
Reigned – 2nd time	6 months
Death	1471 May 21
Age at Death	49

Henry VI succeeded his father Henry V.

In 1445 he married Margaret (b.1430, d.1482), daughter of Rene, Duke of Anjou. They had 1 son.

Family

Uncles, brothers of King Henry V:
Thomas, Duke of Clarence (b.1388, d.1421) killed at the Battle of Bauge. He had no legitimate children.
John, Duke of Bedford (b.1389, d.1435). Married twice but no children. He was Regent of France during Henry VI's minority.
Humphrey, Duke of Gloucester (b.1390, d.1447). Married twice but no children.

THE PLANTAGENETS: KING HENRY VI

The York family

> *Richard. 3ʳᵈ Duke of York (b.1411, d.1460), killed at the Battle of Wakefield. Heir presumptive to the throne from 1447 until Henry VI's son was born in 1453.*
> *Edward, son of 3ʳᵈ Duke of York (b.1442, d.1483). Became King Edward IV 1461, deposed 1470, and restored 1471.*

Henry VI's son

Edward, Prince of Wales (b.1453, d.1471) killed at the Battle of Tewkesbury. In 1470 he married Lady Anne Neville (b.1354, d.1485), daughter of Richard, Earl of Warwick. No children. (Lady Anne Neville married, secondly, King Richard III.)

Grandsons of John of Gaunt, who was a son of King Edward III

John Beaufort, 3ʳᵈ Earl of Somerset, created Duke of Somerset in 1443 (b.1404, d.1444). His grandson became King Henry VII, the first Tudor king.
Edmund Beaufort (b.c.1404, d.1455) succeeded his brother to become 4ᵗʰ Earl of Somerset. In 1448 became Duke of Somerset of the 2ⁿᵈ creation of the title. Killed at the Battle of St Albans.

Persons of note:

John de Mowbray, 3ʳᵈ Duke of Norfolk (b.1415, d.1461). Earl Marshal of England 1432.

Richard Neville, 5ᵗʰ Earl of Salisbury (b 1400, d.1460). Beheaded after capture at the Battle of Wakefield. Father of Earl of Warwick (see below).

Richard Neville, 14ᵗʰ Earl of Warwick (b.1428, d.1471). Known as the 'Kingmaker'. At first on the Yorkist side in the War of the Roses; he proclaimed the 4ᵗʰ Duke of York as King; later changed sides and restored the Lancastrian Henry VI as King. He was killed at the Battle of Barnet, in Hertfordshire.

William de la Pole, Earl of Suffolk (b.1396, d.1450). Elevated Duke of Suffolk. Onetime Lord Chancellor.

Earl of Shrewsbury (d.1460). Killed at the Battle of Northampton. Onetime Lord High Treasurer.

THE PLANTAGENETS: KING HENRY VI

St Joan of Arc (Jeanne d'Arc) (b.c.1413, d.1431). Born at Domreny, Champagne, France. Hearing 'voices in her head' led her to inspire the French to defeat the English and have the Dauphin (the heir to the French throne) crowned King of France.

Henry VI's reign was very eventful, commencing as a baby of nine-months-old, and heir to both the English and French thrones.

His uncles, the Duke of Bedford and the Duke of Gloucester were Regents to govern with a Council of Regency of influential nobles: the Duke of Bedford principally was responsible for France, being Regent and Commander-in-Chief.

The 15-year-old Dauphin, son of the deceased King Charles VI of France, received support of the French to be their monarch. Territorially, France was divided: the English controlled the country north of the Loire and Aquitaine; the rest recognized the Dauphin as their King Charles VII. England had an alliance with the Duke of Burgundy who maintained peace and co-operation in France under the terms of the 1420 Treaty of Troyes.

The Hundred Years' War continued in its intermittent manner. In 1429 an amazing girl of a peasant family inspired and encouraged the French forces with great success against the English. Joan of Arc (Jeanne d'Arc, also known as the Maid of Orleans, a town seventy miles south of Paris) motivated many French victories, enabling the Dauphin, as she had predicted, to be crowned at Rheims (north-east of Paris) as King of France. In May 1430 Joan of Arc was captured at Compiegne (north of Paris), handed-over to the English, tried, found guilty of heresy, and burnt to death at the stake in the market place of Rouen on May 30, 1431.

In England, a 1430 Act of Parliament removed the county franchise from many freemen; the voting rights of the knights were limited to those whose estates were worth forty shillings, so disenfranchising many of the lesser gentry.

Henry, at the age of 10 was taken to Paris to be crowned King of France despite the disapproval of the French population.

At a congress meeting in Arras (one hundred miles north of Paris) in 1453, the French made an offer for the English to abandon Henry's claim to their throne: it was rejected. To complicate the situation, the Duke of Bedford, Henry's Regent and Commander-in-Chief in France, died.

During this period of Regency rule, the Regency Council was divided by various factions, which weakened the rule of England. At a young age Henry regularly attended Council meetings and was involved in the foundation of Eton College, Berkshire, in 1440 and King's College, Cambridge University in 1441. With many people learning to read and write, benefactors were establishing independent schools in addition to the collegiate, cathedral and parish church schools.

THE PLANTAGENETS: KING HENRY VI

In France, many English garrisons were overrun, but eventually peace was negotiated; it was arranged that Henry would marry Margaret of Anjou, a niece of the late King Charles VI of France. When the full details of the peace agreement became general knowledge the Earl of Suffolk and others had the negotiator of the pact, the Duke of Gloucester, arraigned before Parliament, then sitting at St Edmundsbury (now Bury St Edmunds in Suffolk). He was imprisoned for treason and died, possibly murdered, in 1447. When it became known that territory in France had been surrendered, discontentment in England was widespread. The Earl of Suffolk was blamed for the disorder: in 1450 he was impeached. For his safety the King exiled him abroad for five years, but, during his journey the ship was intercepted and he was murdered by beheading.

For the first twenty-five years of his reign, his uncles and his Beaufort cousins guided Henry, the latter being descended from the illegitimate sons of John of Gaunt and his mistress Catherine Swynford (b.1350, d.1403) before their subsequent marriage. They were legitimized by a special Act of Parliament in 1407, during the reign of King Henry IV, but specifically debarred from succession to the throne. Although Lancastrians, there was hostility between them, struggling for influence in the Council of Regency.

At the death of Henry's last uncle, the Duke of Gloucester in 1447 and without any heirs of the uncles, Richard, the 3rd Duke of York, became heir presumptive. Many considered that he had justifiable claims to the throne but there were fears that Henry might amend the 1407 Act to give Edmund Beaufort (4th Earl of Somerset) a claim to the throne, which was considered superior to that of the Duke of York. Concerned, the Duke of York and his allies demanded that he be appointed to the government: to support his claim he raised an army in 1452, mainly from men returning from France, and marched to London, but, realizing that he lacked overwhelming support he declared his loyalty personally to the King who accepted his allegiance and sent him to Calais as Constable for three years.

In 1453 a son was born to Henry and Queen Margaret, displacing the Duke of York as heir presumptive to the Crown. The Duke swore allegiance to the new Prince.

The Hundred Years' War came to an end in 1453. England had lost most of its French territory except the Channel Islands and Calais, but the enormous cost of protecting Calais was equal to one-third of the annual revenue granted to the King by Parliament.

In 1453, Henry had an attack if insanity, an illness that would affect him periodically for the rest of his life. The Duke of York, chosen as Regent during the illness appointed his own supporters into royal positions, displacing many of Henry's appointments including Edmund Beaufort (now elevated Duke of Somerset) whom he imprisoned in the Tower of London. Both Houses of Parliament gave approval to the Duke of York. Henry in due course regained his faculties and restored the Duke of Somerset to his former post and sent the Duke of York back to Calais as Constable.

The Duke of York was no longer a member of the King's Council but when summoned to a Great Council at Leicester in 1455, he feared for his life. Instead of attending he went to Sandal, in Yorkshire, met with the Earl of Warwick and the Earl of Salisbury and joined forces with those of the Duke of Norfolk and the Earl of Shrewsbury to oppose the King's forces (the Lancastrians) at St Albans, in Hertfordshire. The intention was not to seize the Crown; it was a struggle to gain control of the Council. The Duke of York was successful, defeating the Lancastrians, killing Edmund Beaufort (Duke of Somerset) and successfully capturing Henry. The Duke of York declared his allegiance to the detained King: Parliament was summoned to legalize the situation. Henry remained monarch under the control of the Duke, now appointed Regent. Between 1456 and 1459 efforts of reconciliation were attempted: the running of the country continued with the King, under restriction, the Queen, the Duke of York and both factions attending governmental functions together.

The War of the Roses was a civil war between two rival factions of the Plantagenets. Henry was the great-grandson of John of Gaunt (the Duke of Lancaster); Richard (the 3rd Duke of York) was the grandson of Edmund of Langley (the 1st Duke of York); John of Gaunt and Edmund Langley were brothers, the sons of King Edward III. The war was between these families and their supporters not, as is the usual misconception, between the counties of Lancashire and Yorkshire.

Queen Margaret began to assert a strong presence in defending her son's position as heir to the throne, never ceasing to plot against the Yorkists. In September 1459 her forces were defeated at Blore Heath, Staffordshire; it is thought three thousand died in the battle of which two thousand were fighting for Queen Margaret. A month later they were victorious at Ludford Bridge, Ludlow, Shropshire: defeated, the Earl of Warwick and the Earl of Salisbury fled to Calais, the Duke of York to Ireland.

The Yorkists regrouped and returned to England. The Earl of Warwick received papal support together with that of some bishops and both Houses of Parliament. The Yorkists with twenty thousand men defeated the Lancastrians with ten thousand men at Northampton in 1460. Henry, previously having been freed, was recaptured. This time he was forced to agree to humiliating conditions, being that he could remain the monarch for the rest of his life, but that the Duke of York would govern and take the crown on Henry's death, so disinheriting Henry's son and heir, the Prince of Wales.

The Queen and the Prince of Wales remained free at Harlech Castle, in north Wales, where she re-organized her supporters. Later in 1460 the antagonists battled at Wakefield, Yorkshire, where the Yorkists were heavily defeated, having eight thousand troops against the Lancastrians of eighteen thousand. The Duke of York and his 17-year-old son, the Earl of Richmond, were killed. The Earl of Shrewsbury and the Earl of Salisbury were captured and beheaded.

After a battle at Mortimer's Cross, Herefordshire, the second Battle of St Albans in February 1461 resulted in another crushing defeat for the Yorkists. The King was found and released from captivity, but the Earl of Warwick and the

Duke of Norfolk escaped. Queen Margaret, in error, delayed going to London to consolidate the victory and to re-instate Henry as King. This gave the opportunity for the young Duke of York (Edward, the son of Richard) and the Earl of Warwick to reach the capital first, where the people welcomed them with great enthusiasm.

The 18-year-old Duke of York claimed the Crown; was declared King Edward IV on March 4, 1461 with the approval and confirmation of Parliament.

Henry VI was deposed as King of England. He went into hiding.

In 1465 Henry was captured at Clitheroe, Lancashire, and imprisoned. He was released from captivity at the Tower of London and restored as monarch on October 30, 1470, and presented to the people of London as King of England, but he had neither power nor influence.

Within seven months King Edward IV regained the throne; Henry was deposed a second time and died, probably murdered on May 21, 1471. He was buried at Windsor Castle, Berkshire.

PLANTAGENET (YORKIST)

KING EDWARD IV

Born	1442 April 28
Accession	1461 March 4
Age at Accession	18
Deposed	1470 October 30
Restored	1471 April 11
Death	1483 April 9
Age at Death	40
Reigned	22 years

Edward IV seized the throne from Henry VI. Both were descendents of King Edward III, who reigned from 1327 to 1377. He was the second son (the eldest died as an infant) of Richard, the 3rd Duke of York, who was killed at the Battle of Wakefield in 1460. Edward became the 4th Duke of York.

In 1464 he married, a secret kept for five months, Elizabeth Woodville (b.1437, d.1492), a daughter of Sir Richard Woodville, later conferred Earl Rivers. They had 4 sons and 6 daughters. Elizabeth was the widow of Sir John Grey (the Lord Ferrers). (There are various spellings of the surname Woodville.)

Prince George (Duke of Clarence) (b.1449, d.1478), Edward IV's brother, was murdered at the Tower of London.

Prince Richard (Duke of Gloucester) (b.1452, d.1485), Edward IV's youngest brother, became King Richard III in 1483. Killed at the Battle of Bosworth Field, Leicestershire.

Princess Elizabeth of York (b.1466, d.1503), Edward IV's eldest daughter, married Henry Tudor, who became King Henry VII in 1486.

THE PLANTAGENETS: KING EDWARD IV

Persons of note:

Henry Beaufort, 3rd Duke of Somerset (b.1436, d.1464). Killed at the Battle of Hexham, Northumberland.

Edmund Beaufort, 4th Duke of Somerset (b.1438, d d.1471), brother of the 3rd Duke of Somerset. Caught and beheaded at the Battle of Tewkesbury, Gloucestershire.

William Caxton (b.c.1422, d.1491). The first English printer and publisher. Formerly a cloth merchant.

Sir John Conyers (d.1469), a relation by marriage to the Earl of Warwick.

Sir John Grey, (7th Lord Ferrers) (b.1432, d.1460). The 1st husband of Elizabeth Woodville who subsequently secretly married Edward IV in 1464.

Sir William Herbert (d.1469), 1st Earl of Pembroke. Beheaded.

Richard Neville, 14th Earl of Warwick (b.1428, d.1471). Known as the 'Kingmaker'. At first on the Yorkist side in the War of the Roses; he proclaimed the 4th Duke of York as King; later changed sides and restored the Lancastrian King Henry VI as King. He was killed at the Battle of Barnet, Hertfordshire.

John Neville, the Earl of Northumberland and Marquess of Montagu (b.c.1431, d.1471); the earldom was forfeited in 1470. He was the son of 5th Earl of Salisbury. Killed at the Battle of Barnet, Hertfordshire.

George Neville (b.c.1432, d.1476). Archbishop of York and Chancellor.

Lady Anne Neville (b.1456, d.1485), youngest daughter of the 14th Earl of Warwick. She married in 1470 Edward, Prince of Wales, son and heir of King Henry VI. Edward was killed at the Battle of Tewkesbury in 1471, and after Kind Henry's death she married King Richard III.

Sir Ralph Percy (d.1464). Grandson of Sir Henry Percy (see King Henry IV chapter). Killed at the Battle of Hedgeley Moor, Northumberland.

Humphrey Stafford (d.1469). Created Earl of Devon in May 1469; executed in August.

THE PLANTAGENETS: KING EDWARD IV

Sir Richard Woodville, Earl Rivers. His daughter married Edward IV. He was beheaded in 1483.

Edward, the 18-year-old 4th Duke of York, was declared King Edward IV on March 4, 1461, which was confirmed by Parliament.

King Henry VI's French born wife, Queen Margaret, was determined that her husband be returned to the throne and that their son and heir Prince Edward, the Prince of Wales, should not be disinherited from succession. She conspired with anyone who would support their cause. The new King pursued her forces to Towton, south of York, this being one was the fiercest battle of the War of the Roses, and it ended in almost total annihilation of the Lancastrians. In total more than seventy-five thousand troops, almost evenly divided, were involved in the battle.

Three months later on June 28, 1461, the Duke of York was crowned King of England at Westminster Abbey, the first of the Yorkists.

In 1462 with the support of King Louis XI of France, Queen Margaret gained support in the north. Edward IV destroyed the castles inhabited by her supporters in revenge. The Duke of Somerset and Sir Ralph Percy were captured: on swearing allegiances to Edward they were given freedom to retain their estates. Edward often showed mercy to his enemies of noble rank.

The following year, 1463, Sir Ralph Percy betrayed Edward to assist Queen Margaret in the next attempt to regain the throne for her husband, but again the King was victorious. Queen Margaret and the Prince of Wales fled to France whilst Henry hid in the valleys of Cumberland. Again the Queen returned to England, this time she was captured at Northam Castle, Durham; the soldiers wanted her beheaded, but she was allowed to escape. On April 28, 1464, at Hedgeley Moor, near Hexham in Northumberland, the Duke of Somerset changed allegiances to support Henry in the battle, but Edward's forces (the Yorkists) with the support of the Earl of Warwick destroyed the Lancastrians.

On May 15 at the Battle of Hexham, Northumberland, the Duke of Somerset was captured and beheaded. In the following weeks many dozens of Lancastrian supporting noblemen and squires were executed. Henry was captured at Clitheroe, Lancashire, in 1465, and imprisoned at the Tower of London.

Edward had secretly married Elizabeth Woodville in May 1464. He was 22 years of age; Elizabeth was 27 and had two young sons from her previous marriage to Lord Ferrers. Some five months later when Edward's marriage became known there was great consternation.

The Neville family had become paramount. Richard Neville (14th Earl of Warwick), John Neville (Earl of Northumberland), and George Neville (Archbishop of York and Chancellor) now controlled the government. The young King allowed the Nevilles the power to enable him to enjoy a life of pleasure: he had a number of mistresses

The country was not being appropriately governed: Parliament was seldom summoned; the Nevilles and their relatives exerted control over the judges and justices by bribery and intimidation.

Edward began to raise members of the Woodville family to the peerage and appoint them to positions of influence. Gradually, the Nevilles' power began to be undermined. After quarrelling with Edward, the Nevilles approached Edward's brother Prince George (the Duke of Clarence) for support. Soon in 1467 George Neville was dismissed as Chancellor, and Richard Neville (the Earl of Warwick) was sent overseas.

In 1468 Edward's sister, Princess Margaret married Charles the Bold (the Duke of Burgundy) who supported the Lancastrians. In defiance of his brother, Prince George (Duke of Clarence) married Isabel, daughter of Richard Neville (Earl of Warwick) in July 1469.

The country was in turmoil. The House of Commons petitioned the King against the lax and profuse administration: in Yorkshire under the leadership of Sir John Conyers, a relation by marriage to Richard Neville, there was a protest against an obnoxious tax. Edward was forced to counter this rebellion. It gave Richard Neville, George Neville (still Archbishop of York) and Prince George a reason to oppose Edward: now his allies were on the side of the Lancastrians.

In 1469 in a battle at Edgeworth, near Banbury, Oxfordshire, forces led by the Earl of Pembroke and the Earl of Devon, intending to join up with Edward, were overwhelmingly defeated by the Lancastrians, losing nearly two hundred knights and squires. Both of the Earls were captured and beheaded. Soon afterwards at Olney, in Buckinghamshire, Edward realized that he had been captured by his former allies, Richard Neville (the Earl of Warwick) and his own brother, Prince George. At this time, Richard Neville, known as the 'Kingmaker' had both King Henry VI and King Edward IV as prisoners, one in the Tower of London and the other at Middleham, Yorkshire, the home of George Neville (the Archbishop of York).

Edward convinced his captors that he would amend his ways; to pardon all who had conspired against him. He was released only to renew the war again; this time he was victorious in defeating the Lancastrians and having their leaders executed.

March 1470 was the beginning of a tumultuous period of deceit, changing sides and double-dealings. A Lancastrian rebellion in Lincolnshire was repulsed when both the Earl of Warwick and Prince George were betrayed: they refused Edward's summons for treason and fled to France for their safety.

King Louis XI of France persuaded Queen Margaret and the Earl of Warwick to join together in an attempt to restore King Henry VI to the English throne. To seal the alliance it was agreed for the 17-year-old Prince Edward, the Prince of Wales, should marry Lady Anne Neville, the 14-year-old youngest daughter of the Earl of Warwick. In August 1470 they married.

By September 1470, the Earl of Warwick was ready to depose Edward as

King. In the plan, a cousin in Yorkshire started an insurrection to draw Edward's troops to the north of England, leaving the south of England defenceless. From France, the Earl of Warwick landed his forces at Dartmouth, Devon, and marched to London unopposed. Henry was released from the Tower of London and restored to the throne on October 30, 1470; Edward narrowly escaped capture by seeking refuge in France with his brother-in-law, the Duke of Burgundy; Parliament was summoned to reverse the previous legislation that had disinherited Henry, which they did.

King Henry VI was King of England, again.

Because of the uncertain situation it was decided that Queen Margaret and the Prince of Wales would remain in France.

Now it was the deposed Edward's turn to prepare an invasion of England. In a well-planned and co-ordinated scheme in March 1471 his forces landed at several locations on the east coast of England, each with London as their ultimate destination. This time Edward had greater support; at the town of Warwick he proclaimed himself King of England; Prince George had changed sides again, this time to support his brother. Edward and the Yorkists faced their former allies, the Nevilles, and the Lancastrians at the Battle of Barnet, north of London, on April 14, 1471. Richard Neville (Earl of Warwick) was caught and killed.

Meanwhile, Queen Margaret and the Prince of Wales landed at Weymouth, Dorset to travel to Wales to be with their allies. On the journey they were intercepted by the Yorkists. At the Battle of Tewkesbury, Gloucestershire, on May 4, the Prince of Wales was killed on the battlefield; Queen Margaret was captured; Edmund Beaufort (4th Duke of Somerset) was caught and beheaded. Queen Margaret was kept in captivity until Louis XI of France paid a substantial ransom for her release.

King Henry VI was deposed for a second time and died, probably murdered, on May 21, 1471.

King Edward IV was King of England, again.

Parliament provided the finance and urged Edward to invade France with assistance from the Duke of Burgundy, to recover the lost English possessions of western France. The invasion of 1475 had a force of thirteen thousand men, the largest army that had left England, to that time. Edward and the French King really only wanted peace: the Treaty of Picquigny, near Amiens, provided a cash sum and an annuity to Edward.

Therefore, Edward became financially independent and did not need to regularly summon Parliament for his income, which was further supplemented from the sequestrated Lancastrian estates.

The peace in Europe, with law and order restored in England, benefited the country; trade expanded to provide wealth. In 1476 under Edward's patronage, William Caxton established his printing press at Westminster, London.

Edward's brother, Prince George (Duke of Clarence) questioned the validity of Edward's marriage to Elizabeth Woodville: if proved, the two surviving sons, Prince Edward and Prince Richard, would be, *de facto*, illegitimate. In this situation,

Prince George would be heir to the throne. Further, Prince George, now widowed, proposed to marry May, Duchess of Burgundy, which was opposed by Edward.

Fearing that Prince George was planning a rebellion, Edward had Parliament pass a Bill of Attainder: the sentence of death was carried-out secretly at the Tower of London in 1478. He was executed, Shakespeare wrote, by drowning in a butt of Malmesey Wine.

The only real problem facing Edward in his later years was Wales and the Welsh Marches. He was able to control their rebelliousness.

Edward died in April 1483 after ten days of illness, at the age of 40. He was the first king since King Henry II to die without debts, but once again a minor was to inherit the Crown.

Edward rebuilt St George's Chapel, Windsor, Berkshire, towards the end of his reign, where he was buried.

PLANTAGENET (YORKIST)

KING EDWARD V

Born	**1470 November 2**
Accession	**1483 April 9**
Age at Accession	**12**
Deposed	**1483 June 22**
Reigned	**2 months**
Death	**1483**

Edward V succeeded his father Edward IV.

He was unmarried.

Prince Richard (Duke of York) was Edward V's younger surviving brother. Born August 17, 1473, and in 1478 was married to Anne, the daughter of John Mowbray (Duke of Norfolk).

The brothers, Edward V and Prince Richard (Duke of York) were murdered at the Tower of London, about June 23, 1483.

Prince Richard (Duke of Gloucester) (b.1452, d.1485). Youngest brother of King Edward IV, uncle to the princes (above), became King Richard III. Killed at the Battle of Bosworth Field, Leicestershire.

Persons of note:

William Hastings (Lord Hastings) (d.1483). Lord Chancellor 1461. Beheaded.

Henry Stafford (2nd Duke of Buckingham) (b.c.1454, d.1483). Married Catherine Woodville, sister-in-law of King Edward IV, and a descendant of King Edward III. Beheaded.

THE PLANTAGENETS: KING EDWARD V

Sir Richard Woodville, Earl Rivers (d.1483). His daughter Elizabeth married King Edward IV, the mother of Edward V and Prince Richard (Duke of York). Beheaded.

The accession of the 12-year-old Edward V to the throne on the unexpected death of his father created problems for the monarchy and the country. His father's brother, Prince Richard (Duke of Gloucester), questioned the legality of the marriage between King Edward IV and Elizabeth Woodville.

At the time of his father's death, Edward was living with Earl Rivers at Ludlow, Shropshire. It had been arranged that Earl Rivers should take the young King to London for the Coronation.

At Northampton, the Earl and his party were intercepted by the appointed Protector of Edward, Prince Richard (Duke of Gloucester) and the Duke of Buckingham, who then imprisoned most of the group. Edward was taken to London on May 4. When the Coronation was postponed, the concerned members of the King's Council were informed that any disturbances would cause further delay.

Queen Elizabeth (Woodville) took her other children to Westminster for safety. She was persuaded to allow Prince Richard (Duke of York) to join Edward at the Tower of London for companionship.

William Hastings (Lord Hastings), who had been advisor to King Edward IV in the latter part of the reign, was strongly against the power and influence of the Woodville's, but equally concerned that the Protector was gaining too much power. Prince Richard (Duke of Gloucester) aware of this situation, had Lord Hastings arrested and without a trial, beheaded at the Tower of London on June 13, 1483.

The following day Earl Rivers, friends and supporters were all executed.

The final sequence of events of Edward's short reign remains a mystery, but it seems that the peers offered the Crown to Prince Richard (Duke of Gloucester), which he duly accepted and claimed on June 23, 1483.

Edward and his brother, Prince Richard (Duke of York), were never seen alive again. In 1674 two skeletons were discovered of children, of an appropriate age, when the staircase leading to the chapel in the White Tower of the Tower of London was being altered. These remains were interned in Henry VIII's Chapel at Westminster Abbey.

PLANTAGENET (YORKIST)

KING RICHARD III

Born	**1452 October 2**
Accession	**1483 June 23**
Age at Accession	**30**
Death	**1485 August 22**
Age at Death	**32**
Reigned	**2 years**

Richard III, petitioned by Parliament to assume the throne, succeeded his 12-year-old nephew Edward V as King. He was the younger brother of King Edward IV.

In 1472 he married Lady Anne Neville (b.c.1454, d.1485), daughter of Richard Neville (Earl of Warwick). She was the widow of Edward, Prince of Wales (the son of King Henry VI), who was killed at the Battle of Tewkesbury in 1471 at the age of 18. Richard and Anne had 1 son, Edward (b.1471, d.1484), who was created Prince of Wales.

Persons of note:

Henry Stafford (2nd Duke of Buckingham) (b.c.1454, d.1483). Married Catherine Woodville, sister-in-law of King Edward IV, and a descendant of King Edward III. Beheaded.

Henry Tudor (Earl of Richmond) (b.1457, d.1509). Became King Henry VII.

THE PLANTAGENETS: KING RICHARD III

On June 25, 1483 Parliament declared the marriage of King Edward IV and Elizabeth Woodville not to have been valid; consequently their children were deemed illegitimate. Parliament petitioned Prince Richard (Duke of Gloucester), now considered heir to the throne, to assume the Crown. The Coronation was held on July 6.

In September, Richard's 10-year-old son was created Prince of Wales; this virtually confirmed that King Edward V and his brother Prince Richard (Duke of York) were dead.

There was hostility towards Richard, whom many considered responsible for the apparent deaths of his nephews, the Princes.

During October, Henry Stafford (Duke of Buckingham) planned a rebellion to depose the new King and install Henry Tudor (Earl of Richmond), a Lancastrian supporter on the throne. Richard defeated the uprising of his former ally, had him beheaded and many others executed. Henry Tudor escaped to France where previously he had lived in safety for many years. Order in England was restored.

The Dukedom of Norfolk is the oldest *existing* ducal title, which was created in 1483. The present incumbent is the Premier Duke and Earl of England.

In 1484 Richard instituted a series of beneficial reforms in the procedures of government and updated the system for the collection of taxes. The Church was given increased influence in the patronage of education and the endowment of religious foundations.

In April, Richard's only son Prince Edward, Prince of Wales, died at the age of 11. Richard's wife, Queen Anne, died in 1485.

In 1485 Henry Tudor, a distant cousin, and now heir presumptive to the throne, organized another rebellion. Richard responded by issuing decrees that every county throughout England must send a complement of men, to assemble in Nottingham, to form a defensive force.

On August 7, Henry Tudor (Earl of Richmond) landed with troops at Milford Haven, west Wales, and increased the size of his force as men joined in support.

The opposing forces clashed near Market Bosworth, Leicestershire, on Sunday August 21, 1485. Initially, Richard out-numbered Henry Tudor, ten thousand against five thousand, but then three thousand troops from Lancashire and Cheshire changed sides to join Henry Tudor. The King was killed early in the fighting. Henry Tudor, a Lancastrian supporter, won this famous and decisive victory at the Battle of Bosworth Field.

The War of the Roses, commenced thirty years earlier, had almost come to its conclusion. So many Yorkist and Lancastrian noblemen and leaders had been killed and executed there were hardly any left as successors: agreement was reached in which the survivors could be reconciled.

Sir Thomas More and William Shakespeare both depicted Richard as a physical monster, crookbacked and with a withered arm. No one in his lifetime remarked or recorded such details. Richard was the last of the Plantagenet Kings: the crown was passed to a distant cousin.

Richard's reign lasted just over two years, the Yorkist branch of the Plantagenets for twenty-four years. He was 32 years old at his death and was buried at Greyfriars Church, Leicester.

THE TUDORS

Monarch	Reigned	Family
Henry VII	1485 to 1509	Great-great-great-grandson of Edward III
Henry VIII	1509 to 1547	Son of Henry VII
Edward VI	1547 to 1553	Son of Henry VIII
Jane (Lady Jane Grey)	1553	Great-granddaughter of Henry VII
Mary I	1553 to 1558	Daughter of Henry VIII
Elizabeth I	1558 to 1603	Daughter of Henry VIII

TUDOR

KING HENRY VII

Born	**1457 January 28**
Accession	**1485 August 22**
Age at Accession	**28**
Death	**1509 April 21**
Age at Death	**52**
Reigned	**23 years**

Henry Tudor (Duke of Richmond) was proclaimed King Henry VII of England by right of conquest. He was a distant cousin of Richard III, having descended from King Edward III, from John of Gaunt and the Beaufort/Somerset line.

In 1486 he married Elizabeth of York (b.1466, d.1503), eldest daughter of King Edward IV and sister of King Edward V. They had 3 sons and 3 daughters.

The eldest son, Prince Arthur (Prince of Wales) (b.1486, d.1502), married in 1501 Catherine, Princess of Aragon (b.1485, d.1536), daughter of Ferdinand V, King of Castille and Aragon. They had no children. She married, secondly, Prince Arthur's brother, Prince Henry.

Persons of note:

Prince Edward (Earl of Warwick) (b.1475, d.1499), son of Prince George (Duke of Clarence), was the last of the Plantagenet line. He was beheaded.

King James IV of Scotland (b.1473, d.1517). King of Scotland from 1488. Married in 1503 Princess Margaret (b.1489, d.1541), daughter of Henry VII.

Giovanni Caboto (known as John Cabot) (b.c.1450, d.1499). Navigator and explorer who by his voyages in 1497 and 1498 helped lay the foundation for the later English claims to Canada and North America.

THE TUDORS: KING HENRY VII

John Colet (b.1466, d.1519). Theologian and founder of St Paul's School, London, who was one of the chief Tudor humanist and promoted Renaissance culture in England.

Desiderius Erasmus (known as Erasmus of Amsterdam or Dutch Erasmus) (b.c.1466, d.1536). Dutch scholar and humanist who worked to revive classical texts from antiquity.

Francis Lovell (1ˢᵗ Viscount Lovell) (b. and d. unknown). An active Yorkist who made an ineffective attempt to unseat Henry VII.

Sir Thomas More (b.1478, d.1535). Scholar and writer. Knighted (1521), Lord Chancellor (1529 to 1532). He was beheaded. Canonized.

John de la Pole (Earl of Lincoln) (b.1462, d.1487). Eldest son of 2ⁿᵈ Duke of Suffolk. Killed in November 1487.

Lambert Simnel (b.c.1477, d.1534). Fraudulent pretender to the English throne.

Perkin Warbeck (b.c.1474, d.1499). Flemish born impostor. After unsuccessful sieges, he was captured, tried and executed.

Parliament proclaimed Henry Tudor as King of England, Henry VII, by right of his conquest over King Richard III at Bosworth Field, Leicestershire. He gave England the strong and determined leadership it required after years of upheaval during the War of the Roses.

The end of the Plantagenets and the beginning of the Tudors is considered a period of historic change from medievalism transformed into the middle-ages, seeing the emancipation of an educated middle-class with English as the language; an increase in manufacturing, particularly, wool and cloth.

There were several princes who could have made a claim to the throne, but Henry, a Lancastrian, by marrying Elizabeth of York (daughter of King Edward IV), strengthened the monarchy and his own position.

The first serious challenge to Henry came from the Yorkists. An impostor, 10-year-old Lambert Simnel, was purported to be Prince Edward (Earl of Warwick), the son of Prince George (Duke of Clarence).

Supported, amongst others, by the Earl of Lincoln and Viscount Lovell (King Richard III's Chamberlain), an army of eight thousand were defeated by Henry's army of twelve thousand on June 16, 1487 at the Battle of Stoke (East Stoke, near Newark, Nottingham), the final battle of the War of the Roses. Lambert Simnel was pardoned and taken into the King's service. Half of the Earl of Lincoln's army, which included mercenaries from Ireland and Germany, were killed.

A second impostor caused greater problems. From 1492 Perkin Warbeck purported to be Prince Richard (Duke of York), one of the murdered princes in the Tower of London. He received support from discontented Yorkists living in Ireland, the Burgundians, the Kings of France and Scotland, and others. When Perkin Warbeck sought French support, Henry threatened France with war: Parliament was summoned and agreed to raise the necessary taxes.

The French King weakened by being under threat from some of his neighbours made peace with Henry: the Treaty of Estaples (south of Boulogne) provided Henry with a large cash sum and annuity. Further, Perkin Warbeck was banned from re-entering France.

The 1490s was a period of sailing and discovering new lands. The Spanish and Portuguese were the early explorers, especially Christopher Columbus, an Italian employed by the Spanish. In 1493 Pope Alexander VI, by his various papal bulls, divided areas of the 'New World' exclusively between Spain and Portugal for occupation and trade to the disadvantage of other countries including England.

To enforce earlier Acts of Parliament, a new Navigation Act compelled only English ships to be used for foreign trade – importing and exporting – when using English ports.

In Ireland, England's jurisdiction at this time extended to about thirty miles from Dundalk to Dublin. In 1494, Sir Edward Poynings, the Lord Deputy of Ireland, ensured that the Irish Parliament passed laws which made the English Parliament superior and paramount to its own, partly to reduce the powers of the nobles, including Yorkists, who lived in Ireland.

The demand for increased taxes caused disturbances in 1497. In order to control and reduce spending many civic appointments were transferred to the squires and burgesses, e.g. Justices of the Peace, and were or became honorary unpaid positions. This was accepted and continues to the present day, although nowadays Justices of the Peace (JPs) are chosen from the whole population.

Perkin Warbeck's disruption came to an end with his capture in 1497, and two years later, after two failed attempts to escape, he was executed by hanging. Prince Edward (Earl of Warwick) who had been imprisoned all this time in the Tower of London and had been involved in the attempted escapes was executed by beheading in 1499.

In 1497 Giovanni Caboto, known to the English as John Cabot, an explorer from Genoa, Italy, led the first English expedition to what is now known as North America. Under letters patent from Henry, he sailed from Bristol with a crew of eighteen in a small ship known as Matthew, discovering Newfoundland and Nova Scotia, believing it to be part of Asia. Later, he explored the whole east coast of North America as far south as Florida. English claims for territory remained dormant for several generations owing to Henry not wanting to antagonize the Pope over the decrees of the 'New World'.

In religion, there was a small revival of the Lollards: as previously, those who did not retract their beliefs were sent to the stakes for death by burning.

Henry gained confidence to exert his authority: he prohibited personal armies of noblemen; for those who swore allegiance to him their lives and properties were secure.

The King's Council, Parliament (which did not meet regularly during Henry's reign), Common Law, Justices of the Peace and the jury system had declined during the previous fifty years of disruption: these institutions had their powers restored. The King's Council was expanded to have specialist sub-committees, e.g. foreign affairs, financial matters.

The Court of the Star Chamber, consisting of judges who were appointed by the Crown, met regularly at Westminster trying cases that needed special jurisdiction. It was popular because it supported the weak from the strong. The law courts recovered their independence and were no longer intimidated by local influences or persons. Should juries fail to give a satisfactory verdict based on the presented facts, the jury could be called before the Court of the Star Chamber to defend their decisions.

The Italian Renaissance movement was given prominence in England by three friends, Desiderius Erasmus (known at Dutch Erasmus), John Colet (who studied at Oxford and in Italy) and Sir Thomas More. The Old Testament was being studied and taught from the original Hebrew, and the New Testament from the original Greek. In 1505 John Colet was appointed Dean of St Paul's Cathedral and in due course he founded and endowed St Paul's School in London, one of the famous English schools.

As in the past when peace or intrigue was beneficial, marriages were arranged. In 1501, Henry's 15-year-old son and heir, Prince Arthur (the Prince of Wales) was married to Catherine of Aragon, the 16-year-old daughter of Ferdinand V, King of Castille and Aragon (Spain), but Prince Arthur died seven months later. Henry's 14-year-old daughter, Princess Margaret, married the 30-year-old King James IV of Scotland in 1503: it was desired that the marriage would increase English influence in Scotland, to the disadvantage of the French.

It was proposed that the widowed Catherine of Aragon should marry Henry's next son and now heir, Prince Henry. This was not permitted: the laws of the Church prohibited a brother marrying his dead brother's wife, but in 1503, a Papal Bull gave dispensation which implied that as the marriage had not been consummated, Prince Henry and Catherine could marry. This did not occur until Prince Henry became King.

In 1506, Philip of Burgundy, previously an opponent of Henry, was shipwrecked off the English coast and arrested. Before he was released Philip was forced to sign a commercial treaty, which opened the way for increasing the exporting of wool from England.

THE TUDORS: KING HENRY VII

Henry was involved in most aspects in the country's running and development. By the end of his reign of twenty-three years, trade and commercial dealings had made England very prosperous and powerful.

At his death in 1509, Henry was entombed in the Chapel at Westminster Abbey, London, dedicated to his name.

TUDOR

KING HENRY VIII

Born	**1491 June 28**
Accession	**1509 April 21**
Age at Accession	**17**
Death	**1547 January 28**
Age at Death	**55**
Reigned	**37 years**

Henry VIII succeeded his father Henry VII. His elder brother, Prince Arthur (Prince of Wales), born 1486, died in 1502.

Wives

1509, firstly: Catherine of Aragon (Spain), daughter of Ferdinand V, King of Castille and Aragon. She was the widow of Henry's late brother, Prince Arthur. They had 6 children, including 2 sons, but all were either stillborn or died in early infancy, except one daughter, Princess Mary. Their marriage was annulled in 1533. Born in 1485, she died naturally in January 1536.

1533, secondly: Anne, daughter of Sir Thomas Boleyn. They had 2 children, one stillborn and a daughter, Princess Elizabeth. The marriage ended when Anne was beheaded in May 1536. It is thought that she was born in 1507.

1536, thirdly: Jane, daughter of Sir John Seymour. They had 1 son, Prince Edward. Jane was born about 1509 and died in 1537 in childbirth.

1540, fourthly: Anne, daughter of John, Duke of Cleves (in modern day Germany). The marriage was annulled six months later. They had no children. Born in 1515, she died in 1557.

1540, fifthly: Catherine, daughter of Lord Edward Howard. They had no children. She was beheaded in 1542. It is thought she was born in 1523.

1543, sixthly: Catherine, daughter of Sir Thomas Parr. They had no children. She had been twice widowed in 1529 and c.1542 before marrying Henry. After his death she married, a fourth time, but died in childbirth in September 1548. She was born in 1512.

Persons of note:

King James IV of Scotland (b.1473, d.1513). Married Princess Margaret, sister of Henry VIII. James was killed at the Battle of Flodden, south-east of Coldstream, Northumberland.

Thomas Cranmer (b.1478, d.1556). Archbishop of Canterbury, 1533 to 1553. A leading reformer, he worked on the English Prayer Books of 1549 and 1552. Death by burning at the stake.

Thomas Cromwell (Earl of Essex) (b.c.1485, d.1540). English lawyer and statesman who devised the legislation that made the English Church independent of Rome, culminating in the Act of Supremacy (1534). From 1536 he supervised the dissolution of the monasteries. He lost favour of the King, was accused of treason and executed.

Thomas Howard (3rd Duke of Norfolk) (b.1473, d.1554). Soldier and politician. He fought at the Battle of Flodden (1513); president of Henry VIII's King's Council; fell from power after the execution of Catherine Howard, his niece.

Henry Howard (Earl of Surrey) (b.c.1517, d.1547). Son of 3rd Duke of Norfolk (see above). Executed for treason.

Hugh Latimer (b.c.1485, d.1555). English churchman during the Reformation, who became Bishop of Worcester (1535). He was condemned as a heretic and burned at the stake.

Sir Thomas More (b.1478, d.1535). Scholar and writer. Knighted (1521); Lord Chancellor (1529 to 1532); he was beheaded; canonized.

William Tyndale (b.c.1494, d.1536). Protestant reformer and translator of the Holy Bible that became the basis of the Authorised King James version. He was strangled and burnt at the stake at Vilvorde (in modern day Belgium).

Thomas Wolsey (b.c.1475, d.1530). Bishop of Lincoln; Archbishop of York (1514); Cardinal and Lord Chancellor of England (1515); prosecuted (1529); and arrested for high treason (1530).

Henry VIII was 17 years old when he succeeded his father in April 1509. He retained his father's advisors, giving continuity in the governance of England. France was regaining its power; Spain had become influential and was developing its economy; and Calais remained under English rule. The papacy had been quite benign in English affairs for more than a hundred years, although annates, i.e. one year's income and other forms of income paid to Rome by each benefice, were considered a burden.

Henry was well educated in English, Latin, Italian, theology, music, and was a good sportsman in jousting, tennis and hunting. On June 11, 1509, he married Catherine of Aragon: her first marriage to Henry's elder brother, Prince Arthur (Prince of Wales) lasted only seven months before Prince Arthur's death in 1502. The marriage re-affirmed England's friendship with Spain.

Thomas Wolsey came to prominence and was appointed to the King's Council in November 1509, with particular responsibilities as Almoner to the Royal household.

In 1511, Henry was persuaded by his father-in-law to join the Holy League with the Pope against France, whose King wanted to depose the Pope, who in turn wanted to remove the French from Cambria (northern Italy). The following year, Henry took the opportunity to invade Bordeaux to reclaim possessions lost in previous reigns: the attempt failed. In 1513, the Battle of Spurs at Tournai (east of Lille) was successful, but as a diversionary tactic the French persuaded their allies, the Scots, to invade northern England. The Scots were trounced at the famous Battle of Flodden (south-east of Coldstream, then Berwickshire, now Borders, Scotland). England's army of twenty-six thousand, lost four thousand killed; the larger Scottish army of between thirty-five and forty thousand, had ten thousand killed. In the battle, King James IV of Scotland, Henry's brother-in-law, was killed on September 9, 1513.

By August 1514, Thomas Wolsey had negotiated a peace treaty with France, part of which included the marriage between 17-year-old Princess Mary, Henry's younger sister, to the recently widowed 52-year-old King Louis XII of France. Louis died three months later.

England did not have a standing army, but Henry established for the first time in England's history the Royal Navy, with warships of an advanced and revolutionary design. There were new Royal dockyards constructed at Woolwich and Deptford (on the River Thames, London); Trinity House was founded in 1514, an organization to safeguard shipping around the coastline, still in existence and operating today.

Thomas Wolsey, a strong and commanding person, gradually became the foremost and dominant advisor in the first part of Henry's reign. Having been appointed Bishop of Lincoln, he became Archbishop of York in 1514; in 1515 he was elevated to Cardinal, and soon was appointed the Lord Chancellor. Henry being young, relied on Thomas Wolsey, who in 1518 negotiated the Treaty of London which established 'Universal Peace' between the powers of Europe, mainly the Pope, the Holy Roman Emperor (Germany), France and Spain, which made it appear that England was the supreme arbiter in European diplomacy. To seal the bond between England and France, Henry proposed that his very young daughter, Princess Mary, should marry the French King's eldest son, the Dauphin. It did not happen.

Cardinal Wolsey did not trust or need Parliament, principally, because the anti-clericalism in the country was reflected amongst its members. Although Parliament gave allegiance to Henry, it was not summoned for a further eight years. The Court of the Star Chamber grew more active; the government and the enforcement of law became completely arbitrary.

As Henry matured he began to take more responsibilities as King.

In 1520 a most extraordinary and lavish pageant was organized jointly by Henry and the new King of France, Francis I, located between Guinnes and Ardres (just south of Calais). The Field of the Cloth of Gold was an opulent extravaganza with the purpose of the two kings getting better acquainted with each other, but it failed to promote friendship or understanding. Suspicions of each other remained.

By 1521 Cardinal Wolsey's skill, judgment and foresight had begun to falter, both in state and Church matters. When Henry visited Oxford he was astonished to discover that the Cardinal had procured sufficient funds to construct a magnificent college, initially named Cardinal's College, later re-named Christ Church.

In that year, Pope Leo X conferred on Henry the title *Fidei Defensor* (Defender of the Faith). Henry, still a devout Catholic, and his advisors had been pressing for such a religious title to match those of the kings of France and Spain. This title has been in use by English sovereigns (despite being Protestants) ever since. It is shown on the coinage to this day, abbreviated as FD.

Queen Catherine gave birth many times, but Princess Mary, born in 1516, was the only child to have lived for more than a few weeks. Henry did father an illegitimate boy, given the title Duke of Richmond and Somerset, but a male legitimate heir was considered paramount to prevent a disputed succession. (Henry Fitzroy, Duke of Richmond and Somerset, was the son of Henry with Elizabeth Blount. He was born in 1519; he married Mary, daughter of Thomas Howard, Duke of Norfolk; and died in 1536. He was the only illegitimate child Henry recognized.) Queen Catherine, now no longer able to conceive, fell out of favour with Henry who needed, in those times, a son and heir. He wanted a new wife and married Anne Boleyn, believed to have been about 26 years of age.

In the early days of the decade Henry, with other monarchs, wanted to reduce the power of France by defeating it in war, and, subsequently, partitioning it amongst the victors. Henry wanted to become King of France, one of his inherited titles, but taxation to promote the war caused disturbances throughout England.

Eventually peace was reached. France transferred control of Boulogne to England.

In 1529, Henry summoned Parliament to meet for the first time for over a decade. Known as the Reformation Parliament, it met regularly for the next seven years to pass legislation to reform the Church of England. It reduced the clergy income from fees, probates and trading; the clergy were restricted to one benefice (a Church living); if the priest was non-resident it had to be with the approval of the King, not by the Pope as previously; it abolished small monasteries as many had become places of idleness or even vice. Parliament completed the separation of the jurisdiction of the Church in England from Rome, giving supremacy in ecclesiastical matters to the King. Both the country and Henry remained Roman Catholic in faith, but Henry had achieved his aim that the monarchy of England being supreme over foreign jurisdiction, the Pope and the Roman Catholic Church.

The 1531 Convocation (a clerical assembly) acknowledged and confirmed that the monarch was Supreme Head of the Church of England, but with the provision "so far as the laws of Christ allow". Sir Thomas More, loyal to Rome, resigned as Lord Chancellor in objection to the Convocation.

Further, in 1532 the Acts of Annate legislation stopped payments of the 'first-fruit of a benefice', i.e. a one-off payment of a year's income of a benefice to the Pope: any bishop who paid would forfeit its land to the monarch. Legislation was passed authorising the appointment of bishops, with or without the approval of the Pope, whereas, previously the Pope had to approve any such appointments.

In March 1533 Thomas Cranmer became Archbishop of Canterbury with the Pope acquiescing in the appointment, although Thomas Cranmer did swear an oath to the Pope. The 1533 Parliamentary Act in Restraint of Appeals banned all appeals to the Pope regarding wills, marriages and divorces; instead all appeals would be heard by the Upper House of Convocation, which was under Henry's control.

After lengthy consultations over some years, on May 23 Archbishop Cranmer announced that the marriage of Henry to Queen Catherine (of Aragon) was invalid. The Queen had repeatedly refused to be associated with any scheme to end her marriage: eventually she and her daughter Princess Mary were removed from the Royal Court.

A few days later on June 1, Anne Boleyn was crowned Queen of England, and on September 7 a daughter, Princess Elizabeth, was born, the future Queen Elizabeth I. Henry was said to have been furious – no male heir.

Parliament passed the first Act of Succession in 1534 which declared the marriage of Henry and Queen Catherine to be void and that Princess Mary be removed from the succession. In response, the Pope declared Archbishop of Canterbury Cranmer's decision to invalidate the marriage, be annulled. In their turn, Parliament passed the Act of Supremacy declaring the King to be Supreme Head of the Church of England, which the 1531 Convocation had previously declared. An oath was required of all men in the country to "refuse all obedience to any foreign authority". Sir Thomas More (the Lord Chancellor) was imprisoned for refusing to take the oath.

The Statute of Treason, passed by Parliament in 1534, gave great power to

Henry, which he used excessively. In addition to Sir Thomas More, the Bishop of Rochester (John Fisher) and the monks of Charterhouse were all executed in June and July 1535 for refusing to take the oaths of allegiance as set out in the Act of Supremacy.

Shortly afterwards the Pope excommunicated Henry from the Church, which, in theory, deprived him being King of England, but this he ignored and it could not be enforced.

In 1534 Henry began to take greater interest in Ireland, gradually increasing his influence and power. The Irish Parliament voted to recognize him as King of Ireland. As head of the Irish Church he ordered that the monasteries be dissolved and the images in the churches be destroyed. Thomas Cromwell (Earl of Essex) who was Vicar-General and a member of parliament had become very influential. By 1536 he was ruthlessly supervising the dissolution, in fact, the destruction of monasteries throughout England and anything associated with the papacy.

English language was being introduced in the Church. Archbishop Cranmer prepared forms of prayers in English; the King ordered that all children should be taught the Lord's Prayer, the Ten Commandments, and the Articles of Faith in English. The Holy Bible, also in English, became freely available and one had to be installed in every Church.

Queen Catherine (of Aragon) died naturally in January 1536.

Queen Anne (Boleyn), now in disgrace with Henry, was tried and found guilty of adultery with various men and incest with her brother. She was beheaded at the Tower of London on May 19, 1536, not quite three years after her marriage.

The dissolution of the monasteries in addition to other political and social grievances in the north of England, led to a series of rebellions in 1536, known as the 'Pilgrimage of Grace'. The rebels' leader Robert Aske, a lawyer, demanded that the monasteries be restored; that the reforming bishops be removed; and Thomas Cromwell be expelled. Early in the following year the rebellion was crushed; two hundred and fifty of the rebels, including Robert Aske, abbots and monks were hanged; their lands sequestrated and dispersed in small lots to many small landowners.

A few days after Queen Anne's (Boleyn) execution, Henry married Jane Seymour; eighteen months later she gave birth to a boy, Prince Edward, but, two days later she died. Queen Jane was buried with royal honours at St George's Chapel, Windsor, Berkshire.

In 1539 Thomas Cromwell (Earl of Essex) wanted to strengthen the Protestants against the Roman Catholicism of France and Spain by arranging a marriage between Henry and Anne of Cleves (one of the German states). On meeting Anne for the first time Henry was horrified at what he considered to be her ugliness, but Henry felt obligated to keep the marriage promise. The marriage was not consummated; an annulment was arranged; and in the settlement Queen Anne (of Cleves) lived in England for the remaining seventeen years of her life.

As a consequence, Thomas Cromwell was charged with treason, found guilty and executed on July 28, 1540.

Henry married Catherine Howard, whose father was the youngest brother of the Duke of Norfolk, on August 8, 1540, for his fifth marriage. Soon her adultery, including with her cousin Thomas Culpepper, was discovered. Her life ended in February 1542 by beheading, the same as her cousin Queen Anne (Boleyn) before.

By this time Henry had ambitions to control Scotland and form a united kingdom of England, Wales and Scotland. During the latter part of 1542, England and Scotland were at war, the Scots defeating the English at Tevoitdale, south of Hawick in the Borders, but later the Scots were routed at the Battle of Solway Moss, just south of Carlisle.

The Treaty of Greenwich signed in July 1543 between England and the weakened Scotland, brought peace with the agreed betrothal of Prince Edward to the 7-month-old Mary, Queen of Scots. The Scots repudiated the Treaty at the end of the year, and renewed its alliance with France. Henry responded by terrorizing the Scots and having Edinburgh razed to the ground.

Catherine Parr, a 31-year-old, twice married widow, became Henry's sixth wife on July 12, 1543.

Earlier in the year five thousand troops had crossed to Calais to defend the Low Countries because it was thought that France were preparing to invade. In September 1544, the English and allies invaded France, but the Holy Roman Emperor, Charles V, signed a peace treaty with France and withdrew. Also, it was feared the French were planning to invade England; the two navies positioned for battle, but the French disappeared, returning to their ports. The danger was past. The expense incurred for the war and defence of the country was crippling to the King.

The total cost of about £2 million created financial problems for the country: the money was raised by forced loans, heavy subsidies, sale of monastery lands, the selling of church silver and tithes. The currency was devalued, and an attempt was made to raise funds on the Antwerp money markets. Peace was restored between England and France in 1546.

(Of interest, in an attempted French invasion during this period, 1.25 miles from the entrance to Portsmouth Harbour, the warship Mary Rose, the flagship of the Fleet, sank. In 1982 the extensive remains were raised from the seabed. It is on display at the Royal Naval Dockyards, Portsmouth, Hampshire.)

Henry had been empowered by Parliament to settle the succession of the Crown in his Will.

He left the throne first to his son, Prince Edward; if he died without an heir, then Henry's eldest daughter, Princess Mary, would follow; if her line failed then Henry's other daughter, Princess Elizabeth, would take the Crown; finally if there were no heirs the line would pass to the descendents of Henry's youngest sister, Princess Mary.

During his last year, Henry gave thought to the problems of Prince Edward inheriting the throne as a minor. Henry considered that the Catholic Duke of

Norfolk could be a threat to England during a regency period of Prince Edward as King. On December 12, 1506, the Duke of Norfolk and his son, the Earl of Surrey, were arrested and tried for treason. The Earl of Surrey was executed the following month; Parliament passed a Bill of Attainder against the Duke of Norfolk on January 27 that condemned him to death. Henry died the following day, so saving the life of the Duke.

Henry VIII was buried at St George's Chapel, Windsor, Berkshire, near to his queen, Jane Seymour.

TUDOR

KING EDWARD VI

Born	1537 October 12
Accession	1547 January 28
Age at Accession	9
Death	1553 July 6
Age at Death	15
Reigned	6 years

Edward VI succeeded his father Henry VIII. He was the son of Henry's marriage to Jane Seymour.

He did not marry.

Persons of note.

Thomas Cranmer (b.1478, d.1556). Archbishop of Canterbury, 1533 to 1553. A leading reformer, he worked on the English Prayer Books of 1549 and 1552. Death by burning at the stake.

John Dudley, Earl of Warwick (b.1502, d.1553) was Regent to Edward VI. Elevated to Duke of Northumberland during the reign. Lord President of the Regency Council; Lord Protector. The lines of the previous Earls of Warwick and the Dukes of Northumberland had expired.

Hugh Latimer (b.c.1485, d.1555). English churchman during the Reformation, who became Bishop of Worcester (1535). He was condemned as a heretic and burned to death at the stake.

THE TUDORS: KING EDWARD VI

Edward Seymour (b.1506, d.1552) was the brother of Queen Jane (Seymour). He was Lord Protector during the early part of Edward VI's short reign. In 1547 he was elevated to dukedom as the Duke of Somerset, a new creation. He was executed. The line of the Dukes of Somerset, the Beaufort descendents of John of Gaunt had expired.

Edward VI was 9 years old, intellectually precocious, earnest and serious, when inheriting the throne on the death of his father King Henry VIII in 1547. King Henry had nominated a Regency Council comprising both Protestants and Catholics hoping it would keep the *status quo*. It failed.

The intimidation of Scotland continued in an effort to enforce the 1543 Treaty of Greenwich and the proposed marriage between Edward and Mary, Queen of Scots. The so-called 'War of the Rough Wooing' culminated at the Battle of Pinkie Cleugh (south-east of Edinburgh) in 1547. Twenty-three thousand Scots lost to the sixteen thousand English troops that included German mercenaries. This was the last battle between England and Scotland as separate kingdoms. The English attack prompted the French to take retaliatory action by retaking Boulogne, which they had forfeited to England in 1525. Queen Mary (Mary, Queen of Scots) was sent to France for safety, so ruining England's scheme of combining the two thrones and countries.

Edward Seymour (Jane Seymour's brother) was appointed Lord Protector which he used to exert power. Queen Catherine (Parr), King Henry VIII's last wife, married Thomas Seymour (Lord Seymour of Sudeley, in Gloucestershire) who had been appointed the Lord High Admiral. He was very ambitious and plotted against his brother, the Lord Protector. To remove this threat, under the Act of Attainder, Thomas Seymour was arrested, tried for treason and executed on Tower Hill in 1549.

During the year, Thomas Cranmer (Archbishop of Canterbury) produced the first Prayer Book in English, mainly based on his translation from Latin. Meanwhile, Parliament ordered a continuation of King Henry VIII's policy of destroying images, wall pictures, *et al*, all vestiges of Roman Catholicism, in the churches, often in a barbaric manner.

There was unrest in the country. A rebellion in the south-west, mainly Catholic in sympathy against the new Prayer Book, was ruthlessly crushed with over four thousand killed and the leaders hanged. In the east of the country, the enclosure of common land; the change in farming practices; and unemployment resulted in further serious disturbances, a peasants' revolt: five hundred people were killed, not by English troops, but by the hired mercenaries from German states.

Many of the oppressive heresy laws introduced in the previous reign were repealed. Parliament legitimized the marriage of clergymen; it enforced the usage of the first Prayer Book under the Act of Uniformity; and stripped the guilds of properties, so reducing their income that benefited the needy.

Gradually, support for Edward Seymour (the Lord Protector) declined: after a short imprisonment at the end of 1549 when John Dudley (Earl of Warwick) replaced him as Lord Protector (as Lord President of the Regency Council), he was imprisoned at the Tower of London in October 1551. Charged with conspiracy, he was found guilty and executed on Tower Hill in January 1552.

John Dudley, now elevated as Duke of Northumberland, worked hard for the Protestant cause, promoting the Reformation with great enthusiasm. Strasbourg (today part of France) and Switzerland were centres of Protestantism, and places of safety for English exiles: now many felt secure enough to return home to England and to be active in their faith.

In 1552 the second Prayer Book by Thomas Cranmer (Archbishop of Canterbury) was produced. This one was closer to the doctrines of the Reformists, and many ceremonies of the Roman Catholic Church were omitted.

Under the Lord Protector, the first Poor Law in England's history was enacted that stipulated money collections were to be made in every parish for distribution to the poor. In education, Edward VI Grammar Schools were being instituted to be financed from the confiscated lands of the monasteries.

During 1553, it was realized that Edward's health was deteriorating, and John Dudley (Duke of Northumberland) as Lord Protector was planning for the succession. King Henry VIII's Will stated that the next in line for the Crown after Edward, should be his eldest daughter Princess Mary, the daughter of Queen Catherine (of Aragon), who was a staunch Roman Catholic. The Lord Protector advised Edward to make his own Will, advising him to leave the throne to Lady Jane Grey, a granddaughter of King Henry VIII's youngest sister, Princess Mary.

Lady Jane Grey had recently married Lord Guildford Dudley, the fourth son of the Lord Protector: this would have secured the Protestant succession.

Edward died on July 6, 1553 at the age of 15, and was interred at the Henry VII Lady Chapel, Westminster Abbey, London.

TUDOR

QUEEN JANE (LADY JANE GREY)

Born	1537 October
Accession	1553 July 6
Age at Accession	15
Deposed	1553 July 19
Reigned	13 days
Death	1554 February 12
Age at Death	16

Jane succeeded her distant cousin, Edward VI. Her grandmother was King Henry VIII's youngest sister, Princess Mary, whose daughter, Frances, married in 1535 Henry Grey (3rd Marquess of Dorset), later to become Duke of Suffolk, inheriting the dukedom from his father-in-law, on the latter's death in 1545.

In 1553 she married Lord Guildford Dudley, son of John Dudley (Duke of Northumberland and Earl of Warwick). They had no children.

Person of note:

John Dudley (Duke of Northumberland and Earl of Warwick) (b.1502, d.1553), was Lord President of the Council from 1551 to 1553, and father-in-law of Jane. He had been Lord Protector to King Edward VI. The lines of the previous Earls of Warwick and Dukes of Northumberland had expired.

THE TUDORS: QUEEN JANE (LADY JANE GREY)

The 15-year-old Lady Jane Grey was a pawn in the scheme of the Lord Protector (John Dudley, the Duke of Northumberland). He wanted a Protestant on the throne, and in collusion with the Duke of Suffolk, Lady Jane Grey's father, planned for Lady Jane to succeed Edward VI as monarch. This contravened the Will of King Henry VIII.

Lord Guildford Dudley, son of the Lord Protector, had married Lady Jane.

During the final days of King Edward VI's life, the Lord Protector tried to encourage Princess Mary, the rightful heir to the throne to visit her brother. Suspecting a plot she sought protection with the Duke of Norfolk, a staunch Catholic.

Lady Jane Grey was proclaimed Queen on the death of King Edward VI: it was accepted neither by Parliament nor the population. Less than two weeks later on July 19, 1553, Princess Mary, daughter of Queen Catherine (of Aragon) was proclaimed monarch.

Princess Mary, together with her sister Princess Elizabeth, made a triumphant entry through London in the August.

Lady Jane Grey, her husband and her father were imprisoned at the Tower of London.

Seven months later, Lady Jane Grey was executed by beheading on February 12, 1554 at the young age of 16. She was buried at the parish church of the Tower of London, St Peter ad Vincula (St Peter in Chains).

TUDOR

QUEEN MARY I

Born	1516 February 18
Accession	1553 July 19
Age at Accession	37
Death	1558 November 17
Age at Death	42
Reigned	5 years

Mary I succeeded Lady Jane Grey. She was the daughter of Henry VIII and his first wife Catherine of Aragon.

In 1554 she married Philip of Asturias (north-west Spain), heir to the Spanish throne, to which he succeeded in 1556.

Mary was his second wife, he having been married to Maria Manuela for a short time until her death in 1545. The year after Mary's death, he married Elisabeth of Valois, who died in 1568, and married, fourthly, Anne of Austria in 1570 until her death in 1580. Philip was born in 1527, and died in 1598.

Mary and Philip had no children.

Persons of note:

Richard Chancellor (b.1521, b.1556). Navigator; pilot-major to Sir Hugh Willoughby's expedition to the north-east passage (northern Europe) in 1553. He made a second expedition to Russia in 1555, but on his return was drowned when shipwrecked off the Aberdeenshire coast, Scotland, the following year.

Thomas Cranmer (b.1478, d.1556). Archbishop of Canterbury, 1533 to 1553. A leading reformer, he worked on the English Prayer Books of 1549 and 1552. Death by burning at the stake during this reign.

Hugh Latimer (b.c.1485, d.1555). English churchman during the Reformation who was Bishop of Worcester 1535 to 1553. He was condemned as a heretic and burned at the stake during this reign.

Nicholas Ridley (b.c.1500, d.1555). He was appointed Bishop of London in 1550. He assisted in the preparation of the English Prayer Books of 1549 and 1552. He was condemned as a heretic and burned at the stake during this reign.

Sir Thomas Wyatt, the younger (b.1521, d.1554). His godfather was the Duke of Norfolk. Although a Catholic from birth, he supported the Protestant Lady Jane Grey and Princess Elizabeth. He was beheaded.

Mary was the first female monarch of England, other than the thirteen days of Lady Jane Grey, at the age of 37. Her life had been turbulent: at one stage she had been declared illegitimate; her claim to the throne questioned; her life had been threatened and her freedom restricted. She was well educated, as were all of King Henry VIII's children.

Despite her devout Catholicism, her reign began in an atmosphere of popular enthusiasm: King Edward VI had been too young to have had any influence, and their father, although at the end of his reign was anti-Rome and anti-papacy, was in faith a Catholic.

Mary summoned Parliament to repeal the various anti-Catholic laws it had previously passed and to renew the heresy laws. She replaced clergy who were Protestant sympathizers with loyal Catholics; Thomas Cranmer (Archbishop of Canterbury) and Hugh Latimer (Bishop of Worcester) were removed from their sees.

The re-instatement of land to the monasteries, which had been sequestrated by King Henry VIII, was found not to have been possible because it had been divided into small individual lots when sold.

Lady Jane Grey and her husband (Lord Guildford Dudley) and her father (the Duke of Suffolk) were arrested and imprisoned at the Tower of London. The Duke of Suffolk was released because it appeared he was a supporter of Mary. Lady Jane Grey and her husband were arraigned on charges of high treason on November 14, 1553. She pleaded guilty and was sentenced to death together with her husband, but the sentences were suspended.

Mary announced that she was going to marry Philip of Asturias, heir to the King of Spain. Parliament had no constitutional powers to oppose the marriage, but were worried that England would lose its independence by the marriage.

In February 1554 Sir Thomas Wyatt plotted to prevent the marriage; he led a Protestant rebellion to London with the support of the Duke of Suffolk, with the intention of replacing Mary with Princess Elizabeth as monarch. They were defeated: directly as a consequence, at the Tower of London on February 12, Lady Jane Grey and her husband were beheaded. The leaders of the rebellion were captured and executed; the Duke of Suffolk and Sir Thomas Wyatt were beheaded.

Princess Elizabeth although unaware of Sir Thomas's scheme was sent to the Tower of London, where she feared for her life. Within a few months she was released but kept under surveillance.

Mary's marriage took place on July 25, 1554. To appease Parliament, a marriage treaty stated that Mary would have sole control over England; that no foreigners would command the army or navy; if she had a child and heir, in due course, it would be monarch of England, Burgundy and the Spanish Netherlands. The danger being that treaties were often broken.

Richard Chancellor, seeking a north-east passage through northern Russia to China, visited the Tsar of Russia, Ivan IV (Ivan the Terrible), in Moscow. His successful negotiations with the Tsar resulted in the formation of the Muscovy Company in 1553, the first joint-stock company, which gave it a monopoly of Russian trade.

In accord with her faith, Mary returned England's allegiance and obedience to the Church of Rome. The consequences were that Thomas Cranmer, Hugh Latimer and Nicholas Ridley were all tried on charges of heresy and found guilty. Hugh Latimer and Nicholas Ridley were burned at the stake in Oxford in October 1555; Thomas Cranmer, having been approved by a Pope on his appointment as Archbishop, it required the current Pope to give authorisation for execution, which he did. Thomas Cranmer died by burning at the stake at Oxford on March 21, 1556. During Mary's reign about three hundred martyrs were executed: she became known as 'Bloody Mary'.

Mary had hoped that the persecutions would damage the Protestant support: it had the opposite effect and she lost the loyalty of her subjects.

Parliament continued to be active in many fields of reform; they removed the corrupt practices created during the Protectorate of King Edward VI's short reign.

In 1557, the French prepared for war. Requests by the English garrisons in France for reinforcements to resist the anticipated attacks were not met. At the beginning of January 1558 overwhelming French forces invaded and regained Calais for the first time since 1347, and soon overran nearby Guinnes.

Mary was childless. She feared that her Protestant sister, Princess Elizabeth, and heir presumptive to the throne would succeed her as monarch and would destroy the re-establishment of Roman Catholicism in England.

An ill Mary died in London on November 17, 1558 at the age of 42. She was buried at the Henry VII Lady Chapel, Westminster Abbey, London.

TUDOR

QUEEN ELIZABETH I

Born	**1533 September 7**
Accession	**1558 November 17**
Age at Accession	**25**
Death	**1603 March 24**
Age at Death	**69**
Reigned	**44 years**

Elizabeth I succeeded her sister Mary I, was the daughter of Henry VIII and his second wife, Anne Boleyn.

She did not marry.

Mary, Queen of Scots (b.1542, d.1587), daughter of King James V of Scotland; became monarch at 6 days of age; she abdicated in 1567; beheaded in 1587.
Marriages:
Firstly, April 1558 to Francis (b.1544, d.1560), Dauphin to King Henry II of France. He succeeded his father as King in 1559, but died in December 1560.
Secondly, July 1565, to Henry Stuart (Earl of Darnley) (b.1545, d.1567). They had 1 son who became King James VI of Scotland and King James I of England. Her third husband murdered Henry Stuart, probably.
Thirdly, May 1567 to John Hepburn (Earl of Bothwell) (b.c.1536, d.1578).
Acquitted of the murder of Henry Stuart (Earl of Darnley). The marriage lasted only a few weeks. He died in prison.

THE TUDORS: QUEEN ELIZABETH I

Persons of note:

Anthony Babington (b.1561, d.1586). Catholic courier for Mary, Queen of Scots. He was hanged.

William Cecil (b.1520, d.1598). Elizabeth's most influential and important administrator during her reign. Created Baron Burghley in 1571.

Robert Devereux (2ⁿᵈ Earl of Essex) (b.1566, d.1601). He was a favourite of Elizabeth, until in disgrace he was beheaded for treason. Stepson of Robert Dudley (Earl of Leicester).

Sir Francis Drake (b.c.1540, d.1596). The first Englishman to have circumnavigated the World, in 1580. He was vice-admiral of the fleet, which destroyed the Spanish Armada in 1588.

Robert Dudley (1ˢᵗ Earl of Leicester) (b.c.1532, d.1588). Brother of Lord Guildford Dudley, husband of Lady Jane Grey. A favourite of Elizabeth.

Sir Martin Frobisher (b.c.1535, d.1594). He made three voyages to the Canadian Arctic in 1576, 1577 and 1578, seeking a north-west passage to Asia.

Sir John Hawkins (b.1532, d.1595). Sailor and slave-trader. Treasurer of the Royal Navy 1585 to 1588. He was a commander in the defeat of the Spanish Armada in 1588. Died at sea off the coast of Puerto Rico on November 12, 1595.

Thomas Howard (4ᵗʰ Duke of Norfolk) (b.c.1535, d.1572). Son of the Earl of Surrey, whose father had been executed.

Charles Howard (2ⁿᵈ Baron Howard of Effingham, later Earl of Nottingham) (b.1536, d.1624). High admiral of the fleet that defeated the Spanish Armada in 1588, and involved in the capture of Cadiz (Spain) in 1596.

Ben Jonson (b.1573, d.1637). Poet and dramatist who developed the comedy of humour. Poet Laureate 1619 to 1637.

Ignatius Loyala (b.1491, d.1556). Spanish priest who founded the Society of Jesus (the Jesuits). He was canonized in 1622.

Christopher Marlowe (b.1564, d.1593). Dramatist who influenced William Shakespeare. His early death was due to a tavern brawl.

Charles Neville (6th Earl of Westmorland) (b.c.1542, d.1601). After the Earls Rebellion he went into hiding. His estates were confiscated, and he died in poverty.

Matthew Parker (b.1504, d.1575). Archbishop of Canterbury from 1559 until his death. A book of his is said to have been the first book privately printed in England.

Thomas Percy (7ᵗʰ Earl of Northumberland) (b.1528, d.1572). Mary I re-created the earldom, it having been extinct for this family. He was beheaded.

Reginald Pole (b.1500, d.1558). The Roman Catholic Archbishop of Canterbury from 1556 until his death. Became a cardinal. He opposed King Henry VIII's divorce from Queen Catherine (of Aragon), and went abroad in exile in 1532 for a period.

Sir Walter Raleigh (b.c.1554, d.1618). Explorer, admiral and writer. He introduced tobacco and potatoes to England. Served long periods as a prisoner in the Tower of London, with his family. He died by execution.

William Shakespeare (b.1564, d.1616), born Stratford-upon-Avon, Warwickshire. England's greatest poet and dramatist. He went to London at the height of the English Renaissance and soon became connected with the Globe Theatre as an actor and playwright.

Edmund Spenser (b.c.1552, d.1599). Poet Laureate. Chiefly known for his allegorical epic romance 'The Faerie Queene'.

Sir Francis Walsingham (b.c.1532, d.1590). Politician and spymaster. Principal Secretary of State to Elizabeth.

The Protestant Elizabeth succeeded her Catholic sister in accordance with the Will of their father, King Henry VIII. Mary I, near to death, recognized Princess Elizabeth as heir to the throne.

Elizabeth was well educated; able to speak English, Greek, Latin and other languages, also enjoyed hunting, archery, hawking, dancing and music. She was fortunate in having a very sound advisor in William Cecil who guided her until his death in 1598. He kept a tight control over the country's finances and gave good advice on domestic and foreign matters through the various positions he held as Secretary of State, Lord High Treasurer and the leadership of the Privy Council.

England's finances were not very strong owing to the debts incurred during previous reigns and the subsequent interest being paid. Parliament considered it could not impose a high level of tax on the country, consequently, Elizabeth's own income was modest throughout her reign, but some of her revenue came directly from 'monopolies', from people and businesses being licensed to have the right to trade.

The great concern of many in England was the need to have a Protestant heir to Elizabeth: many times she was encouraged to marry, but always refused. If she was childless at the time of her death, the Will of her father stated that the succession should pass through the line of his youngest sister, Princess Mary, but in accordance with primogeniture, the heir to an unmarried Elizabeth should be through the line of King Henry VIII's eldest sister, Princess Margaret. She had married King James IV of Scotland, and their eldest son, King James V of Scotland, was father of Mary, Queen of Scots, a Catholic, who had succeeded to the Scottish throne as a one-week-old baby in 1542. Early in 1558 Mary, Queen of Scots married the heir to the French throne: in the event of her death without children she had assigned the throne of Scotland to her husband as well as any claim to the English throne.

He died in 1560 not long after succeeding his father as King of France. To complicate matters for Mary, Queen of Scots, Scotland was turning Protestant; their Parliament in 1560 sanctioned the establishment of the Reformed Church and the abolition of papal jurisdiction.

The papacy had refused to accept the annulment of King Henry VIII's marriage to Queen Catherine (of Aragon): therefore, the marriage of Queen Anne (Boleyn) was not considered valid. Elizabeth should not inherit the English throne because they considered her to be illegitimate. Their influence was minimal in this matter and was ignored, but it gave support to Catholic supporters in England.

Many Acts of Parliament were passed in the early years of Elizabeth's reign dealing with religious matters. The 1559 Act of Supremacy appointed the Queen as Supreme Governor of the Church of England. This has remained the legal authority of every monarch since, including the present time. The Oath of Supremacy of the same year, imposed on everyone taking public or church office in England to swear allegiance to the monarch as Supreme Governor of the Church of England. Failure to do so was treated as treasonable. The Oath was later extended to include members of parliament and those studying at universities. The allegiance to Rome by Queen Mary I was repealed so abolishing papal authority in England.

The 1559 Act of Uniformity set the order to be used in Church of the Book of Common Prayer, Thomas Cranmer's second Prayer Book of 1552. Anyone, including Roman Catholics, who did not attend a Protestant Church for a Mass once a week, had to pay a fine of one shilling or the family rate of one pound a month, quite a sum of money in those times.

A Convocation of the Church in 1563 established the Thirty-nine Articles of Religion, which summarizes the dogma of the Church of England. In 1571,

Parliament made the Articles a legal requirement.

The Roman Catholic Archbishop of Canterbury, Reginald Pole, died in 1558, so giving the opportunity to appoint a Protestant: Matthew Parker was appointed and remained Archbishop until his death in 1575.

English adventurers and traders began to explore the World, finding new markets for their goods, mainly wool and manufactured cloth. This was the age of oceanic exploration, piracy, smuggling and legal trading: but the ships were quite small and conditions on board very basic. Sir John Hawkins became the first Englishman to trade outside of England, between Africa and Spanish America, including the transportation of Africans into slavery.

The English Muscovy Company became the first European company to trade with the interior of Russia and the first important joint-stock company was granted a charter by Elizabeth. She became one of its shareholders.

Much of the population were skilled by trade. Apprenticeships were important for England to develop, and standards were set by the 1563 Statute of Artificiers (referred to as the Statute of Apprentices).

In 1564 William Shakespeare, to become England's greatest poet and dramatist, was born at Stratford-upon-Avon, Warwickshire.

The widowed Mary, Queen of Scots returned to Scotland to marry her cousin Henry Stuart (the Earl of Darnley) in 1565 and their one child would become King James VI of Scotland just a year later at one year of age. Henry Stuart was murdered, probably, by James Hepburn (the Earl of Bothwell) whom Mary, married in May 1567. The Scottish Protestants disapproved of this marriage and rebelled at Pinkie (south-east of Edinburgh); her husband escaped but Mary, Queen of Scots was captured and sent to prison at Loch Levan, Kinross, from where she escaped to Solway. Two days later she crossed the border into England. She abdicated her throne in favour of her young son on July 24, 1567. Now in England, she was placed under supervision at Bolton Castle, Yorkshire.

She became a focus for the Catholics in their endeavours to return England to Catholicism. A plot occurred in 1569 by the northern families of the Percys (led by the Earl of Northumberland) and the Nevilles (led by the Earl of Westmorland), but the 'Rising of the North', also referred to as the 'Earls Rebellion', failed. Many of the rebels were hanged in Durham and Yorkshire.

At about this time, two separate and extreme religious groups were beginning to be prominent. The Puritans, who were Protestants, were most intolerant of non-Puritans, those who differed from their own distinct views: they challenged the authority of the Church of England and the State. The Society of Jesus, the Jesuits, founded by Ignatius Loyala, a Spanish priest, came to England to promote the counter-reformation policies of the Roman Catholic Church.

By now, under the influence of the Jesuits, the Pope was regarded as the temporal ruler for most of Ireland, except around Dublin, which was under English control.

THE TUDORS: QUEEN ELIZABETH I

Pope Pius V issued a Papal Bull in 1570 which excommunicated Elizabeth from the Roman Catholic Church: in an attempt to undermine her authority it freed the people from their obedience to her.

Further plots against the Queen were discovered: in 1572 Thomas Howard (4th Duke of Norfolk) was executed for treason; in the following year leaders of other plots also were executed.

English sailors were gaining experience of oceanic travel, and trading companies were being established. Parliament and the Queen realized the benefits of commerce to the country. Sir John Hawkins was appointed Treasurer and Councillor of the Royal Navy in 1573; Francis Drake set sail in the 'Pelican' (later renamed 'The Golden Hind') to circumnavigate the World, a three-year voyage, commencing in 1577. On his return Elizabeth knighted him on board his ship at Deptford, London; but both of these captains were really pirates who attacked the Spanish merchant shipping and plundered Spanish towns and their settlements. Sir Martin Frobisher was granted a licence to search for gold in North America and to explore for a north-west passage to Asia, from 1576 onwards. The Queen granted charters to the Eastland Company in 1579 to trade in the Baltic, importing grain and timber and exporting woollen products. The Levant Company in 1581 was granted a charter for trading in the eastern Mediterranean Sea with the sole right to trade with the Ottoman Empire.

In 1584 Parliament passed an Act which made it illegal for anyone to support a claimant to the throne, and those accused would be tried by a royal commission: this was to stop support for Mary, Queen of Scots. Elizabeth followed this with an alliance with James VI of Scotland, the Protestant son of Mary, for the mutual defence of their religion.

Although under supervision Mary was able to correspond with friends and supporters. The Catholic Anthony Babington, a member of the English royal court, organized a plot to murder Elizabeth: letters were intercepted by the spymaster Sir Francis Walsingham, implicating Mary. She was tried for treason and found guilty. Parliament petitioned for an immediate execution, and although Elizabeth resisted at first, she eventually acceded to their demands. In February 1587 Mary, Queen of Scots at the age of 45 was beheaded at Fotheringhay Castle, Northamptonshire, near Peterborough.

Whilst Mary, Queen of Scots was a prisoner in England for twenty years, her supporter King Philip II of Spain was reluctant to stop the English pirates attacking his ships, towns and settlements: the losses in ships and goods (mainly gold and silver) from Spanish America were considerable, depriving them of great wealth to the advantage of England. Mary in her Will bequeathed her domain and her claim to the English throne to Philip.

Over the years Elizabeth had sent small armies to the continent to defend the Protestants in their attempt to remove the Spanish from the Netherlands as part of the Dutch Revolt, the Eighty Years' War (1568 to 1648).

Now Philip regarded himself as Elizabeth's heir and decided she should be overthrown. His plans for an invasion became known: England needed time to prepare for war. Sir Francis Drake was sent to attack the Spanish fleet in Cadiz Harbour and to interfere with Spain's coastal and Mediterranean Sea shipping, so delaying their preparations.

By the following year, 1588, Spain was ready with 130 ships, 8,000 seamen and about 20,000 soldiers. Their plan being to sail to the Netherlands (being under Spanish rule), collect a further 20,000 to 30,000 soldiers, invade southern England, install Philip on the throne, and re-impose the Catholic faith in England.

England prepared its defences both on land and at sea; Robert Dudley (Earl of Leicester) commanded an army of 20,000 at Tilbury, Essex; Charles Howard (Baron Howard) the High Admiral, commanded the Royal Navy with the experienced captains Sir John Hawkins, Sir Francis Drake and Sir Martin Frobisher. Sir John Hawkins had re-designed naval ships making them faster and installed new longer-ranged guns, so making obsolete the traditional methods of grappling hand-to-hand combat between opposing soldiers when their ships were next to each other at sea.

With the blessing of Pope Sixtus V, the Spanish Armada sailed from Lisbon (in 1581 Philip II had invaded Portugal and held it for sixty years) on May 20. It put into La Coruna, northern Spain, and left on July 12. It was observed off the Lizard Point, Cornwall, seven days later. The English fleet, having been at sea, had just put into Plymouth, Devon, for re-supplies. The Armada sailed by unimpeded. The English fleet quickly left Plymouth, and with their faster ships caught up with the Spanish. The traditional system of sending warning messages by the lighting of beacons across the country had been arranged; soon after the warning 7,000 men gathered in
London; and Elizabeth went to Tilbury to support her troops.

In the English Channel the English caused damage to the Spanish; the English fleet sustained little damage. The out-gunned Armada was forced to take refuge in the vicinity of Calais. On the evening of July 28, the English sent eight fire-ships packed with explosives into the Spanish fleet causing havoc, confusion and destruction. The resultant battle lasted eight hours.

The weather changed to the English advantage. The Armada ceased fighting to return to Spain, but the storm-winds forced the ships northwards to the North Sea. In the Spanish Netherlands, the plans fell into disarray: the Protestant Dutch created blockades to prevent movements by the soldiers, but, also, the tides were too low to launch ships. They played no part in the attempted invasion. The Armada sailed around Scotland and Ireland on their return to Spain but lost many more men and ships in the storms than fighting the English. Overall, the English lost about 60 men; the Spanish lost half of their ships. The immediate danger of invasion had passed.

Four outstanding poets and dramatists were writing during Elizabeth's reign. William Shakespeare, England's greatest poet and dramatist, born at Stratford-upon-Avon, Warwickshire, commenced writing in the early 1590s, and acted in London. Christopher Marlowe, born about the same time as Shakespeare, wrote from the 1580s. It is thought that he and Shakespeare may have co-operated in writing some dramas. Edmund Spenser whose greatest work was 'The Faerie Queene': the first three books were printed in 1589, the second three in 1596. Ben Jonson, another playwright, his works were performed at the Globe Theatre in London. This theatre was erected in about 1595 in the shape of a circular building with a thatched roof only covering the audience; the central stage was open to the weather. A replica was built in the 1990s on the banks of the River Thames, London.

The Court of High Commission had responsibility for ecclesiastical offences, and in the period 1590 to 1593 many Presbyterians, Puritans and Catholics were hanged as seditionists, or burned at the stake as heretics.

By the mid-1590s there were further problems with Spain. In 1596 Robert Devereux (Earl of Essex) and Sir Walter Raleigh were sent to Cadiz and successfully destroyed the Spanish fleet and the town; later Robert Devereux was given orders to destroy the formation of another threatening Armada being prepared off the coast of western Spain. He missed the fleet, but fortunately the Armada was destroyed by bad weather.

In 1601, Robert Devereux was involved in a plot against Elizabeth: he was arrested, tried for treason, found guilty and beheaded.

Parliament passed the Poor Law Act of 1601 to strengthen the Poor Law Acts of 1552, 1563, 1572, 1576 and 1597 that were parish based. The new Act created a common national system. Apprenticeships were to be provided for the orphaned and for those children whose parents were unable to support them; working materials to be provided; relief to be supplied to the 'deserving poor'; children to be responsible for the care of their elderly parents; assistance to be given to the 'deserving unemployed'; the sick to be cared for in hospitals. A rate was levied on each property to meet the costs.

In the same year the country's economy had become strong enough for a new coinage to be minted to replace the debased old coinage.

Parliament was becoming more confident with the House of Commons gradually gaining importance. The number of burgesses representing the chartered boroughs and towns had increased to 379 in the House of Commons by the end of Elizabeth's reign. Although not an executive body, Parliament was beginning to express its opinions on matters previously outside its authority, including questioning the Queen's right to grant 'monopolies', regulating and licensing the commercial economy of the country.

A reign of 44 years was nearing its end. England had become a strong commercial country with its ships trading and exploring the then unknown World; peace with the now Protestant Scotland; and the Church of England free from papal control.

Throughout her reign, Elizabeth governed with caution, balancing the demands from her potential opponents both at home and abroad, but never afraid to enforce strong action when required.

Elizabeth, the Good Queen Bess of the Great Elizabethan Age, the last of the Tudor monarchs, died at the age of 69 on March 24, 1603. She was interred at the Henry VII Lady Chapel, Westminster Abbey, London, alongside King Edward VI and Queen Mary I.

THE STUARTS

Monarch	Reigned	Family
James I	1603 to 1625	Great-great-grandson of Henry VII
Charles I	1625 to 1649	Son of James I

Commonwealth	1649 to 1660	

THE STUARTS RESTORED

Monarch	Reigned	Family
Charles II	1660 to 1685	Son of Charles I
James II	1685 to 1688	Son of Charles I
William III and	1689 to 1702	Nephew of James II
Mary II	1689 to 1694	Daughter of James II
Anne	1702 to 1714	Daughter of James II

STUART

KING JAMES I

Born	1566 June 19
Accession	1603 March 24
Age at Accession	36
Death	1625 March 27
Age at Death	58
Reigned	22 years

James I, who succeeded Elizabeth I, was the great-great-grandson of King Henry VII.

He was the only child of Mary, Queen of Scots and her second husband Henry Stuart (Earl of Darnley).

He succeeded his mother, who had abdicated, to the Scottish throne in 1567 at the age of one, as King James VI of Scotland.

In 1589 he married Anne (b.1574, d.1619), daughter of Frederick II, King of Denmark. They had 3 sons and 4 daughters.

Persons of note:

Sir Robert Cecil (1ˢᵗ Earl of Salisbury) (b.1563, d.1612), son of William Cecil (Baron Burghley). Succeeded his father as Secretary of State to Queen Elizabeth I and continued in that role under James I. Created Earl in 1605.

Guy Fawkes (b.1570, d.1606). One of the Catholic conspirators who attempted to kill James by detonating explosives in the crypt of the Houses of Parliament. Born at Stonegate, Yorkshire, he was executed (hanged, drawn and quartered) at the Old Palace Yard, Westminster, London.

THE STUARTS: KING JAMES I

Sir Walter Raleigh (b.c.1554, d.1618). Explorer, admiral and writer. He introduced tobacco and potatoes into England. Served long periods as a prisoner in the Tower of London, with his family. Found guilty of treason by James I, but he was released from the Tower for an expedition to South America, only to be executed on his return.

Henry Stuart (Earl of Darnley) (b.1545, d.1567). He married Mary, Queen of Scots, being her second husband. Their son became James VI of Scotland and James I of England. Henry Stuart was murdered by James Hepburn (Earl of Bothwell), probably.

The Tudor line ended with the death of Queen Elizabeth I. Her successor was King James VI of Scotland, a Stuart, descended from King Henry VII's eldest daughter Princess Margaret. She had married King James IV of Scotland, whose son was King James V, who was the father of Mary, Queen of Scots, James VI's mother. Crowned as King James I of England, he was the first monarch of both England and Scotland: the two kingdoms remained separate and independent of each other, although James spent the greater part of his time in England.

Despite his mother being a devout Roman Catholic, James had been brought up under Calvinism, the religious doctrines of John Calvin, a French Protestant theologian. James had not met his mother since the day she left Scotland when he was only one-year-old.

Queen Elizabeth I's chief minister towards the end of her reign, Sir Robert Cecil, had negotiated a peaceful and smooth accession, but there were at least three plots against James in the early part of his rule: one implicated Sir Walter Raleigh who was condemned to death for conspiracy in 1603, later reprieved but detained with his family within the confines of the Tower of London.

Technically, England and Spain were still at war, since the attempted invasion by the Spanish Armada in 1588, but the alliances and friendships of Scotland with France and Spain over the centuries, made it quite straightforward for James to sign a treaty of peace in 1604.

The Puritans presented a Millenary Petition to the King, although its title suggests a thousand, it was signed by eight hundred clergy who listed their demands for changes within the Church of England. At the subsequent Hampton Court Conference, James refused to make any changes to the Elizabethan Church Settlement, other than agreeing to the preparation of a new version of the Holy Bible.

James believed that a King had the Divine Right to rule as he decreed: this occasionally caused tensions with Parliament. In the Parliament of 1604, the House of Commons had become more representative of the country with many squires, merchants and lawyers; the Puritans were well represented; it was very anti-Catholic; and it wanted to determine its position *vis-à-vis* the new monarch.

It was accepted that Acts of Parliament required the approval of the King; that Parliament could only meet when summoned by the monarch and could not sit once he had it dismissed. James emphasized that his prerogative could override Parliament; he accepted that he required Parliamentary approval for his income from taxes. Parliament revived the rights of impeachment and it upheld the liberty of free speech in Parliament.

In a court ruling, the judges ruled that James had the right to change custom duties at all ports as they were under his personal and sole jurisdiction, as they had been with previous monarchs. This gave James an income which was not controlled by Parliament.

Initially, James was fairly tolerant towards Catholics, who took this as an opportunity to encourage priests from abroad to come to England, including the Jesuits. James responded by re-imposing fines for recusancy (fines for not attending Church of England mass) that previously he had allowed to lapse. This angered the Catholics.

In 1605 the infamous Gunpowder Plot was discovered. Explosives that had been placed in the crypt of the House of Lords were to be detonated when the King and members of both Houses of Parliament had assembled in the Chamber for the opening of the new session. It was hoped that the anticipated death of the Protestant James would encourage rebellion leading to the re-establishment of Catholicism in England. The plan was foiled by the discovery of the explosives together with one of the conspirators, Guy Fawkes. In response Parliament passed laws of extreme severity against Roman Catholics, banning them from the professions, appearing at Royal Court and limiting their presence within London.

James had little understanding of the importance and need for the Royal Navy, allowing it to decline. Holland was becoming a strong and prosperous country through its overseas trading: it began to interfere with England's commercial shipping dominance, even pushing the English trawlers from their own fishing areas.

In 1611 the authorised Version of the Holy Bible was published. Known as the King James Version, it remains the accepted Holy Bible to this day. It was the combined work of forty-seven scholars.

Only three children of James lived to adulthood. Prince Henry (the Prince of Wales) died in 1612 at the age of 18; Prince Charles, born 1600, became heir to the throne; Princess Elizabeth married in 1613 at the age of 16 to the Protestant 17-year-old Elector Frederick V, Count of the Palatine of the Rhine.

During his reign, James re-distributed land in Ireland: the poor quality went to the Irish, the best half-a-million acres to settlers from England, Scotland, the City of London and its twelve City companies.

The East India Company, founded by a group of merchants in 1600, established its first factory in Surat (Gujarat, north-west India) in about 1615.

In 1616, thirteen years after his loosely controlled imprisonment within the confines of the Tower of London, Sir Walter Raleigh was released to sail to a region of South America (nowadays modern Venezuela) to search for gold.

Whilst there he had a confrontation with the local Spanish, which was reported to their King, who informed James of his displeasure. At this time negotiations had commenced with the possibility of Prince Charles marrying the Spanish Infanta. To appease the Spanish King, on his return to England, Sir Walter Raleigh was arrested, tried and found guilty of treason. He was beheaded in Palace Yard, Westminster, on October 29, 1618.

Some Puritans wanting freedom to conduct their lives in accordance with their own philosophies, negotiated with James for permission to travel to the New World, i.e. North America. Thirty-five Puritans, who had been living in exile in Holland for twelve or more years, and sixty-five others mainly from the south-west of England, left Plymouth, Devon, in September 1620. Known as the Pilgrim Fathers they sailed in the Mayflower, and after a two-and-a-half month voyage arrived safely and found a site that they named New Plymouth, situated in Cape Cod Bay (in Massachusetts).

The complex religious and vicious Thirty Years' War (1618 to 1648), fought mainly in the Holy Roman Empire (Germany), did not involve England directly, although it involved James's son-in-law, Frederick and his Spanish allies. James summoned Parliament in 1621, the first for seven years, which granted him money for the war, but they were confused at how it was to be used.

Parliament, having been summoned, was very active in its duties, and, objected to the possibility of Prince Charles, heir to the throne, marrying the Catholic Spanish Infanta: James forcefully informed Parliament that it was not of their concern, only of the monarch. As a consequence, James dissolved Parliament in February 1622. The marriage did not proceed.

Agreement was reached in December 1624 for the marriage between Prince Charles to Princess Henrietta Maria, the Catholic 15-year-old daughter of the late King Henry IV of France, but it was delayed by the death of James.

James died on March 27, 1625 at his country residence, Theobalds Park, Hertfordshire, and is buried at Westminster Abbey, London.

STUART

KING CHARLES I

Born	1600 November 19
Accession	1625 March 27
Age at Accession	24
Death (Execution)	1649 January 30
Age at Death	48
Reigned	23 years

Charles I succeeded his father James I.

In 1625 he married Princess Henrietta Maria (b.1609, d.1669), daughter of the late King Henry IV of France, and sister of King Louis XIII of France. They had 4 sons and 5 daughters; only 2 sons and 1 daughter lived to adulthood.

Charles I was the second son of James I. The eldest son Prince Henry (Prince of Wales) died at 18 years of age.

Persons of note:

Oliver Cromwell (b.1599, d.1658). Puritan; Member of Parliament for Huntingdon; founder of the New Model Army in 1644; Lord Protector 1653 to 1658.

Sir John Eliot (b.1592, d.1632). Member of Parliament; knighted in 1618. For opposing Charles in Parliament, he was imprisoned at the Tower of London in 1629 where he died three years later.

William Harvey (b.1578, d.1657). Physician who discovered the circulation of the blood. He was physician to King James I and Charles. His treatise 'On the

THE STUARTS: KING CHARLES I

Motion of the Heart and Blood' (1628) accurately described the circulation of blood via heart, lungs, arteries and veins.

William Laud (b.1573, d.1645). Archbishop of Canterbury 1633 until his death. His attempt with Charles to introduce the Book of Common Prayer into Scotland led to the Bishops' Wars. He was beheaded for treason.

John Milton (b.1608, d.1674). Poet and author. During the Civil War he supported the Parliamentarians. After he became blind he wrote the epic poem 'Paradise Lost'.

Sir Thomas Pride (b.?, d.1658). Colonel in the Parliamentary army; commanded the troops 'Pride's Purge' which prevented members of parliament who supported Charles from admission to the House of Commons. Appointed to the High Court of Justice and was one of fifty-nine signatures of the King's death warrant. Oliver Cromwell knighted him.

George Villiers (created Duke of Buckingham in 1623) (b.1592, d.1628). Royal favourite of King James I from 1623, and continued with Charles.

Charles succeeded to the throne on the death of his father King James I, who at the end of his reign had reached an agreement for Charles to marry the Catholic 15-year-old daughter of the late King Henry IV of France, and sister of King Louis XIII: the marriage with Princess Henrietta Maria took place seven weeks after his accession. Like his father he believed in the Divine Right of Kings, which made a difficult relationship with Parliament.

His first Parliament met in 1625 but acrimony arose immediately. In 1626 he summoned Parliament again, only for it to be dissolved within a few months because it wished to impeach his friend George Villiers (the Duke of Buckingham) for the naval failure against the Spanish at Cadiz.

Charles next sent George Villiers's army into France to protect the Huguenots (French Protestants) from their King, but the expedition was inconclusive. In 1628 when preparing for another excursion into France, George Villiers was attacked and stabbed to death in Portsmouth.

When the King refused to explain his foreign policy, Parliament refused to authorise any further taxes. Therefore, he levied forced loans throughout the country that were most unpopular and judged to be illegal. The Parliament of 1628 decided to control the abuses of Charles: they passed the Petition of Right, really a restatement of past legislation, in order for them to control taxes; to make illegal the procedure of arbitrary imprisonment; to control the billeting of soldiers in private houses (then a practice); and to limit the use of martial law. Eventually

Charles consented to these limitations of his power, but Parliament in 1629 accused him of ignoring the Petition.

Fearing dissolution by the King, a demonstration occurred when members of the House of Commons restrained the Speaker, Sir John Finch, in his chair to enable Eliot's 'Three Resolutions', dealing with religion and taxes, to be passed. Parliament was attempting to establish control over the monarch, including the appointment of ministers: the King refused, dissolved Parliament and sent Sir John Eliot and eight others to the Tower of London for imprisonment.

Parliament was not summoned for another eleven years: a period known as the 'Personal Rule of Charles'. He made peace with both France and Spain.

Trade within England and overseas was developing and expanding: coal-mining and other industries were gaining in importance; London as the capital and trading centre was becoming wealthier.

In 1627, Capt. Henry Powell landed a party of English settlers on Barbados to colonize this most easterly of the Caribbean islands. The English colonized Antigua, another island in the eastern Caribbean in 1632, which had been discovered by Christopher Columbus in 1493.

Charles introduced new forms of taxation that did not require Parliamentary approval, e.g. ship-money. Ship-money was raised to expand the Royal Navy: in 1634 it was levied only on coastal towns; in 1635 it was levied throughout the whole country. At first the tax was accepted, but by 1639 only about twenty percent paid the demands.

The Archbishop of Canterbury, William Laud, with the support of the King, enforced uniformity in the Church and persecuted those who did not conform. In doing so the High Anglicans and the Puritans were alienated. Meanwhile, many thousands of Puritans were emigrating to North America.

Constitutionally, the State was superior to the Church in England, whereas, in Scotland, the Church controlled the State. Charles did not really understand the two different systems and upset the Scots with his interferences. In 1637, together with the Archbishop of Canterbury, he sought to impose a version of the English Book of Common Prayer on the Scots, even by force. The Scots responded by sending a covenanting army into England in March 1639, the first of the so-called Bishops' Wars at York, although there was no fighting. A truce to leave the Scots alone was signed in the June at Berwick-on-Tweed.

By 1640 the 'Personal Rule of Charles' in England, and with Scotland intriguing with the French, the situation persuaded Charles to summon Parliament. Known as the Short Parliament, it met from April 13 to May 5. The King needed to raise money to subdue the Scots. Parliament refused; it was dissolved. Then the Scots invaded and took control of Northumberland and Durham in the August, purporting to support the English Parliament and the Puritans.

Under pressure Charles summoned another Parliament in the November.
(This Parliament is referred to as the Long Parliament because, technically, in a form, it sat for the next twenty years until 1660).

THE STUARTS: KING CHARLES I

Parliament exerted its power over a weakened King: it defined the powers of the Monarch and of Parliament which Charles was forced to accept. It abolished the arbitrary powers of the monarch; the Triennial Act stated that Parliament had to be summoned at least every three years; Parliament could not be dissolved without its own consent; Prerogative Courts (e.g. Star Chambers and the Court of High Commission) were abolished; all trials had to be heard by a jury; taxes such as ship-money were declared illegal; tonnage and poundage could be set only with Parliamentary approval; and there should be a Parliamentary reformation of the Church on Erastian-Presbyterian principles (i.e. submitting the Church to civil authority in all matters). All were given overwhelming Parliamentary support. The Act for the abolition of Episcopacy (the system in which bishops were the chief ministers of the Church government) – the Root and Branch Act – was passed by a small majority, as was the Grand Remonstrance to the King, that required the King's Councillors to be approved by Parliament.

At the beginning of January 1642, with Parliament intending to impeach the Catholic Queen Henrietta Maria, the King without precedent, entered Parliament with about four hundred men with the intention of arresting one member of the House of Lords and five leading members of the House of Commons, but, having received warning, the six had escaped earlier. The threatening anger of the people, forced Charles and his Court officials to flee to Hampton Court, then to Newmarket, to Nottingham and to York, leaving London under the control of Parliament. Previously, the Queen had travelled to Holland for safety.

Some months later in June, when calm had been restored, Parliament presented a list of propositions to Charles which included that Parliament should appoint all ministers of the government; it should control the militia; and a Church settlement should be determined by Parliament, all of which effectively gave Parliament supremacy over the monarch in matters of both state and Church.

Society was changing: Puritans were predominant in Parliament; High Anglican churchmen were dominant in the Royal Court; merchants and manufacturers wanted power which was held by the aristocracy and hereditary landlords. The country was divided, all causing turmoil and Scotland unsettled.

Should the King or Parliament be supreme in ruling the country? Civil War seemed inevitable. The divided country erupted in August 1642.

Charles made his headquarters, first in Shrewsbury and then in Oxford. The first confrontation between the two sides was inconclusive at the Battle of Edgehill, in Warwickshire, on October 23, 1642; by midsummer 1643 the Royalist had successes with the capture of Bristol (then England's second city to London); victory at Adwallan Moor, in Yorkshire; and the capture of Lincoln: but with the Royalist losing at Gloucester, Charles returned to Oxford. After the September Battle of Newbury, in Berkshire, the fortunes changed in favour of the Parliamentarians. At the end of the month, Parliament signed a Solemn League and Covenant with Presbyterian Scotland for them to join the war against Charles. The Scots crossed into England in January 1644. A significant Roundhead (a name used for the Parliamentarians, the Puritans, in this civil war) victory was achieved near York at Marston Moor on July 2, by far the largest confrontation of the Civil War where the Royalists lost nearly three thousand men, but then the Royalists were victorious at Lostwithiel, in Cornwall, at the beginning of September 1644.

Oliver Cromwell, Cambridge University educated and a member of parliament for Huntingdon from 1628, came into prominence after serving with the East Anglian regiments for the Parliamentary forces. In Parliament he had become influential in Roundhead politics: he criticized the manner the war was being conducted; he proposed a New Model Army based on his own East Anglian regiment. With the Parliamentary army re-organized, he was appointed General of the Horse, so becoming dominant in Parliament and the Army.

In June 1645, the Royalists were comprehensively defeated by the New Model Army at Naseby (south of Market Harborough) in Northamptonshire, under the command of Sir Thomas Fairfax, a major turning point in the Civil War. Between the September and the following June the Parliamentarians defeated the Royalists at Langport, in Somerset, followed by victories in Bristol and Stow-on-the-Wold, Gloucestershire. The King's headquarters in Oxford soon fell.

William Laud, Archbishop of Canterbury, was beheaded in January 1645 on Tower Hill after Parliament had passed the Bill of Attainder accusing him of treason; in reality it was for his support of Charles.

Charles had a French agent negotiate with the Scottish covenanters (Presbyterians) for his protection, despite their support for the Parliamentarians. He joined them at Newark, Nottinghamshire, at the beginning of May 1646, and they moved north in January 1647, and the next month handed Charles over to the English Parliamentary Commission. On the journey south, the people greeted him rapturously, causing considerable consternation to his escorts. In June he was moved to the army headquarters at Newmarket and then to Hampton Court where he was re-united with two of his children.

The Puritans, dominant in the Long Parliament, passed legislation to imprison Baptists; to prohibit laymen preaching in public; and to dismiss all independent officers of the New Model Army.

During this period Parliament and the King corresponded on constitutional matters although agreements were never reached. In 1647 the New Model Army was in dispute with Parliament over many issues including pay and, with the Civil War over, their threatened demobilisation. The army, now known as the Ironsides, still considered the monarch as their head and appealed to him over their grievances. The King sent a message to Parliament asking them to support the Ironsides: it agreed to do so but reversed its decision when the people intervened. The Ironsides were restive, but discipline was maintained.

Many people were changing allegiances to support the King, even some Parliamentarians. Charles escaped from imprisonment at Hampton Court: his plan to reach France failed; he arrived at Carisbroke Castle, on the Isle of Wight, where he remained for a year.

These disruptive conditions led to a second Civil War that was short. The whole country and institutions turned against the Ironsides, but the strength of its forces prevailed. Charles was taken to Hurst Castle, in Hampshire, at the end of 1648 and then to Windsor Castle, Berkshire, in December.

By this time Oliver Cromwell was in control. On December 6, Colonel Pride with his musketeers, known as 'Pride's Purge', prevented those members of parliament who were opposed to proceedings against the King, from admittance to the House of Commons. The remaining ninety or so members agreed to have a tribunal to try Charles for treason. He was brought to London, tried and found guilty at the trial held at Westminster Hall.

His beheading on January 30, 1649 was at the Banqueting Hall at Whitehall, London. A week later he was buried at Windsor, Berkshire.

COMMONWEALTH   1649 TO 1660

Commonwealth Governed by a Council of State   1649 January 30

Oliver Cromwell: **Commander-in-Chief**
at the age of 49   **1649 March**

Lord Protector   **1653 December 16**

Richard Cromwell: Lord Protector   **1658 September until**
at the age of 32   **1659 May**

Persons of note:

Oliver Cromwell (b. April 25, 1599, d. September 3, 1658). Educated at Cambridge University; Member of Parliament for Huntingdon; Puritan; founder of the New Model Army in 1644; Lord Protector 1653 to 1658.

Richard Cromwell (b. October 4, 1626, d. July 12, 1712). Son of Oliver Cromwell. Lord Protector 1658 to 1659. He officially abdicated May 25, 1659.

George Monck (1ˢᵗ Duke of Albemarle, created in 1660) (b.1608, d.1670). Professional soldier. He fought for King Charles I, the Commonwealth, then for the restoration of the monarchy.

John Bunyan (b.1628, d.1688). Writer and preacher. As a Puritan he served in the Parliamentary army. Whilst in prison for his religious preaching, from 1660 to 1672, he wrote 'The Pilgrim's Progress'.

William Harvey (b.1578, d.1657). Physician who discovered the circulation of the blood. He was physician to King James I and King Charles I. His treatise 'On the Motion of the Heart and Blood' (1628) accurately described the blood circulation via heart, lungs, arteries and veins.

John Milton (b.1608, d.1674). Poet and author. During the Civil War he supported the Parliamentarians. After he became blind he wrote his epic poem 'Paradise Lost'.

THE COMMONWEALTH

At the execution of King Charles I, the monarchy was replaced by the Commonwealth of England with a Council of State appointed to rule the country, both domestic and foreign affairs. During the following years, many changes were made to the various ruling bodies: initially Parliament elected members to the Council of State; Oliver Cromwell was its first chairman and was appointed Commander-in-Chief of the New Model Army.

The country was in disruption: those peers taken prisoner during the short second Civil War were beheaded; of the judiciary, six of the twelve judges refused to co-operate, but, nevertheless, Common Law was maintained.

The so-called Long Parliament, convened by King Charles I in 1640, continued to sit in a 'rump' form. It was not representative of the country; it was republican in tone; it pursued any policy it wished; and it could not be dissolved without its own consent. Its opponents were ruthlessly suppressed and heavy fines were imposed on the defeated Royalists and Roman Catholics.

Prince Charles Stuart, son and heir of the executed King Charles I was prevented from being crowned King by the Puritan army and Parliament. He was a loyal Protestant, despite his mother's Catholicism. In Scotland he received support and was proclaimed King Charles II under conditions, which he considered objectionable. The conditions of the covenant were extremely anti-Catholic, anti-Anglican, pro-Presbyterian. For supporting Prince Charles Stuart an angered Oliver Cromwell sent troops into Scotland, inflicting defeat on them at Dunbar, east Lothian in September 1650.

In 1650 Oliver Cromwell amalgamated some private regiments to form the Regiment of Foot, the direct predecessor of the Coldstream Guards (Coldstream, then in Berwickshire, now Borders, Scotland), under Colonel George Monck. (This is the oldest regiment in the United Kingdom army, and is still in existence.)

A Scottish force supporting Prince Charles Stuart invaded England the following year, but it was completely routed at Worcester on September 3. The Prince, involved in the invasion, escaped capture by hiding in an oak tree at Boscobel, Shropshire. Six weeks later he reached France for security. That was the last serious attempt to regain the throne until 1660.

The strength and size of the Royal Navy had declined during the last reign, which was rectified by the Commonwealth Government. England regained its position as a strong naval power. The 1651 Navigation Act, similar to previous Acts since the time of King Richard II, stated that all goods brought into England had to be transported by English ships or ships belonging to the country from which the goods originated.

The Dutch had become dominant in commercial shipping, including trading in the Baltic, the Indian spice trade, and the herring fisheries. They objected to the implementation of the Navigation Act, and declared war against England in May 1652. One thousand, four hundred Dutch ships were captured and their shipping dominance was ended. Eventually, a peace treaty was signed in 1654: England now controlled shipping in the English Channel.

In Ireland, a rebellion against the English that started in 1641 was finally crushed in April 1653, by the army commanded by George Monck. One third of the population had died as a result of the uprising and Catholicism had been suppressed. Vast acreage of land was transferred to officers of the New Model Army and the Protestant settlers.

Oliver Cromwell was dissatisfied with the Rump Parliament and he physically locked its doors, ending the session on April 20, 1653. A new nominated Parliament, the Barebones Parliament, named after the parliamentarian 'Praise-God Barbon', had members appointed from England, Wales. Scotland and Ireland, the first time all four countries had been represented in a form of Parliament. It dissolved itself within a few months, after appointing Oliver Cromwell to the position of Lord Protector.

The New Model Army drafted a constitution, the 'Instrument of Government'. It proposed: the Lord Protector to have executive power; a single House of Parliament to have legislative powers; the Lord Protector to have power over the parliament: in theory, the Council of State had power over the Lord Protector.

The first Protectorate Parliament met in 1654, but immediately a hundred of the appointed members were excluded for refusing to swear allegiance to the Commonwealth and the Lord Protector. The remaining members wanted a different constitution; to reduce the size of the army; and to abolish toleration towards religious opponents. This Parliament was dissolved fairly quickly.

Oliver Cromwell, as Lord Protector, could now dictate and implement his own policies. He divided the country into eleven districts, each to be administered by a major-general with responsibilities for policing and public order, the collection of special taxes from the Royalists, and strict enforcement of Puritan morality.

In 1655, with Spain at war with France over the control of the Spanish Netherlands, Oliver Cromwell took the opportunity in an attempt to weaken the Catholic influence in the Americas, by sending a force of twenty-five thousands, transported in forty ships, to the Caribbean. They failed to capture Hispaniola (now Haiti and the Dominican Republic), but the nearby island of Jamaica, discovered by Christopher Columbus in 1494 and settled by the Spanish from 1509, was poorly defended. The English troops invaded and took possession of the island. In other actions, the English at Cadiz in 1656 and Tenerife in 1657 destroyed the Spanish fleets.

Prince Charles Stuart summoned his two thousand troops fighting for France under the command of his brother, Prince James (Duke of York), to transfer to the Spanish, to oppose Oliver Cromwell's actions against the Spanish. One of his senior regiments in 1656 became the Royal Regiment of Guards and another eventually became the Life Guards regiment. (The former is the direct predecessor of the Grenadier Guards, the most senior regiment of Foot Guards, and the latter was the most senior regiment in the army, until it was amalgamated with the Blues and Royals.)

Oliver Cromwell sought peace. An Anglo-French alliance was signed in March 1657 for England to join France in the war over the Spanish Netherlands, which ended inconclusively.

Agreements were reached between France and Spain in October 1659, and England and Spain in September 1660, to stop the conflicts. In this agreement, Jamaica remained an English possession.

In 1657 the second Protectorate Parliament was selected and, again, a hundred of its members were excluded; the remaining members presented to the Lord Protectorate the Humble Petition and Advice, under which they proposed that the Council of State should be abolished; Cromwell be made King and given increased powers, including the right to name his successor; and that there should be two Houses of Parliament. The New Model Army was against kingship, but agreed with the other proposals.

A new House of Lords was installed and many of Oliver Cromwell's loyal supporters were transferred from the House of Commons to the new House of Lords, and the hundred members, previously excluded, were permitted to return to the House of Commons. Yet again following further difficulties: the Lord Protector dissolved Parliament in February 1658.

The Lord Protector's rule and control of the country and its enforcement by the major-generals were much resented. All gaiety, fun, sport, drunkenness and swearing was punished. There was some religious freedom: the Quaker movement (the full title 'The Religious Society of Friends') was founded in England around 1650, and Jews were allowed to return to the country, having been expelled from England in 1290. Many schools were founded under the Puritan influence.

Oliver Cromwell, the Lord Protector, died on September 3, 1658 and was buried at Westminster Abbey, London.

His son, Richard Cromwell, was immediately proclaimed the new Lord Protector. The New Model Army did not support Richard Cromwell, and demanded that England become a republic. Eighteen months of crises followed.

In 1659 the English East India Company took possession of the strategically placed island of St Helena in the south Atlantic Ocean. The Dutch had annexed the island in 1633.

The New Model Army dismissed Richard Cromwell and recalled the Rump Parliament in May 1659. General George Monck, the Commander-in-Chief of Scotland, led forces into England to restore order that had disintegrated under the weak Richard Cromwell; also he re-instated members to the Parliament who previously had been excluded by Pride's Purge in 1648. On March 16, 1660, the Long Parliament was dissolved and new elections were held. The so-called Convention Parliament met for the first time in April 1660.

Negotiations were held with Prince Charles Stuart to become King of England. On advice from General George Monck, the Prince moved from the Catholic Spanish Netherlands to the Protestant Netherlands, and with three principal advisors prepared the Declaration of Breda of 1660. It contained four constituent points: indemnity; free pardon to those who would swear allegiance to the Crown; land tenure; and a religious settlement.

Copies of the Declaration of Breda were sent to the House of Lords, the House of Commons, the New Model Army, the Royal Navy, and the City of London. Prince Charles Stuart insisted that it should be placed before the newly elected Parliament for their decision. The members of both Houses of Parliament were mainly Royalists and Presbyterians: they unanimously approved the Declaration on May 1, 1660.

On May 24, 1660 Richard Cromwell formally resigned as Lord Protector. General George Monck received and welcomed Prince Charles Stuart at Dover, Kent.

The Commonwealth Government had ended, and the monarchy was about to be restored.

STUART – RESTORATION

KING CHARLES II

Born	**1630 May 29**
Accession	**1660 May 29**
Age at Accession	**30**
Death	**1685 February 6**
Age at Death	**54**
Reigned	**24 years**

Charles II succeeded to the throne when the monarchy was restored after the Commonwealth Government period of rule. He was the eldest son of Charles I.

In 1662 he married Catherine of Braganza, Princess of Portugal (b.1638, d.1705), daughter of John IV, King of Portugal. They had no children.

Persons of note:

John Bunyan (b.1628, d.1688). Writer and preacher. As a Puritan he served in the Parliamentary army. Whilst in prison for his religious preaching, from 1660 to 1672, he wrote 'The Pilgrim's Progress'.

Earl of Clarendon (Edward Hyde, created Earl in 1661) (b.1609, d.1674). Statesman, lawyer and historian; minister to King Charles I and Lord Chancellor to Charles II. His daughter, Anne, married Prince James, the future King James II.

Earl of Danby (Sir Thomas Osbourne) (b.1632, d.1712). Statesman. Chief Minister 1673 to 1679, and 1690 to 1694; impeached 1678; Royal pardon which Parliament declared illegal and sent him to the Tower of London until 1684 without trial.

John Dryden (b.1631, d.1700). Poet and dramatist; political satirist. Poet Laureate 1668 to 1688.

Nell Gwynn (b.1650, d.1687). She was an actress from the age of fifteen and performed at the Drury Lane Theatre, London. John Dryden wrote characters especially for her to play. She became the mistress of Charles II and they had 2 sons.

John Milton (b.1608, d.1674). Poet and author. During the Civil War he supported the Parliamentarians. After he became blind he wrote his epic poem 'Paradise Lost'.

George Monck (1st Duke of Albemarle, created 1660) (b.1608, d.1670). Professional soldier. He fought for King Charles I, the Commonwealth, and then for the restoration of the monarchy.

Duke of Monmouth (James Scott) (b.1649, d.1685). Pretender to the throne; illegitimate son of Charles II with Lucy Walter. After 1662 he lived at Court; created Duke in 1663.

Titus Oates (1649, d.1705). His anti-Catholic preaching and activities caused considerable unrest in the country. He was deceitful and a liar. Sent to prison in 1681; in 1685 stripped of his 'clerical dress'. He was pardoned in 1688.

Samuel Pepys (b.1633, d.1703). Diarist and naval administrator. His diaries from 1660 to 1669 were in cipher; not deciphered until 1825.

Sir Christopher Wren (b.1632, d.1723). Architect. After the Great Fire of London in 1666, he rebuilt St Paul's Cathedral and over fifty other churches. He helped to found the Royal Society.

Parliament, known as the Convention Parliament, considered the conditions for the restoration of the monarchy in England and the Declaration of Breda, which Charles had prepared and submitted. Parliament unanimously approved the Declaration on May 1, 1660.

General George Monck received Prince Charles Stuart at Dover on May 25, 1660 and he entered London as King Charles II on his thirtieth birthday, having been in exile mostly since the age of 15.

The Declaration of Breda's four conditions were:
(i)   Arrears of pay promised to the soldiers to be paid;

(ii)   A general amnesty to Commonwealth supporters for those swearing allegiance to the Crown;

(iii)   Security of tenure to those who had obtained land under the Commonwealth;

(iv)   Liberty of conscience over religious matters.

Parliament approved (i), followed by the army being disbanded except for the Regiment of Foot (later re-named the Coldstream Guards). The Act of Indemnity and Oblivion became law in the August: some exceptions were made to (ii) as thirteen regicides were executed and twenty-five others imprisoned for life, whilst Oliver Cromwell's body was exhumed from its burial place in Westminster Abbey, to be hanged at Tyburn and afterwards buried beneath the gallows, the site now of Connaught Square, London. The clause (iii) proved to be very complicated, the outcome not being satisfactory. The fourth clause (iv) was delayed for a future parliament to act.

The monarchy was restored.

Nevertheless, Parliament generally retained the powers it had previously gained over the monarch, who could no longer tax on his own or in any form without the consent of Parliament. Their decisions and the enforcement of Common Law were absolute.

At the restoration, Charles's Royal Regiment of Guards was renamed the King's Own Regiment of Foot Guards.

The East India Company that received its charter from Richard Cromwell to govern the south Atlantic Ocean island, St Helena, received the Royal charter from Charles in 1661.

The Convention Parliament was dissolved in December 1660 and the so-named Cavalier Parliament was elected in May 1661. In the next few years four radical Acts were passed, entitled the Clarendon Code, named after the Lord Chancellor, the Earl of Clarendon.

The Corporation Act of 1661: Corporations were the local authorities, which governed the towns and controlled the elections to Parliament. To be a member of the corporation required an oath of allegiance to the King and to be a communicant of the Church of England. The Act was an attempt to deprive Puritans from holding positions in the towns and Parliament.

The Act of Uniformity of 1662: All the clergy had to be ordained by a bishop; all schoolmasters to be licensed by a bishop; both clergy and schoolmasters had to take the oath of allegiance to the King and to use and accept the Book of Common Prayer. Over two thousand clergy who refused to conform to the Act were deprived of their livings.

The Conventicle Act of 1664: This prohibited religious assemblies of more than five people, except under the auspices of the Church of England. Punishment for this offence could lead to transportation from England to the colonies.

THE STUARTS – RESTORATION: KING CHARLES II

The Five Mile Act of 1665: All non-conformists were prohibited to live or travel within five miles of any town. Although this may appear to have been severe, towns in 1665 were very far apart, not very large in size, and the majority of the population lived in rural locations.

These Acts of the Clarendon Code helped to re-establish the supremacy of the Church of England, mainly, to the disadvantage of the Puritans.

In 1662, Charles married Princess Catherine of Braganza, the daughter of the King of Portugal. The dowry secured two useful possessions for England – Bombay (now Mumbai) in India, and Tangier in Morocco – the latter giving English shipping an untroubled access to the Mediterranean Sea. Marriage to Catherine did not preclude Charles's extra-marital relationships, especially with his famous mistress Nell Gwynn, his 'Protestant Whore'.

'The Royal Society of London for the Promotion of Natural Knowledge', generally known as the Royal Society, was founded in 1660 and received its Royal charter in 1662. It is one of the oldest scientific societies in the World.

The King issued his first Declaration of Indulgence in 1663, aiming to introduce a degree of religious tolerance in taking oaths of allegiance. The House of Commons objected and declared it void.

In 1663 the English attacked a Dutch west African trading base, and the following year in North America the town of New Amsterdam was overrun. In retaliation the Dutch attacked the Caribbean island of Barbados. At sea the great Four Days' Battle, one of the longest naval engagements in history, ended with both sides claiming victory. Finally, the Dutch inflicted a heavy defeat on the Royal Navy at Medway, the mouth of the River Thames. The second Dutch War (the first being in 1652) ended with the signing of the Treaty of Breda in 1667. The Dutch kept control of some of its captures, secured its trading routes, and the Navigation Act of 1651 was amended. England kept its conquests in North America, being parts of New England and the town of New Amsterdam, soon to be re-named New York, named after Charles's brother Prince James, who also had the title Duke of York.

Two major catastrophes occurred in 1665 and 1666. The Great Plague, having spread across Europe, had a devastating effect in England killing twenty percent of Londoners and many throughout the country. The Great Fire of London in 1666 started in a bakery in Pudding Lane, ultimately destroying thirteen hundred houses, ninety churches, many warehouses and stores, altogether two-thirds of all buildings in the capital.

As a condition for increasing his income, Charles agreed in 1667 that Parliament would audit his expenditure, ensuring that grants made to him were being used for the intended purposes.

King Louis XIV of France (the Great, born in 1638 and who reigned from 1643 to 1715) had become a threat to France's smaller neighbours, so in 1668 a Protestant Triple Alliance of England, Holland and Sweden was formed to counteract France. This unlikely Alliance ended with Sweden's defection; also, there were problems between England and Holland. Negotiations between Charles and Louis concluded with the secret Treaty of Dover in 1670, in which Charles would receive an annual income from the French, on the condition that he would declare himself a Roman Catholic, at an appropriate time, and to join France in a war against Holland. With the substantial increase in income, Charles strengthened and rebuilt the Royal Navy.

In 1670, the Regiment of Foot was re-named the Coldstream Guards in recognition of its march from Coldstream (then in Berwickshire, now Borders, Scotland) to London in support of the restoration of the monarchy.

The history of modern Canada began in 1497 when John Cabot reached the north-east coast of that continent; Jacques Cartier claimed it for the French in 1534, and the actual establishment of New France began in 1604. In 1670, the English Hudson's Bay Company established itself in Canada for trading.

During March 1672 Charles issued his second Declaration of Indulgence, proposing to protect non-conformist and recusants (those who were fined for not attending Church of England mass) from discrimination. Parliament refused to accept the Declaration because it was at variance with legislation passed since the restoration of the monarchy. Charles withdrew the Declaration and agreed to the 1673 Test Act, later to the 1678 Test Act, both of which precluded a person from holding an office of state unless they were regular communicants of the Church of England. The Acts resulted in the removal of several ministers of the Government, some advisors, and Charles's Catholic brother, Prince James (the Duke of York), who was the Lord High Admiral.

The College of Physicians founded by King Henry VIII's charter in 1518, acquired its 'Royal' prefix in 1674.

Prince James's daughter, the Protestant Princess Mary, married her first cousin Prince William of Orange in 1677. Prince William's mother was the Princess Royal, sister to both Charles and Prince James.

The existence of a popish plot to re-establish Catholicism in England was made in a statement to magistrates by the Anglican priest Dr Titus Oates in 1678. Although no real evidence of a plot could be found, it caused considerable unrest in the country, particularly, as the heir presumptive was a Catholic. Also, it was revealed that a leading parliamentarian, the recently ennobled Earl of Danby, had been in negotiations with the French King. Parliament decided to impeach the Earl. Dr Titus Oates, in punishment for perjury, received three thousand four hundred lashings administered over a period of three days.

By the end of 1678, the King dissolved Parliament after its existence of eighteen years. The next Parliament was concerned about Charles's now obvious Catholic sympathies. To counter this he allowed the Earl of Danby to be imprisoned at the Tower of London, as Parliament wished, and sent Prince James (Duke of York) abroad in exile.

In Parliament, two main opponents derogatory name-called each other. The names 'stuck' and the groupings became known as the Tories and Whigs. The Tories were mainly Anglicans, the Whigs mainly non-conformists, with the latter being in the majority in the House of Commons.

THE STUARTS – RESTORATION: KING CHARLES II

It was in 1679 that a most important and lasting piece of legislation was passed: the Act of *Habeas Corpus*, to ensure that the prosecuted were brought to court for trial before a jury, and as early as possible.

This Parliament and the following two (all three sat between 1679 and 1681) attempted to pass the Exclusion Bill that would have debarred the heir presumptive, Prince James (Duke of York), from succeeding his brother as King. It was claimed that the Duke of Monmouth (the illegitimate son of Charles) could have been considered legitimate, but Charles rejected these moves. Because of these attempts, all three Parliaments were dissolved, the last having been held in Oxford in order to avoid the agitation of Londoners.

Prince James returned from exile in May 1682. The following year a plot was uncovered to assassinate both Charles and Prince James at Rye House, Hoddesdon, Hertfordshire, when they would have been returning from horseracing at Newmarket, Suffolk.

After 1681 Charles decided to rule without Parliament. He made changes to the charter of London and the charters of sixty-five towns in England, so allowing him to nominate the men to run the corporations – the local authorities – which in turn elected members to the House of Commons.

Bermuda, situated about 700 miles off the coast of south-east United States of America, was discovered by the Spanish in c.1503. In 1612 ships of the Virginia Company were windblown off-course to Bermuda, which they claimed. In 1684 Bermuda became a colony administered by the Crown.

Charles had a stroke and died on February 6, 1685 at the age of 54. His friend the Roman Catholic priest Father Huddleston, who helped him escape from Worcestershire in 1651, administered the last Sacrament, so indicating Charles to be a communicant of the Roman Catholic Church. He was buried at Westminster Abbey, London.

STUART

KING JAMES II

Born	**1633 October 14**
Accession	**1685 February 6**
Age at Accession	**51**
Deemed to have abdicated	**1688 December 11**
Reigned	**3 years**
Death	**1701 September 6**
Age at Death	**67**

James II, who succeeded his brother Charles II, was the second son of King Charles I.

In 1659 he married, firstly, Anne (b.1637, d.1671), daughter of the 1ˢᵗ Earl of Clarendon. They had 4 sons and 4 daughters, only two survived childhood, Princess Mary and Princess Anne.

In 1673 he married, secondly, the 15-year-old Mary (b.1658, d.1718), daughter of Alphonsus IV, the Duke of Modena, Italy. Of the children born, only one lived beyond the age of five. He was James Francis Edward, known as 'The Old Pretender' (b.1688, d.1766). He had a son Charles Edward Louis Philip Casimir, and he was known as 'The Young Pretender' (b.1720, d.1788).

Persons of note:

Earl of Argyll (Archibald Campbell) (b.1629, d.1685). He was an active Protestant and joined the conspiracy to place the Duke of Monmouth on the throne.

John Dryden (b.1631, d.1700). Poet and dramatist; political satirist. Poet Laureate 1668 to 1688.

Edmund Halley (b.1656, d.1742). Astronomer Royal 1720 until his death. He published observations on the planets and comets, being the first to predict the return of a comet. He made the magnetic survey of the oceans 1698 to 1700.

Judge George Jeffreys (b.c.1648, d.1689). Known as 'The Hanging Judge'. Chief Justice under James II. Created Baron Jeffreys. When James II was overthrown, Judge Jeffreys was imprisoned in the Tower of London where he died.

Duke of Monmouth (James Scott) (b.1649, d.1685). Pretender to the throne; illegitimate son of King Charles II with Lucy Walter. After 1662 he lived at Court; created Duke in 1663; beheaded in 1685 on Tower Hill, London.

Sir Isaac Newton (b.1642, d.1727). Scientist. His three great discoveries included the theory of gravitation.

William Sancroft (b.1617, d.1693). Appointed Dean of St Paul's Cathedral in 1664 and greatly assisted in the rebuilding after the Great Fire of London of 1666. Archbishop of Canterbury 1678 to 1691.

Sir Christopher Wren (b.1632, d.1723). Architect. After the Great Fire of London in 1666, he rebuilt St Paul's Cathedral and over fifty other churches. He helped to found the Royal Society.

The people enthusiastically received James II on his accession to the throne, succeeding his brother King Charles II.

The new Parliament, elected on the basis of the corporations remodelled by King Charles II, was dominated by the Tories, who being loyal monarchists voted James a large income. He had converted to Roman Catholicism in 1669, although in politics he had always been a leading Anglican Tory.

King Charles II's illegitimate son, the Duke of Monmouth, and the Earl of Argyll planned to overthrow James. Separately they departed from Holland: the Earl to Scotland and the Duke to south-west England. The Earl of Argyll was arrested at Inchinnan, near Glasgow, taken to Edinburgh and was beheaded on June 30, 1685. The Duke of Monmouth arrived at Lyme Regis, Dorset, on June 11 and several thousand local people from Dorset and Somerset joined in support, but were easily defeated at Sedgemoor, Somerset. The Duke was captured, and in July was executed by beheading.

The Chief Justice, Judge Jeffreys, was sent to the west country where he sentenced more than three thousand opponents of James to be hanged and eight hundred transported to the Caribbean islands into slavery, at the so-called 'Bloody Assizes'.

James was determined to have Roman Catholics in the important posts of government; at Oxford University; in the judiciary; the county Lord Lieutenancies; the officers of the army; to suspend the Test Acts and the Act of *Habeas Corpus* of 1679. He prorogued Parliament in July 1685 after a disagreement, and then ruled without one.

Contrary to the law, James revived the Court of High Commission, mainly, to prevent Anglican clergy preaching against Catholicism. In May he issued a Declaration of Indulgence to be read by the clergy in every church stating that the laws against Roman Catholics and Protestant Dissenters should be suspended. He always linked the non-conformists Dissenters' causes in his depositions as a distraction whilst intending to give increased power to the Catholics. Archbishop of Canterbury William Sancroft and some bishops were prosecuted for sedition for refusing to read the Declaration of Indulgence in their churches. They were committed to the Tower of London, but acquitted of the charges. The country did not convert to Catholicism as James had hoped and expected.

Bombay (now Mumbai) in India, transferred to England in 1662 as part of the dowry of King Charles II's marriage, became the seat of English rule in India in 1687.

King Louis XIV's maltreatment of the French Protestants resulted in many of them migrating, bringing their skills in business and industry to the benefit of England.

On June 10, 1688 the succession of the monarchy changed, causing great concern. After fifteen years of marriage a healthy son was born to James and Queen Mary; previously she had given birth ten times. Protestants accepted James's Catholicism knowing that Princess Mary, his eldest daughter was heir presumptive and a strong Protestant. Now the birth of a boy prince changed the situation.

Archbishop Sancroft concurred with some Whigs and Tories, in an appeal to the Protestant Prince William of Orange (Holland), inviting him to invade England in order to overthrow James. Prince William of Orange was the husband of Princess Mary, the eldest daughter of James.

Prince William of Orange accepted: he landed forces at Torbay, in Devon, on November 5, 1688 and was well received by the population. Prince William had 14,000 soldiers transported in 500 ships and escorted by 60 warships. James had a large, well equipped army of 27,000 men and a better navy, and felt confident of victory. Disaster occurred for James when the Royal Navy defected to Prince William and many regiments of the army deserted. His attempt at a reconciliation with the Parliamentary leaders failed.

James's wife, Queen Mary, and their young son had escaped to France. His efforts to follow the Queen to France on December 11 failed and he threw the 'Great Seal' of his office into the River Thames at Vauxhall, London. The seal was the symbol of kingship: this action was deemed to have been his abdication. He was captured, and then escaped to France on Christmas Day.

The 'Glorious Revolution' of 1688 was bloodless: a settlement of the religious and political differences was accomplished. James's reign of less than four years of turbulence, created by himself, ended peacefully.

James died at Saint-Germain-en-Laye, France, on September 6, 1701 where he was buried.

STUART

KING WILLIAM III & QUEEN MARY II

	WILLIAM III	MARY II
Born	1650 November 4	1662 April 30
Accession	1689 February 13	1689 February 13
Age at Accession	38	26
Death	1702 March 8	1694 December 28
Age at Death	51	32
Reigned	13 years	5 years

William III and Mary II succeeded James II after his deemed abdication of December 11, 1688.

William III was the son of Princess Mary (the Princess Royal), sister of James II. Princess Mary had married William II, Prince of Orange of the Netherlands.

Mary II was the daughter of James II and his first wife Anne, daughter of the 1st Earl of Clarendon. She had been heir presumptive until 1688.

William III and Mary II were first cousins, both grandchildren of King Charles I. They had no children.

Persons of note:

John Dryden (b.1631, d.1700). Poet and dramatist; political satirist. Poet Laureate 1668 to 1688. He was hostile to the Glorious Revolution of 1688.

THE STUARTS: KING WILLIAM III & QUEEN MARY II

Edmund Halley (b.1656, d.1742). Astronomer Royal 1720 until his death. He published observations of the planets and comets, being the first to predict the return of a comet. He made the magnetic survey of the oceans 1698 to 1700.

Charles Montagu (1ˢᵗ Earl of Halifax) (b.1661, d.1715). Chancellor of the Exchequer 1694 to 1699.

Sir Isaac Newton (b.1642, d.1727). Scientist. His three great discoveries included the theory of gravitation.

Jonathon Swift (b.1667, d.1745). Irish born satirist. Took Anglican religious orders; involved in politics. He wrote 'Gulliver's Travels' in 1726.

Sir Christopher Wren (b.1632, d.1723). Architect. After the Great Fire of London in 1666, he rebuilt St Paul's Cathedral and over fifty other churches. He helped to found the Royal Society.

King James II was deemed to have abdicated on December 11, 1688 when he threw the 'Great Seal' of his office into the River Thames at Vauxhall, London, the Seal being the symbol of kingship.

Previously, the Protestant William of Orange (Holland) had been invited by sympathizers to overthrow and replace the Catholic King James II, which commenced when he landed with his forces at Torbay, Devon, on November 5, 1688.

His wife Princess Mary (the eldest daughter of King James II) had been heir presumptive to the throne until her father had a son in 1688. William of Orange and Princess Mary were first cousins and grandchildren of King Charles I.

On February 12, 1689, the Convention Parliament (there were three so-called Convention Parliaments in 1399, 1660 and 1689) declared King James II had abdicated, and invited the cousins to be joint-monarchs, with William having executive power. They were crowned on April 11. The Glorious Revolution of 1688 established the Protestant monarchy in England.

The Whigs and Tories used this period as an opportunity to increase the role of Parliament and to reduce the power of the monarchy. The Bill of Rights of 1689 declared that the Crown could be held only by a Protestant; the Crown would no longer have the power to suspend the laws or have independent powers, recently used; all prerogative courts would be illegal; Parliament to be freely elected with members having freedom of speech; no taxes to be raised without its consent; a standing army would be illegal and troops could not be armed for longer than twelve months. Some of these clauses reiterated previous legislation which often had been ignored by past monarchs.

THE STUARTS: KING WILLIAM III & QUEEN MARY II

The Toleration Act of the same year began the process of freedom to worship, although some restrictions of employment and the holding of office under the Test Act (1673) and the Corporation Act (1661) remained. In 1690 the Whigs tried and failed to amend various provisions. William, still having the power to dissolve Parliament, did so and the following February elections gave the Tories a majority.

William, still responsible for Dutch affairs as stadholder of the United Provinces of the Netherlands, spent periods away from England during his reign, mainly opposing the French. King Louis XIV of France, the long reigning monarch, continued his desire to dominate and rule his neighbouring countries, including Holland and the adjacent Spanish Netherlands (nowadays Belgium and Luxembourg). There were intermittent battles on land and sea, involving many thousands of troops, but neither side won a battle decisively between 1689 and 1697.

In a complicated situation, with the Pope against King Louis XIV but supporting William and with the French King wanting to distract and weaken William by expanding the area of his war, he made an attempt to facilitate the return of King James II to the English throne by opening up divisions in Ireland.

The attempt on July 1, 1690 (the later introduced Gregorian calendar amended the date to July 12) culminated in the Battle of the Boyne, probably Ireland's most famous battle. (The battle site was near to Drogheda on the River Boyne, about twenty miles north of Dublin, today in the Republic of Ireland.) King James II's army of about 30,000 troops of Irish, English, Dutch, German and French origin was opposed by the better trained and equipped William's army of Irish, English, Scottish, Dutch, French Huguenots, Germans, Swiss, Italian, Scandinavian and Polish, totalling about 36,000 troops. William defeated King James II, but was merciful in victory, for those times, for only about 2,000 were killed, two thirds being King James's forces.

Taxes were insufficient to finance further fighting. A new scheme, the National Debt, was instituted to encourage people to loan money to the government in return for interest payments. The following year, 1694, the Chancellor of the Exchequer, Charles Montagu, founded the Bank of England, a joint-stock company, which was to work in partnership with the Government.

In December 1694 Mary died of smallpox, leaving William to reign as sole monarch. Mary was buried at Westminster Abbey, London.

The Licensing Act (a statute to regulate authors and publishers) was required to be renewed annually by Parliament, but in 1695 this procedure was ended, so giving the press a wider degree of liberty, although the libel laws and the Sedition Acts remained in force.

The French were exhausted by their eight years of war. In the 1697 peace Treaty of Rijswijk, in Holland, King Louis XIV recognized William of Orange as King of England.

William and Mary were childless and the heir presumptive was Princess

THE STUARTS: KING WILLIAM III & QUEEN MARY II

Anne, Mary's sister. Princess Anne's only child to have survived infancy, the Duke of Gloucester, died in 1700 at the age of ten from smallpox. Parliament passed the Act of Settlement in 1701, decreeing that the succession after William would be Princess Anne, followed by Princess Sophia of Hanover, whose mother Princess Elizabeth was the daughter of King James I. (Princess Elizabeth had married Frederick V, Count of Palatine of the Rhine, Elector, King of Bohemia. Princess Sophia had married Ernst Augustus, the Duke of Brunswick-Lunenburg, King of Hanover, and Elector.) Also, the Act specified that every future sovereign of England must be a communicant of the Church of England.

London with a population of about half-a-million people had become the centre of commerce, industry and finance. The generated wealth substantially increased trade in both imports and exports.

From the 1680s to 1702 saw the formation of many army regiments raised by individuals for the country, such as Lord Lucan, the Duke of Beaufort and Sir William Clifton. This set the precedent throughout the 18th and 19th centuries. Nearly all of the regiments of the 21st century can trace their origins to this period.

On September 16, 1701 the abdicated King James II died in France. King Louis XIV now reneged on the Treaty of Rijswijk by publicly recognizing King James II's son, James Francis Edward, as King James III of England.

King Louis XIV was beginning to prepare new plans to increase the territories under his rule: the death of King Charles II of Spain without an heir was the start of the War of the Spanish Succession in 1701. French troops entered the Spanish Netherlands; English shipping was threatened in the English Channel and the Mediterranean Sea.

Parliament's efforts to provide funds to enlarge the size of the army and the Royal Navy were not sufficient to satisfy William, so he dissolved Parliament. The newly elected House of Commons retained its Tory majority, but, nevertheless, England prepared for another war against France.

William had a horse-riding accident from which the complications of his injury caused his death on March 8, 1702 at the age of 51. He was buried at Westminster Abbey, London.

STUART

QUEEN ANNE

Born	1665 February 6
Accession	1702 March 8
Age at Accession	37
Death	1714 August 1
Age at Death	49
Reigned	12 years

Anne who succeeded her cousin William III was the second surviving daughter of King James II.

In 1683 she married George, Prince of Denmark (b.1653, d.1708), the son of Frederick III, King of Denmark and Norway. They had many children; all except one died at birth or infancy. The one surviving child, the Duke of Gloucester, died in 1700 at the age of 10 from smallpox.

Persons of note:

1ˢᵗ Duke of Marlborough (John Churchill) (b.1650, d.1722). Soldier and statesman. He served under King James II at the defeat of the Duke of Monmouth, and was made a Baron in 1685. He supported William of Orange against King James II in the Glorious Revolution of 1688, receiving an Earldom. Created Duke in 1702. He served in the War of the Spanish Succession with victories at Blenheim (1704), Ramillies (1706), Oudenaarde (1708), and Malplaquet (1709). Dismissed for alleged corruption in 1711, he fled to Holland and returned to England in 1714.

THE STUARTS: QUEEN ANNE

Edmund Halley (b.1656, d.1742). Astronomer Royal 1720 until his death. He published observations on the planets and comets, being the first to predict the return of a comet. He made the magnetic survey of the oceans 1698 to 1700.

Sir Isaac Newton (b.1642, d.1727). Scientist. His three great discoveries included the theory of gravitation.

Jonathon Swift (b.1667, d.1745). Irish born satirist. Took Anglican religious orders; involved in politics. He wrote 'Gulliver's Travels' in 1726.

Sir Christopher Wren (b.1632, d.1723). Architect. After the Great Fire of London in 1666, he rebuilt St Paul's Cathedral and over fifty other churches. He helped to found the Royal Society.

Anne succeeded to the throne on the death of King William III in accordance with the conditions of the 1689 Bill of Rights and the 1701 Act of Settlement. She was the younger sister of Queen Mary II and cousin to King William III.

The War of the Spanish Succession dominated the whole of Anne's reign, with King Louis XIV (the long reigning French monarch from 1643 to 1715) determined to rule and dominate France's neighbours, including interfering in the succession of the Spanish throne, although England, the Dutch republic and France had conspired from 1698 to divide Spain and its possessions at the death of their king, Philip II. By 1702 France had overrun the Spanish Netherlands (nowadays Belgium and Luxembourg) that created a threat to the Netherlands. In Parliament the Tories were dominant, although Anne disagreed with their policy of fighting the war.

England, now a World trading country was increasing its strength in maritime, commercial and financial affairs. Its interests needed to be protected, particularly from France and Spain, rivals for control of the English Channel and the Mediterranean Sea.

On April 13, 1704 the Duke of Marlborough, one of England's most successful generals, achieved one of England's greatest victories at the Battle of Blenheim (Blindheim, north-west of Munich, Germany). This major defeat of the French was the first they had experienced for more than fifty years. It was very brutal: of 52,000 troops of the English and Austrian allies 12,000 were killed or wounded; of the French and Bavarian enemy 18,000 were killed or wounded out of 60,000 troops. The victory prevented Austria and the small German states being invaded and occupied: just as importantly it destroyed the apparent invincibility of the French and re-established the military prestige of England.

The Anglo-Dutch forces then captured Gibraltar, in southern Spain; so giving some control to England of the narrow entrance to the Mediterranean Sea.

In 1706 the Duke of Marlborough led the armies of the Anglo-Dutch troops to victory at the Battle of Ramillies, south-east of Brussels, on May 23; France lost control of the whole north and east of the Spanish Netherlands. The allies had 5,000 killed and wounded; the French had 17,000 killed, wounded and captured, each side having about 60,000 troops in the battle.

1707 was one of the most important years in English history when England and Scotland joined together with the passing of the Act of Union in both Parliaments. From 1603 when King James VI of Scotland became the King of England as James I, both countries were ruled by the same monarch with each country keeping its separate Parliament and legal system, etc. The Scottish Parliament voted for Union on January 16, 1707; the Act came into effect on May 1. The Act of Union constituted one Parliament to govern both countries: the Scots were allocated forty-five seats in the House of Commons and sixteen peers in the House of Lords. Scotland retained their own legal system; Presbyterianism was recognized as Scotland's state religion; there would be free trade between both countries; now Scotland would be able to trade directly with the English colonies for the first time. Anne became Queen of Great Britain.

The Whigs had gained some posts in the Government and in 1708 they took control when the remaining Tory ministers resigned.

On July 11, 1708 the French forces were defeated again by the allies under the command of the Duke of Marlborough at the Battle of Oudenaarde, west of Brussels, leading to the complete capture of the Spanish Netherlands. Again the casualties were in the thousands.

Great Britain captured the island of Minorca in the Mediterranean Sea that became a naval base.

The Duke of Marlborough led the Anglo-Dutch forces, together with other nationalities, to victory at the Battle of Malplaquet, ten miles south of Mons, over the French forces with their other nationalities, involving the largest number of troops and the bloodiest battle of the eighteenth century. The battle started at Mons the previous week and finished on September 11, 1709. The allied army totalled 100,000, the enemy 90,000. The allies had 22,000 killed and wounded; the enemy had 12,000 killed and wounded. Mons was finally overrun on October 26.

The 1710 election was won by the Tories: wanting peace they dismissed the Duke of Marlborough from his command, but were unable to persuade the allies to pursue peace.

Roman Catholics and non-conformists could qualify for public offices by occasionally taking Holy Communion in the Church of England. This was in contravention of the Corporation Act of 1661 and the 1673 Test Act. In 1711 the Occasional Conformity Act was passed to prevent this practice.

Eventually, Great Britain and France negotiated peace with the signing of the Treaty of Utrecht (Netherlands) in 1713. By the treaty, France recognized that the succession to the British throne must be a Protestant; agreed to expel James Francis Edward (the Old Pretender), the son of the late King James II, from

France; agreed the transfer of various territories in North America and the West Indies (Caribbean) to Great Britain. By the treaty Spain agreed that Great Britain should retain its conquests of Minorca and Gibraltar; for thirty years to have the right to transport Africans to the slave colonies of Spanish America; and the Spanish Netherlands to be transferred to Austrian control. The War of the Spanish Succession from 1701 ended in 1714. Philip V, grandson of King Louis XIV of France, was confirmed as the King of Spain.

The Schism Act of 1714 made it a requirement for educational teachers to be licensed by a bishop: this stopped Dissenters from running their own schools.

When it was realized that Anne was dying, the country was alerted in case France reneged on the Treaty of Utrecht. Garrisons were prepared, the Royal Navy ordered to patrol the English Channel, and the French ports were kept under observation for threatening activity.

The Act of Settlement of 1701 decreed that Anne's successor would be through the line of Princess Sophia of Hanover, the daughter of Princess Elizabeth, whose father was King James I. Princess Sophia died two months before Anne on June 8, 1714 at the age of 83; her 54-year-old son Georg Ludwig became heir to the throne. Anne appointed Charles Talbot (Duke of Shrewsbury) to attend to the accession to the Protestant Hanoverian.

Anne died at Kensington Palace, London on August 1, 1714, and was buried at Westminster Abbey, London.

THE HANOVERS

Monarch	Reigned	Family
George I	1714 to 1727	Great-grandson of James I
George II	1727 to 1760	Son of George I
George III	1760 to 1820	Grandson of George II
George IV	1820 to 1830	Son of George III
William IV	1830 to 1837	Son of George III
Victoria	1837 to 1901	Granddaughter of George III

HANOVER

KING GEORGE I

Born	1660 May 28
Accession	1714 August 1
Age at Accession	54
Death	1727 June 11
Age at Death	67
Reigned	12 years

George I succeeded his distant relative Anne: both were great-grandchildren of King James I. His mother Princess Sophia had been decreed heir presumptive by the 1701 Act of Settlement, but died on June 8, 1714 at the age of 83. Georg Ludwig, Duke of Brunswick-Lunenburg, Elector of Hanover, being her eldest son became heir presumptive to the English throne.

In 1682 he married his first cousin Sophia Dorothea (b.1666, d.1726). They were divorced in 1694. They had 1 son and 1 daughter.

Persons of note:

Edmund Halley (b.1656, d.1742). Astronomer Royal 1720 until his death. He published observations of the planets and comets, being the first to predict the return of a comet. He made the magnetic survey of the oceans 1698 to 1700.

Sir Isaac Newton (b.1643, d.1727). Scientist. His three great discoveries included his theory of gravitation.

Jonathon Swift (b.1667, d.1745). Irish born satirist. Took Anglican religious orders; involved in politics. He wrote 'Gulliver's Travels' in 1726.

THE HANOVERS: KING GEORGE I

Sir Robert Walpole (1ˢᵗ Earl of Orford) (b.1676, d.1745). Statesman and politician. Regarded as Great Britain's first prime minister (the post was not officially designated until 1905).

Sir Christopher Wren (b.1632, d.1723). Architect. After the Great Fire of London in 1666, he rebuilt St Paul's Cathedral and over fifty other churches. He helped to found the Royal Society.

The 54-year-old Georg Ludwig arrived at Greenwich, London, on September 1, 1714 to become King George I of Great Britain, the first Hanoverian.

He did not speak English; he communicated in French with his officials and parliamentarians; he adapted to the constitutional and parliamentary system of his new country. During his reign, George divided his time between England and Hanover, where he was the Elector. His son and heir, Prince George, was created Prince of Wales on September 27.

Parliament governed without too much interference from George. From the 1714 election the Whigs had become dominant and remained in power for the following forty-five years. They were tolerant in religious matters by repealing the Occasional Conformity Act of 1711 and the Schism Act of 1714.

A Jacobite (the Latin equivalent of the name James) scheme to install James Francis Edward (known as the Old Pretender), son of the late King James II, to the throne commenced with attempted insurrections in Scotland and northern England, known as the 15, or 1715 Rebellion. A small force of Scottish and English supporters was defeated at Preston, in Lancashire, on November 13. The leaders found guilty of treason had their estates confiscated; Lord Derewentwater and Lord Kenmure were beheaded on Tower Hill, London; others were transported into slavery to North America or West Indian (Caribbean) colonies; the Old Pretender returned to France. It would be thirty years before another serious attempt would be made to usurp the throne for a Catholic monarch.

The Septennial Act of 1716 extended the Parliamentary term to seven years, its purpose being the strengthening of the monarchy and giving continuity in the country to prevent any further Catholic aggression.

The Bahamas, a group of islands to the south-east of Florida, United States of America, were discovered by Christopher Columbus in 1492. They were occupied by the English in the 17ᵗʰ century and in 1717 became a Crown colony.

The following year the Quadruple Alliance (the Treaty of London) was signed by Great Britain, Austria, Dutch Republic and France in an attempt to prevent Spain breaking the 1713 Treaty of Utrecht. King Philip V of Spain was determined to regain Spain's lost possessions in Italy and Gibraltar. During the subsequent war, Spain invaded Sicily: the British fleet, commanded by Admiral Sir George Bing, destroyed the Spanish Mediterranean fleet off Cape Passaro,

Sicily, Italy, on August 11, 1718. In April 1719 a Spanish Jacobite force landed at Eilean Donan Castle on the west coast of Scotland. It was destroyed by the Royal Navy a month later. The Quadruple Alliance ended in 1720 when peace was concluded at The Hague, Holland.

In 1719, the South Sea Trading Company, incorporated in 1711 to trade throughout the World, persuaded many to invest by buying shares in the company, which rapidly increased in value. So much money had been invested in the company it was agreed it could take over the National Debt, which was quite considerable. With no actual business conducted, and with the company insisting that profits "were just around the corner", in September 1720, the company collapsed into bankruptcy, the famous South Sea Bubble had burst. In the aftermath of the collapse, the Bank of England accepted a large percentage of the South Sea Trading Company's capital; the National Debt was restructured; and the issuing of company shares became illegal until 1825.

By 1721 Sir Robert Walpole had become the dominant parliamentarian and was considered to be head of the government, whom George, unfamiliar with the British Parliamentary system and being frequently away in Hanover, relied upon. The title of First Lord of the Treasury is part of the full title of Prime Ministers since, and Sir Robert Walpole is recognized as being the first Prime Minister of Great Britain, although the term 'Prime Minister' was not official until 1905. He formed his own Cabinet, choosing ministers only from the Houses of Commons and Lords: the Cabinet members had to accept the need for an agreed policy, nowadays referred to as 'collective responsibility'. Previously, the monarch appointed ministers to implement the monarch's policies. George approved these changes as it relieved him of day-to-day responsibility of government. Now the King was advised, rather than advising.

The Most Honourable Order of the Bath is the second highest Order of Chivalry in England, was established by George under the Great Seal, dated May 18, 1725. Similar orders and the purification ceremonies were associated with earlier reigns.

Various Acts of Parliament continued to affect Ireland in employment and religious matters, to its disadvantage.

At the age of 67, George had a stroke at Osnabruck, Hanover, and died on June 11, 1727. He was buried at Herrenhausen, Hanover, Germany.

HANOVER

KING GEORGE II

Born	1683 October 30
Accession	1727 June 11
Age at Accession	43
Death	1760 October 25
Age at Death	76
Reigned	33 years

George II succeeded his father George I as King of Great Britain and Elector of Hanover.

In 1705 he married Caroline (b.1683, d.1737), daughter of John Frederick, Margrave of Brandenburg-Ansbach. (Margrave was a hereditary title of certain princes in the Holy Roman Empire.) They had 3 sons and 5 daughters.

The eldest son Prince Frederick Louis, Prince of Wales, born 1707, died in 1751 aged 44. He married Augusta (b.1719, d.1772), daughter of Frederick II, Duke of Saxe-Gotha-Altenburg. They had 5 sons and 4 daughters. Their eldest son succeeded George II as King.

James Francis Edward (the Old Pretender) (b.1688, d.1766) was the son of King James II and his second wife Mary (b.1658, d.1718), daughter of the Duke of Alphonso IV, Duke of Modena. Being a Roman Catholic debarred him from the English throne.

Charles Edward Louis Philip Casimir (the Young Pretender) (b.1720, d.1788), also known as Bonnie Prince Charlie. He was the son of the Old Pretender. He married in 1772 Louisa Maximiliana (d.1824), daughter of Gustavus Adolpohus, Prince of Storberg-Gedern. They had no children.

THE HANOVERS: KING GEORGE II

Persons of note:

Sir Richard Arkwright (b.1732, d.1792). Inventor. His water frame (run by water power) was an early development in the industrialism of the country.

Lancelot Brown (b.1716, d.1783), known as 'Capability Brown'. Landscape gardener. He designed many parks and gardens in imitation of the natural landscape.

Thomas Chippendale (b.1718, d.1779). Designer of furniture. His designs were shown in 'The Gentleman and Cabinet Maker's Director' of 1754. His name is synonymous with the Anglicized Rococo style of furniture.

Thomas Gainsborough (b.1727, d.1788). Landscape and portrait painter. His portraits are marked by informality and grace.

Edmund Halley (b.1656, d.1742). Astronomer Royal 1720 until his death. He published observations of the planets and comets, being the first to predict the return of a comet. He made the magnetic survey of the oceans 1698 to 1700.

George Hepplewhite (b?, d.1786). Cabinet-maker whose name is identified with the style that followed the Chippendale period.

Sir Joshua Reynolds (b.1723, d.1792). Portrait painter. He was a sympathetic painter of children. First president of the Royal Academy 1768 until his death.

Jonathon Swift (b.1667, d.1745). Irish born satirist. Took Anglican religious orders; involved in politics. He wrote 'Gulliver's Travels' in 1726.

Josiah Wedgwood (b.1730, d.1795). Potter who at his works in Hanley, Stoke-on-Trent, produced a new ware pottery to classical designs.

Rev John Wesley (b.1703, d.1791). Evangelist preacher. Founder of Methodism. With his brother Charles (b.1707, d.1788) produced their first hymnbook in 1739.

Sir Robert Walpole (1st Earl of Orford) (b.1676, d.1745). Statesman and politician. Regarded as Great Britain's first prime minister (the post was not designated until 1905).

First Lords of the Treasury (Prime Ministers)	Party	Took Office
Sir Robert Walpole (b.1676, d.1745).	Whig	1721 April
Spencer Compton (b.1673, d.1743). Created Earl of Wilmington in 1730	Whig	1742 February
Henry Pelham (b.1696, d.1754).	Whig	1743 August
Thomas Pelham-Holles (b.1693, d.1768). Created Duke of Newcastle upon Tyne in 1714 and Duke of Newcastle-under-Lyme in 1756	Whig	1754 May
William Cavendish (b.1720, d.1764). 4th Duke of Devonshire	Whig	1756 November
Thomas Pelham-Holles (see above)	Whig	1757 July

George II who succeeded his father was the last British monarch not to have been born in England. Unlike his father, he understood the constitution and his position within it. Sir Robert Walpole and the Whig government continued in office after the accession.

The Spanish made efforts to reclaim Gibraltar again from 1725; peace was agreed with the Treaty of Seville in 1729, concluding the Anglo-Spanish War. Great Britain had continued plundering Spanish ships sailing from their colonies so depriving Spain of great wealth.

In gratitude for his leadership of the country, George presented to Sir Robert Walpole, as a personal gift, 10 Downing Street, Whitehall, London. He accepted it only on the condition it was an official gift. The house, now popularly known as 'Number 10', became and continues to be the official London residence of prime ministers. The building has been altered extensively over the years since being built in 1530.

Trading regulations were being liberalized: overseas trade increased between Great Britain and the colonies; colonies were permitted to trade between each other; and foreign countries allowed to trade directly with the colonies. The country was flourishing: industry, commerce and financial successes continued to create wealth and prosperity, but the downside being the poor living conditions in the cities and towns.

Smuggling had become extensive as a means to avoid paying duty on imports. In 1733 the Government introduced the Excise Bill in order to control this situation, but it was very unpopular in Parliament and with the people. The

Bill was withdrawn.

John Wesley, an evangelical preacher, with others, tried to start a reform movement at Oxford in 1729. He began his evangelism in 1738; founded the Methodist society, and built his first chapel in 1739 in Bristol. He remained an ordained priest of the Church of England until his death. In the country, non-conformists and Dissenters were being permitted in official posts in towns and corporations, despite the laws forbidding their employment still in force.

Dick Turpin, probably the most famous highwayman, born in 1706 was executed by hanging at York on April 7, 1739 for his crimes.

The antagonism between Great Britain and Spain continued. Spain's rebuilt navy was controlling and interfering with foreign shipping, including the English ships trading with the Spanish American colonies. The disruption to shipping and the Spanish illegal searching and sequestration of goods forced the Government to respond. Negotiations between the two governments failed: Parliament forced the Government to declare war in October 1739.

During this period the Whigs were re-elected to govern, but opposition within his own party, obliged Sir Robert Walpole to resign as head of the government after twenty-one years leadership.

The War of the Austrian Succession was a conglomeration of related wars, including this one declared against the Spanish. Now it involved Great Britain against the French over both countries' colonial possessions. The allies of the British, Hanoverians, Hessians and Austrians defeated the French at the Battle of Dettingen, near Aschaffenburg (south-west of Frankfurt, Germany) in June 1743. George and his 22-year-old son Prince William (Duke of Cumberland) commanded the troops; the last occasion a British King would lead an army in battle.

In 1745, Charles Edward Louis Philip Casimir (the Young Pretender) son of James Francis Edward (the Old Pretender), with the support of France, made an attempt to claim the British throne, known as the 45, or 1745 Rebellion. Landing in Scotland his troops marched south as far as Derby, in England, before being forced to return to Scotland. His force of 7,000 opposed by 8,000 English troops commanded by Prince William (Duke of Cumberland), were defeated at the Battle of Culloden, near Inverness, on April 16, 1746. This was the last battle ever to be fought on British soil. The Young Pretender escaped dressed as a woman, and with the help of Flora MacDonald returned to France. This was the last occasion an effort was made to usurp the throne by Roman Catholics.

The Treaty of Aix-la-Chapelle (now Aachen, between Brussels and Cologne) in October 1748 brought the war to a conclusion. It was an inconclusive war; none of the colonial or other conflicts between Great Britain and France were resolved.

Until 1751 army regiments were named after their colonels who virtually had complete control over them. From 1751 regiments became numbered, e.g. the regiment raised by the Duke of Beaufort in 1685 was renamed the 11th Regiment of Foot.

THE HANOVERS: KING GEORGE II

Prince Frederick (the Prince of Wales) the heir to the throne died on March 20, 1751 at the age of 44. Prince Frederick's eldest son, the 12-year-old Prince George, now heir to the throne, became the new Prince of Wales. The Government attempted to introduce a Regency Bill to appoint a Regent and Regency Council should Prince George become King as a minor. Parliament would not accept the Bill which was withdrawn.

Pope Gregory XII in 1582 introduced a new calendar, the Gregorian Calendar, to correct a miscalculation in the previous Julian Calendar. It was not until September 1752 that Great Britain introduced the change. Parliament ordered that the day after September 2, 1752 would be September 14, 1752, so wiping out eleven days. Also, the legal year was altered to commence on January 1 instead of March 25.

In 1756, the Seven Years' War commenced when the Austrians attempted to regain Silesia, which they had lost at the conclusion of the War of the Austrian Succession. With France supporting Austria, and Great Britain leading the opposition, the fighting spread to the colonies of both Great Britain and France, although the conflict in North America had commenced two years earlier. Casualties were many thousands killed; Great Britain lost control of the island of Minorca in the Mediterranean Sea, to France; and with France about to invade England in 1757, the Royal Navy succeeded in defeating them. By late 1759, France had lost most of its possessions in India, Canada and the West Indies; England became dominant in northern India (nowadays Pakistan).

At the age of 76, George died on October 25, 1760 and was buried at Westminster Abbey, London.

HANOVER

KING GEORGE III

Born	**1738 May 24 (Julian Calendar)** **June 4 (Gregorian Calendar** **from 1752)**
Accession	**1760 October 25**
Age at Accession	**22**
Death	**1820 January 29**
Age at Death	**81**
Reigned	**59 years**

George III succeeded his grandfather, George II. He was Elector of Hanover 1760 to 1814, and King of Hanover 1814 until his death. His father, Prince Frederick Louis (Prince of Wales) died in 1751.

In 1761 he married Sophia Charlotte (b.1744, d.1818), daughter of Charles I, Duke of Mecklenburg-Strelitz. They had 9 sons (2 died young) and 6 daughters.

The eldest son and heir, Prince George (b.1762) was appointed Prince Regent from February 5, 1811.

Persons of note:

1ˢᵗ Viscount Horatio Nelson (b.1758, d.1805). Admiral who commanded the fleet in the successful Battle of Trafalgar, in which he was killed. Previously, he had lost an eye at Calvi (1794) and an arm at Santa Cruz (1797).

Arthur Wellesley, 1ˢᵗ Duke of Wellington (b.1769, d.1852), also known as the Iron Duke. Soldier and statesman. He became Prime Minister 1828 to 1830.

THE HANOVERS: KING GEORGE III

William Wilberforce (b.1759, d.1833). Politician and social reformer. Member of Parliament (1780 to 1825) campaigned for the abolition of the slave trade, achieved in 1807, and the abolition of slavery, achieved in 1833.

Sir Richard Arkwright (b.1732, d.1792). Inventor. His water frame (run by water power) was an early step in the industrialism of the country.

Jane Austen (b.1775, d.1817). Novelist with the ability to create characters with incisive social satire, irony, wit and gracious manners.

Lancelot Brown (b.1716, d.1783), known as 'Capability Brown'. Landscape gardener. He designed many parks and gardens in the imitation of the natural landscape.

George Gordon Byron (6th Baron Byron, known as Lord Byron) (b.1788, d.1824). Romantic poet. One of the leading figures of the English Romantic movement.

Thomas Chippendale (b.1718, d.1779). Designer of furniture. His designs were shown in 'The Gentleman and Cabinet Maker's Director' of 1754. His name is synonymous with the Anglicized Rococo style of furniture.

John Constable (b.1776, d.1837). Leading landscape artist of Suffolk. 'The Hay Wain' is his best-known work.

Captain James Cook (b.1728, d.1779). Navigator and explorer. He made voyages of discovery to Australia and New Zealand. In 1770 he named Botany Bay (nowadays Sydney, Australia) because of the interesting plants found on the shores.

Sir Humphrey Davy (b.1778, d.1829). Chemist. Invented the miners' safety lamp which bears his name. President of the Royal Society in 1820.

Michael Faraday (b.1791, d.1867). Chemist and physicist, discoverer of electromagnetism, leading to modern development in physics and electronics.

Thomas Gainsborough (b.1727, d.1788). Landscape and portrait painter. His portraits are marked by informality and grace.

George Hepplewhite (b?, d.1786). Cabinet-maker whose name is identified with the style that followed the Chippendale period.

Edward Jenner (b.1749, d.1823). Physician who discovered the smallpox vaccination in 1796, laying the foundation of modern immunology.

John Nash (b.1752, d.1835). Architect who planned Regent Street, London; laid out Regent's Park; enlarged Buckingham Palace; designed Marble Arch and the Brighton Pavilion, et al.

Sir Joshua Reynolds (b.1723, d.1792). Portrait painter. He was a sympathetic painter of children. First President of the Royal Academy 1768, until his death.

Thomas Sheraton (b.1751, d.1806). Cabinet-maker whose 'Cabinetmaker's Book' promoted new classical designs.

Joseph Mallord William Turner (b.1775, d.1851). Landscape painter, a master of light and colour. He bequeathed his works to the nation.

Josiah Wedgwood (b.1730, d.1795). Potter who at his works in Hanley, Stoke-on-Trent, produced a new ware pottery to classical designs.

Rev John Wesley (b.1703, d.1791). Evangelist preacher. Founder of Methodism. With his brother Charles (b.1707, d.1788) produced their first hymnbook in 1739.

William Wordsworth (b.1770, d.1850). Poet. He was influenced by his early life in The Lake District, Cumbria. He was Poet Laureate 1843 until his death.

First Lords of the Treasury (Prime Ministers)	*Party*	*Took Office*
Thomas Pelham-Holles (b.1693, d.1768). Created Duke of Newcastle upon Tyne in 1714 and Duke of Newcastle-under-Lyme in 1756	*Whig*	*1757 July*
John Stuart (b.1713, d.1792). Succeeded as 3rd Earl of Bute in 1723. First Lord of the Treasury from Scotland after the Union	*Tory*	*1762 May*
George Granville (b.1712, d.1770).	*Whig*	*1763 April*
Charles Watson-Wentworth (b.1730, d.1782). Succeeded as 2nd Marquess of Rockingham in 1750	*Whig*	*1765 July*

THE HANOVERS: KING GEORGE III

William Pitt (b.1708, d.1778). Known as Pitt the Elder. Created Earl of Chatham in 1766   *Whig*   *1766 April*

Augustus Fitzroy (b.1735, d.1811). Succeeded as 3ʳᵈ Duke of Grafton in 1757   *Whig*   *1768 December*

Frederick North (b.1732, d.1792). Succeeded as 2ⁿᵈ Earl of Guildford in 1790. (Normally referred to as Lord North)   *Tory*   *1770 February*

Charles Watson-Wentworth (see above)   *Whig*   *1782 March*

William Petty (b.1737, d.1805). Succeeded as 2ⁿᵈ Earl of Shelburn in 1761   *Whig*   *1782 July*

William Cavendish-Bentinck (b.1738, d.1809). Succeeded as 3ʳᵈ Duke of Portland in 1762   *Coalition*   *1783 April*

William Pitt (b.1759, d.1806). Known as Pitt the Younger, a son of the above. Youngest ever First Lord of the Treasury/Prime Minister   *Tory*   *1783 December*

Henry Addington (b.1757, d.1844). Created 1ˢᵗ Viscount Sidmouth in 1805   *Tory*   *1801 March*

William Pitt (see above)   *Tory*   *1804 May*

William Grenville (b.1759, d.1834). Created 1ˢᵗ Baron Grenville in 1790   *Whig*   *1806 February*

William Cavendish-Bentinck (see above)   *Tory*   *1807 March*

Spencer Perceval (b.1762, d.1812). Only First Lord of the Treasury/Prime Minister to have been assassinated.   *Tory*   *1809 December*

Robert Jenkinson (b.1770, d.1828). Succeeded as 2ⁿᵈ Earl of Liverpool in 1808   *Tory*   *1812 June*

THE HANOVERS: KING GEORGE III

George III was the first Hanoverian monarch to have been born and educated in England. The 22-year-old succeeded his grandfather, King George II, as King. During the first two decades of his reign he involved himself in the administration of the Government of the country. He appointed prime ministers, ministers and in two instances, presided at Cabinet meetings. This behaviour created instability in government and frequent changes in the First Lords of the Treasury, i.e. Prime Ministers.

His personal estate, the Crown Estates, which generated a considerable amount of income, was transferred to Parliament; in return George received an income from the Civil List.

On September 8, 1761 George married Sophia Charlotte of Mecklenburg-Strelitz, whom he met for the first time on their wedding day. He had taken advice for a suitable lady to become his wife and Queen.

The Seven Years' War ended in 1763 with the signing of the Treaty of Paris. France ceded to Great Britain its possession in Canada and all of its territory to the east of the Mississippi River in North America. Spain ceded Florida to Great Britain. The cost of the war nearly doubled the National Debt and heavy taxes were imposed.

In 1769 Captain James Cook explored the islands of New Zealand that previously had been discovered and named by the Dutch explorer Abel Tasman in 1642. The following year Captain Cook claimed Australia for Great Britain: the Dutch had earlier landed in northern Australia at the Gulf of Carpentaria.

In need of income to finance the National Debt, successive governments introduced tax-raising scheme in the increasingly prosperous colonies of North America. These were resisted: most of the taxes were repealed except one, the taxation on tea. This was the catalyst that united thirteen colonies to sign the Declaration of Independence in 1775 in Philadelphia, and led to their War of Independence. France and Spain interfered, not necessarily to help the colonies, but as an attempt to break the power of Great Britain.

The laws that prohibited Roman Catholics buying land in Ireland were repealed in 1778, and in England two years later. Parliament repealed various discriminatory laws against the Roman Catholics, but opposition in London by the Protestants, led by the agitator Lord George Gordon, lasted for four days until the King ordered troops to disperse the rioters.

Great Britain was changing: machinery was expanding the growth of industrialization; more people were moving from the villages to the expanding cities and towns for work; the population was increasing; and demands were being made for reform in many aspects of life.

In sport, one of the classic English horse races, the Derby, dates from 1780. It was named after Edward Stanley, the 12th Earl of Derby. It is raced annually at Epsom Downs racecourse in Surrey for 3-year-old horses. It has been copied by many countries as an important event. In 1787, the Marleybone Cricket Club, better known by its initials, MCC, was founded to govern the game; it being the World's most famous cricket club.

THE HANOVERS: KING GEORGE III

A reorganization of the army commenced in 1782: many regiments began to add the name of their location to their number, e.g. 11th Regiment of Foot, became the 11th (North Devonshire) Regiment of Foot.

In the same year, Ireland was granted an independent Parliament.

Peace in the American colonies was eventually achieved after their victory over the British forces, by the signing in Paris of the Treaty of Versailles in 1783, which granted independence to each of the thirteen colonies. In the treaty, Spain regained Florida, and in the Mediterranean Sea, the island of Minorca: France regained some of the West Indian islands they had previously lost to Great Britain under the 1763 Treaty of Paris; the island of St Vincent (discovered by Christopher Columbus in 1498) had temporarily been under French control, was returned to the British. The thirteen colonies, now independent states, commercially suffered by losing the right to trade with Great Britain and the other British colonies outside of North America. Lancashire suffered by losing its sources of supply for its cotton industry.

After ten First Lords of the Treasury (Prime Ministers) in twenty-three years since George ascended to the throne, William Pitt (Pitt the Younger), at 24 years of age, became Prime Minister in December 1783, the youngest ever in this country.

George succumbed to mental health problems, which affected him periodically for the rest of his life. He attended to governmental matters less, therefore, giving government ministers greater independence to influence and control affairs.

The East India Company had ruled India independently until the India Act of 1784 which brought their administration under the supervision of the British Government.

The Reform Bill of 1785 to increase the representation of the new and enlarged cities and towns, and to reduce the representation of the 'rotten boroughs' was defeated in Parliament.

In Australia in 1788, a penal colony was established at Port Jackson, now Sydney. (Over the years until 1839 more than 160,000 convicts were sent from Great Britain to Australia to serve their prison sentences.) In the same year, Freetown, Sierra Leone (west coast of Africa) was founded as a British colony for Africans who had served in the army and for those who had escaped from slavery in the Americas.

The French Revolution of 1789, at first, did not unduly concern the Government, but within four years revolutionary France had become a threat to all of its neighbours, including England. Alliances were made, then broken: countries being against France then becoming allies of the French: Great Britain had to defend its trade, shipping fleet, colonies, and itself.

Meanwhile, in 1791 Canada was granted representative government.

Increasing discontent with the Prime Minister's autocracy gave birth to the Radical movement, forcing the Government to take drastic action after rioting in several towns. The *Habeas Corpus* Act was suspended in 1794 to allow imprisonment without trial; in 1795 public meetings were restricted; and it became illegal to incite against the Government. In 1796 following a period of disturbances, the Irish rebellion failed and was subdued.

France planned an invasion of Egypt in order to interfere with Great Britain's trade routes and to usurp India. Rear-Admiral Sir Horatio Nelson (knighted in 1797) commanded the Royal Navy in the Mediterranean Sea and destroyed the French fleet, commanded by Napoleon Bonaparte, on August 1, 1798, at Alexandria, Egypt, at the Battle of the Nile. Great Britain lost 213 killed and 677 wounded, many of those died. The French had 600 wounded and at least 1,400 killed, but it is considered the actual number was between 2,000 and 5,000 killed and wounded.

The next year the British ousted the French from the Mediterranean Sea island of Malta. In a further attempt to limit British trade, the French restricted British merchant shipping from entering continental ports. To re-open the trade route to the Baltic Sea ports, the successful 1801 Battle of Copenhagen was another victory commanded by Horatio Nelson, by now promoted to Vice-Admiral. After this victory he was created a Viscount.

Parliament passed two Combination Acts in 1799 and 1800 making trade unionism illegal. The Acts prohibited any working man to combine with another working man in order to gain an increase in wages or a decrease in working hours, etc.

In 1801 the first census was taken: the population of England and Wales was just under nine millions, of Great Britain as a whole it was about twelve millions. (Thereafter, a census has been taken every ten years except in wartime 1941.)

The Act of Union between Great Britain (England, Wales and Scotland) and Ireland became effective on January 1, 1801, having been passed by both the British and Irish Parliaments in 1800. Ireland was allocated one hundred elected members to sit in the House of Commons, four Anglican bishops and twenty-eight peers to be created to sit in the House of Lords. Ireland kept its own Courts of Justice and civil service. George created a serious problem by refusing to allow Roman Catholics to be members of either House, as it was contrary to his Coronation Oath. As a consequence William Pitt resigned as head of the government.

By 1802 Great Britain and France had been at war for almost ten years: the fighting which had incurred large debts for both countries, came to an end with the signing of the Treaty of Amiens (northern France) by Great Britain (now the United Kingdom), France, Spain and the Dutch. The treaty conditions included Ceylon (now Sri Lanka) ceded by the Dutch, and Trinidad (in the West Indies) ceded by Spain, both being transferred to the United Kingdom. (Ceylon had been a Portuguese colony from 1618, a Dutch colony from 1658 to 1798, then occupied by the British. Trinidad was discovered by Christopher Columbus in 1498, and colonized by Spain in 1532.)

The first recorded regiment of the Marines was in October 1644: marine regiments were formed in time of war, and then disbanded after the war ended.

From 1755 there had been a regiment of Marines: in April 1802 in recognition of their service to the country George granted the style Royal Marines, which has been its title ever since.

The Treaty of Amiens only brought peace for a year because Napoleon Bonaparte, now Emperor of France, wanted to destroy British shipping and trade dominance; wanted to dominate Europe and to invade England. Spain allied itself to France.

On October 21, 1805, Vice-Admiral, the Viscount Nelson achieved for the United Kingdom the famous victory at the Battle of Trafalgar, in southern Spain adjacent to the Strait of Gibraltar. (Nelson was mortally wounded in the battle.) The fleets of France and Spain were almost completely destroyed. In the battle Britain had 27 ships, France and Spain had 33; the British had 1,500 killed and wounded, the enemy never revealed their figures, but it is considered to have been about 14,000 casualties.

In revenge, the ports of France and its allies were declared out-of-bounds to British merchant shipping. In retaliation, the United Kingdom used its naval superiority to physically blockade their ports so causing widespread ruin to the economies of those countries.

Slavery had been a fervent cause of William Wilberforce during his parliamentary career. After many setbacks and disappointments, eventually, he achieved having legislation passed in Parliament in 1807, for the prohibition of transporting Africans into slavery.

As part of the continuing Napoleonic Wars, the Peninsular War (the Iberian peninsula of Spain and Portugal) commenced in 1809; France had overrun both countries. Sir Arthur Wellesley (he was knighted in 1804, and created Duke of Wellington in 1814) commanded the allies to victory against the French forces. Many thousands were killed and wounded in the numerous battles. The French were forced from Iberia.

The war extended to the Indian Ocean; the islands of Mauritius and Seychelles were surrendered by the French forces to the British in 1810.

George's mental illness made him incapable of his monarchical duties. From February 1811 his son and heir, Prince George, was appointed Prince Regent, and the Queen to have custody over her husband. George often recovered from these bouts of illness to resume his duties and responsibilities.

Modern industrial innovations and methods were being introduced, e.g. John Macadam in 1811 demonstrated new surfaces for roads. In factories new machinery and methods were displacing workers. The rising unemployment led to rioting between 1811 and 1816 by the Luddites, a group of workers who opposed the industrial and technical advancements.

The Prime Minister, Spencer Perceval, was shot dead in the lobby of the House of Commons in June 1812. John Bellingham, a bankrupt businessman from Liverpool, was hanged for the murder. Spencer Perceval is the only British prime minister to have been assassinated.

The United Kingdom's policy of controlling foreign merchant shipping by stopping and searching ships on the 'high seas' was the cause of the war with America in 1812. The United States of America used this war as an opportunity to invade and attempt to usurp Canada, but in 1814 the United Kingdom was able to transfer troops involved in the Napoleonic War, from Europe to Canada to oppose the Americans. When the war finished 1,600 British and 2,260 Americans had been killed. The British forces had entered Washington, the new capital of the United States of America, destroyed the Capitol (the legislative assembly), and the White House (the residence of the President). The peace Treaty of Ghent, then in the Netherlands, was signed on Christmas Eve of 1814.

Napoleon was forced to abdicate as Emperor of France in 1814 and exiled to the island of Elba, off the Italian coast of Tuscany. In 1815 he secretly returned to France: with orders to defeat Napoleon, the Duke of Wellington commanded the allied forces. On June 22, 1815, the Duke's greatest victory was achieved at the Battle of Waterloo, then in the Netherlands, now Belgium. Each of the combatants' strength was about 100,000 troops; at the end of the fighting the total killed and wounded for each side were about 25,000. The French defeat secured peace in Europe for many decades and brought an end to the Napoleonic Wars, and Napoleon's 'Hundred Days' of return ended in exile.

The 1814 Treaty of Paris, confirmed by the Congress of Vienna of 1815, returned to independence the countries overrun by France under Napoleon. The United Kingdom kept its war conquests of Malta (recaptured from the French), Mauritius and the Seychelles (captured from the French). The Cape of Good Hope (now South Africa), Tobago and British Guiana (now Guyana), both in the Caribbean, were ceded by the Dutch; Dominica and St Lucia, in the West Indies, were ceded by France; all to the United Kingdom.

Napoleon Bonaparte was exiled to the British island of St Helena in the south Atlantic Ocean, where he died in 1821.

The Royal Regiment of Foot Guards, having been renamed in 1685 as the 1st Regiment of Foot Guards, after defeating the Grenadiers of the French Imperial Guards at Waterloo in 1815, was renamed the Grenadier Regiment of Foot Guards. At this time, the Royal Navy was supreme throughout the World: there were 140,000 naval and Royal Marine personnel and 713 ships in commission.

In 1815, the Prince Regent decided to abolish many of the rites of the Most Honourable Order of the Bath, and to enlarge its membership to include many officers of the army and the Royal Navy who had fought in the Napoleonic Wars.

The industrialization of the United Kingdom, particularly England, was progressing rapidly, with bigger and deeper coalmines; canals constructed for the transportation of coal and manufactured goods from inland towns to coastal ports and to larger rivers, e.g. Liverpool Docks and the River Mersey; roads were constructed; improved agricultural farming practices; the invention of the Spinning Jenny which mechanized weaving for the cloth and woollen industries; and in 1815 George Stephenson's first successful steam locomotive.

The Government introduced in 1815 the Corn Law to protect England's cereals from cheap imports; this caused anger throughout the country, for many of the unemployed and poor could not afford the higher prices for local produce, e.g. bread.

Income Tax, introduced during the Napoleonic Wars, was abolished in 1816.

Increasingly, there were demands from the working population for better housing, better working conditions, and a fairer representation in Parliament. In 1817, in response to the lawlessness these demands caused, the Government suspended the *Habeas Corpus* Act: rioters were tried for treason and pirates for sedition. The 1819 Six Acts, commonly called the Gag Acts, forbade certain public meetings; duties were increased on printing which subsequently increased the costs of newspapers; and private houses were allowed to be searched with impunity.

In 1818, Sir Stamford Raffles, the Lieutenant-Governor of Bencoolen (south-west coast on the island of Sumatra, Indonesia) was given approval to establish a trading-post in the region and decided on the island of Singapore.

The Most Distinguished Order of St Michael and St George was founded in 1818 by the Prince Regent to commemorate the British protectorate over the Ionian Islands (a chain of Greek islands) and Malta.

A protest meeting organized by the Radicals, a reformist movement, was held on August 16, 1819 at St Peter's Field, Manchester, to demand Parliamentary reform. The yeomanry (the local militia) were summoned initially to organize and afterwards to disperse the crowd, estimated to have been about 50,000. In the melee the militia opened fire and killed eleven people and injured four hundred. Using the name Waterloo, this disturbance was named the Peterloo Massacre.

George died on January 29, 1820 at Windsor Castle, having been monarch for fifty-nine years, to that date the longest reign of an English monarch. He was buried at St George's Chapel, Windsor, Berkshire. Although he had several German titles, Elector of Hanover and King of Hanover, he never visited Germany.

HANOVER

KING GEORGE IV

Born	**1762 August 12**
Accession	**1820 January 29**
Age at Accession	57
Death	**1830 June 26**
Age at Death	67
Reigned	**10 years**

George IV succeeded his father George III. He had been appointed Prince Regent with full monarchical powers in 1811 because of his father's mental incapacity. Also, he succeeded his father as King of Hanover in 1820.

In 1795 he married Caroline Amelia Elizabeth (b.1768, d.1821), his cousin, daughter of the Duke of Brunswick. They had 1 daughter, Princess Charlotte Augusta (b.1796), who married Prince Leopold of Saxe-Coburg-Saalfeld. She, and her child, died in childbirth in 1817.

Persons of note:

Jane Austen (b.1775, d.1817). Novelist with the ability to create characters with incisive social satire, irony, wit and gracious manners.

George Gordon Byron (6th Baron Byron, known as Lord Byron) (b.1788, d.1824). Romantic poet. One of the leading figures of the English Romantic movement.

John Constable (b.1776, d.1837). Leading landscape artist of Suffolk. 'The Hay Wain' is his best known work.

Sir Humphrey Davy (b.1778, d.1829). Chemist. Invented the miners' safety lamp which bears his name. President of the Royal Society in 1820.

Michael Faraday (b.1791, d.1867). Chemist and physicist, discoverer of electromagnetism, leading to the modern development in physics and electronics.

Edward Jenner (b.1749, d.1823). Physician who discovered the smallpox vaccinations in 1796, laying the foundation of modern immunology.

John Nash (b.1752, d.1835). Architect who planned Regent Street, London; laid out Regent's Park; enlarged Buckingham Palace; designed Marble Arch and the Brighton Pavilion, et al.

Sir Robert Peel (b.1788, d.1850). Parliamentarian who instituted the first police force. Held many posts in a successful political career.

George Stephenson (b.1781, d.1848). Engineer and locomotive designer. His 'Rocket' train in 1829 won a £500 prize for exceeding 30 mph.

Joseph Mallord William Turner (b.1775, d.1851). Landscape painter, a master of light and colour. He bequeathed his works to the nation.

William Wilberforce (b.1759, d.1833). Parliamentarian who was leader of the campaign against the slave trade and slavery itself.

William Wordsworth (b.1770, d.1850). Poet. He was influenced by his early life in the Lake District, Cumbria. Poet Laureate 1843 until his death.

First Lords of the Treasury (Prime Ministers)	Party	Took Office
Robert Jenkinson (b.1770, d.1828). Succeeded as 2nd Earl of Liverpool in 1808	*Tory*	*1812 June*
George Canning (b.1770, d.1827).	*Tory*	*1827 April*
Frederick John Robinson (b.1782, d.1859). Created Viscount Goderich in 1827	*Tory*	*1827 September*
Arthur Wellesley (b.1769, d.1852). Created Duke of Wellington in 1814	*Tory*	*1828 January*

THE HANOVERS: KING GEORGE IV

George IV had been Prince Regent for almost nine years before he became King on the death of his father, King George III. Also, he became the King of Hanover.

The civil unrest in the country continued, and, in 1820 a group of reformist planned to assassinate the monarch and leading members of the Government; to seize control of the Tower of London; and to set up a republic. The Cato Street Conspiracy (named after their meeting place, a street off Edgware Road, London) was discovered. On the evidence of conspirators who had been given assurances of immunity from prosecution, Arthur Thistlewood, William Davidson, James Ings, Richard Tidd and John Brunt were tried, found guilty and hanged at Newgate Prison on May 1, 1820.

George made an attempt to divorce his estranged wife: a Bill was introduced in Parliament to allow this action but was withdrawn after Queen Caroline had been cross-examined for ten days in the House of Lords. George refused to permit his wife to be crowned Queen at the Coronation on July 19, 1821. She died shortly afterwards on August 7, 1821.

The colonies of Botany Bay, New Holland and New South Wales became known as Australia about 1820. At this time the Gold Coast (now Ghana, west Africa) came under British administration: the indigenous Ashanti people strongly objected and resisted the British presence for the next eighty years.

Parliament responded to the changing times by amending previous legislation that had become out-dated. In 1823 the various Navigation Acts since 1651 were modified to allow merchant shipping from foreign countries to transport goods into British ports. Importation duties on many goods were reduced. The Combination Acts of 1799 and 1800, which had prohibited trade union membership and strikes, etc., were repealed in 1824.

Penalties for quite minor offences continued to be severe, e.g. stealing livestock or pick-pocketing could be punished by death; poaching punishable by transportation to a penal colony (in 1819 ten thousand convicts were sent to Botany Bay in Australia, to serve their prison sentences) and over two hundred people were hanged for such offences. The penal code was amended: the death penalty was restricted mainly for murder or treason, and other penalties were modified.

Industry and commerce continued to flourish and grow. In 1825, George Stephenson's Stockton to Darlington (County Durham) railway-line was opened to transport coal from the mines.

The 1673 Test Act was partially repealed in 1828, to remove restrictions of non-conformist taking public office. Roman Catholics continued to be debarred.

In July 1828, Daniel O'Connell, the victor at a parliamentary by-election for County Clare in Ireland, was not permitted to take his seat in the House of Commons because he was a Roman Catholic. There were differing opinions between and within the Tories and Whigs, but eventually it was accepted that the law had to be changed. In 1829 the Catholic Relief (or Emancipation) Act became law giving Roman Catholics equality, admitting them to Parliament and high office.

THE HANOVERS: KING GEORGE IV

In 1829 the first civilian police in England was inaugurated in London. The Metropolitan Police Force was formed to replace the militia that had been responsible for controlling order. The Police were popularly known as 'Peelers' or 'Bobbies', nick-named after Sir Robert (Bobby) Peel, the Home Secretary, responsible for the change.

The first Boat Race between the Universities of Oxford and Cambridge was held in 1829. Cambridge challenged Oxford; 20,000 people at Henley-on-Thames, Oxfordshire, saw Oxford win.

Agitation for a fairer representation in Parliament was growing. The right to vote in the shires (counties) was based on the value of freehold land; in the cities and towns there were a variety of qualifications; some newly enlarged cities and towns had no representation. Demands for change were made by the middle and lower classes.

With a deteriorating civil situation, George died on June 26, 1830 at Windsor Castle. He was buried at St George's Chapel, Windsor, Berkshire.

HANOVER

KING WILLIAM IV

Born	**1765 August 21**
Accession	**1830 June 26**
Age at Accession	**64**
Death	**1837 June 20**
Age at Death	**71**
Reigned	**7 years**

William IV was the third son of King George III, and succeeded his brother King George IV. Also, he became King of Hanover.

In 1818 he married Adelaide (b.1792, d.1849), daughter of George I, Duke of Saxe-Meiningen. They had 2 daughters, both of whom died in infancy.

George IV's one child, a daughter, died in 1817, without an heir.

King George III's second son, Frederick Augustus, Duke of York and Albany, had married, but died without an heir in 1827.

Persons of note:

Mary Anning (b.1799, d.1847). Pioneering palaeontologist who discovered early fossilised remains of dinosaurs.

Charles Babbage (b.1801, d.1871). Mathematician who invented the difference engine, a machine that was the forerunner of the modern digital computer.

Isambard Kingdom Brunel (b.1806, d.1859). Civil engineer of ocean liners, railways and bridges.

John Constable (b.1776, d.1837). Leading landscape artist of Suffolk. 'The Hay Wain' is his best-known work.

Charles Robert Darwin (b.1809, d.1892). Naturalist, who revolutionized biological theory after a voyage to South America and the Pacific Ocean islands on board HMS Beagle, a five-year journey from 1831 to 1836. His books 'The Origin of Species' (1859) and 'The Descent of Man' (1871) caused great controversies.

Michael Faraday (b.1791, d.1867). Chemist and physicist, discoverer of electromagnetism, leading to the modern development in physics and electronics.

Sir William Huskisson (b.1770, d.1830). Politician. President of the Board of Trade. First person to be killed in a railway accident.

Sir Edwin Henry Landseer (b.1802, d.1873). Painter specializing in animals. Designed the lion statues in Trafalgar Square, London.

John Nash (b.1752, d.1835). Architect who planned Regent Street, London; laid out Regent's Park; enlarged Buckingham Palace; designed Marble Arch and the Brighton Pavilion, et al.

Sir Robert Peel (b.1788, d.1850). Parliamentarian who instituted the first police force. Held many posts in a successful political career.

George Stephenson (b.1781, d.1848). Engineer and locomotive designer. His 'Rocket' train in 1829 won a prize of £500 prize for exceeding 30 mph.

Joseph Mallord William Turner (b.1775, d.1851). Landscape painter, a master of light and colour. He bequeathed his works to the nation.

William Wilberforce (b.1759, d.1833). Parliamentarian who was leader of the campaign against the slave trade and slavery itself.

William Wordsworth (b.1770, d.1850). Poet. He was influenced by his early life in the Lake District, Cumbria. Poet Laureate 1843 until his death.

THE HANOVERS: KING WILLIAM IV

First Lords of the Treasury (Prime Ministers)	Party	Took Office
Arthur Wellesley (b.1769, d.1852). Created Duke of Wellington in 1814	Tory	1828 January
Charles Grey (b.1764, d.1845). Succeeded as 2nd Earl Grey in 1807	Whig	1830 November
William Lamb (b.1779, d.1848). Succeeded as 2nd Viscount Melbourne in 1829	Whig	1834 July
Sir Robert Peel (b.1788, d.1850).	Tory	1834 December
William Lamb (see above)	Whig	1835 March

William IV was the third son of King George III and brother of King George IV whom he succeeded, and became the last English monarch to have been King of Hanover.

During William's reign of seven years, Parliament enacted much social legislation in welfare, employment of the young, and education; more people were entitled to vote, and some restrictions on trade unionism lifted.

In 1830 the World's first regular rail passenger service commenced between Liverpool and Manchester. Sir William Huskisson, the President of the Board of Trade and one of the government's foremost supporters of the railway, became the first railway death. On September 15, invited guests were given a ride on the 'Northumbrian' train. Afterwards, Sir William Huskisson, crossing the railway-line, was knocked-down by the 'Rocket' train, and with severe injuries he died in hospital.

The Whig Government in 1831 wanted to reform and expand the franchise to vote throughout the country, but owing to the resistance for change in both the House of Commons and the House of Lords, it resigned. An election was held and the Whigs were returned to Government with a large majority. The House of Commons passed a Reform Bill only for it to be defeated in the House of Lords. This constitutional crisis incensed the country: London and Bristol had violent rioting; and Birmingham threatened to send 20,000 men to London. Another Bill was introduced, but the House of Lords amended it so much as to destroy it. Another crisis: the Prime Minister resigned, but there was no support for a successor.

The Prime Minister wanted William to create sufficient new peers to give the Whigs a majority in the House of Lords. At first he declined, but because of the discontentment throughout the country, he gave his authorisation. With the threat of losing their majority in the House of Lords, the Tories abstained from voting, so allowing the Bill to be passed. This Reform Act of 1832 was the first Act in a process to widen the franchise: this one modestly increased those entitled to vote from about half-a-million to just under one million, mainly of the middle class. Some, 'rotten boroughs' were abolished; cities and towns were given representation in the House of Commons according to the size of population. The industrial midlands and the north of England gained, the rural south lost; householders obtained the vote, landowners lost.

According to the 1831 census, the population of England and Wales had increased to 13.9 millions and Scotland was 2.36 millions.

In 1833 the Factory Act prohibited the employment of children under the age of nine; those between nine and thirteen years of age were limited to a maximum of 48 hours a week; and those under eighteen were limited to a maximum of 13.5 hours a day.

The 1833 Slavery Abolition Act, twenty-six years after the 1807 Act that prohibited the transportation of Africans into slavery, abolished the keeping of slaves in the British colonies, mainly in Jamaica and South Africa. A transitional period of five years was allowed to implement the new law; slave owners received compensation of £20 million. William Wilberforce, the leader of this campaign, just lived long enough to see his aims and objectives achieved.

The same year the Government granted £20,000 a year to two private societies (the Church of England and the non-conformists) to educate working children for at least two hours a day.

The Poor Law Amendments Act of 1834 changed the poor-relief system. It included the setting up of Workhouses for the poor, initially considered to be beneficial, but soon proved to be unsatisfactory because families were split up.

Trades Unions were developing and beginning to organize the working population, but their activities were limited by past legislation. An attempt to form an agricultural workers' branch in Dorset, the Friendly Society of Agricultural Labourers, in which each member was required to take an oath of allegiance to the union, a process forbidden by the Six Acts of 1819, resulted in six labourers being found guilty of breaking the law. In March 1834, the famous Tolpuddle Martyrs of Dorset, James Brine, James Hammett, George Loveless, James Loveless, Thomas Standfield, and John Standfield were found guilty and sentenced to seven years transportation to Australia. Because of public agitation they were pardoned, five in 1836 and James Hammett the following year.

In 1834 the south Atlantic Ocean island of St Helena was brought under direct governmental rule of the Crown, i.e. the Government. Free settlers had established in Australia the colonies of New South Wales (1786), Tasmania (1825), Western Australia (1829) and in 1834 South Australia.

In 1834 a terrible fire almost completely destroyed the Palace of Westminster, it being the Parliament building of the House of Commons and the House of Lords.

HMS Beagle had departed from Plymouth, Devon, at the end of 1831 for a voyage that lasted until October 1836, mainly for hydrographic purposes of the Pacific Ocean. The naturalist Charles Robert Darwin used the voyage to examine and observe the diverse plant and animal life of South America and the Pacific Ocean islands.

The rural areas of England had been under the jurisdiction of the Justices of the Peace for many centuries: now the Municipal Corporations Act of 1835 introduced a uniform system of elected councils to administer the rural and urban areas.

On June 20, 1837, William died at Windsor Castle and was buried in St George's Chapel, Windsor, Berkshire.

HANOVER

QUEEN VICTORIA

Born	**1819 May 24**
Accession	**1837 June 20**
Age at Accession	**18**
Death	**1901 January 22**
Age at Death	**81**
Reigned	**63 years**

Victoria succeeded her uncle William IV.

Victoria's father was Prince Edward Augustus, Duke of Kent and Strathearn (b.1767, d.1820), the 4th son of King George III.

Her mother was Princess Victoire (Victoria) (b.1786, d.1861), daughter of the Duke of Saxe-Coburg-Saalfeld. She married, firstly, Carl Friedrich Wilhelm Emich, Prince of Leiningen (b.1763, d.1814). They had 1 son and 1 daughter. She married, secondly, the Duke of Kent and Strathearn.

In 1840 she married Prince Albert of Saxe-Coburg and Gotha (b.1819, d.1861). He was created Prince Consort in 1857. They had 4 sons and 5 daughters. All survived to adulthood.

Persons of note:

Elizabeth Garrett Anderson (b.1836, d.1917). One of the first English women to have entered the medical profession, and the first woman to be a town mayor.

Mary Anning (b.1799, d.1847). Pioneering palaeontologist who discovered early fossilised remains of dinosaurs.

Charles Babbage (b.1801, d.1871). Mathematician who invented the difference engine, a machine that was the forerunner of the modern digital computer.

Sir Charles Barry (b.1795, d.1860). Architect of the Houses of Parliament, which were rebuilt in 1860 after fire destroyed the old Palace of Westminster in 1834.

William Booth (b.1829, d.1912). Founder and first General of the Salvation Army, in 1878.

Isambard Kingdom Brunel (b.1806, d.1859). Civil engineer of ocean liners, railways and bridges.

Lewis Carroll (Charles Lutwidge Dodgson) (b.1832, d.1898). Author whose works include 'Alice's Adventures in Wonderland' and 'Through the Looking-Glass'.

Charles Robert Darwin (b.1809, d.1892). Naturalist, who revolutionized biological theory after a voyage to South America and the Pacific Ocean islands on board HMS Beagle, a five-year journey from 1831 to 1836. His books 'The Origin of Species' (1859) and 'The Descent of Man' (1871) caused great controversies.

Frederick Delius (b.1862, d.1934). English born composer of German parentage. Composed operas, concertos, orchestral music and chamber music.

Charles Dickens (b.1812, d.1870). Novelist with capacity for vivid storytelling, e.g. 'Pickwick Papers', 'Oliver Twist', and 'Great Expectations'.

Michael Faraday (b.1791, d.1867). Chemist and physicist, discoverer of electromagnetism, leading to the modern developments in physics and electronics.

Sir William Schwenk Gilbert (W.S. Gilbert) (b.1836, d.1911). Humorist and librettist of the Gilbert and Sullivan light operas. (See below)

James Keir Hardie (b.1856, d.1915). Scottish Labour political leader. One of the founders of the British Labour Party. In 1892 he was the first socialist Member of Parliament.

Thomas Hardy (b.1840, d.1928). Novelist and poet. His Wessex novels, set in the south of England, include 'Far From the Madding Crowd'.

Rudyard Kipling (b.1865, d.1936). Writer who portrayed contemporary British rule in India. Received the Nobel Prize for Literature in 1907.

Sir Edwin Henry Landseer (b.1802, d.1873). Painter specializing in animals. Designed the lion statues in Trafalgar Square, London.

Karl Marx (b.1818, d.1883). German founder of international communism. In exile, he lived in London from 1849 until his death. Buried in Highgate Cemetery, London.

William Morris (b.1834, d.1896). Poet and political activist. In 1861 he founded a firm of decorators to combat mass-produced goods. In 1884 he was a founder member of the Socialist League.

John Henry Newman (b.1801, d.1890). Anglican priest who converted to Roman Catholicism (1845); elevated to Cardinal (1879); founder of the Oxford Movement in 1833.

Florence Nightingale (b.1820, d.1910). Nurse and pioneer of hospital reform. Called 'The Lady of the Lamp' by the British soldiers in the Crimean War In 1907, she was the first woman to receive the Order of Merit (OM).

Emmeline Goulden Pankhurst (b.1858, d.1928). Suffragette, with her daughters Christobel and Sylvia, worked for women's suffrage. Founder of the Women's Social and Political Union in 1903.

Samuel Plimsoll (b.1824, d.1898). Politician and social reformer. He was instrumental for the Merchant Shipping Act of 1876 that imposed the safety loading-line on ships.

7th Earl of Shaftesbury (b.1801, d.1885). Philanthropist and politician mainly responsible for legislation to protect children and women working in industry.

George Stephenson (b.1781, d.1848). Engineer and locomotive designer. His 'Rocket ' train in 1829 won a £500 prize for exceeding 30 mph.

Sir Arthur Seymour Sullivan (A. S. Sullivan) (b.1842, d.1900). Composer, mainly known for the music he wrote for light operas with W.S. Gilbert. (See above)

Alfred Tennyson (Alfred, Lord Tennyson, b.1809, d.1892). Poet. Many poems mirrored the times of his life. Poet Laureate 1850 until his death.

William Makepeace Thackeray (b.1811, d.1863). Novelist, famous for 'Vanity Fair'.

Joseph Mallord William Turner (b.1775, d.1851). Landscape painter, a master of light and colour. He bequeathed his works to the nation.

Herbert George Wells (H.G. Wells) (b.1866, d.1946). Author achieved success with science-fiction works such as 'The Time Machine' in 1895.

William Wordsworth (b.1770, d.1850). Poet. He was influenced by his early life in the Lake District, Cumbria. Poet Laureate 1843 until his death.

First Lords of the Treasury (Prime Ministers)	*Party*	*Took Office*
William Lamb (b.1779, d.1848). Succeeded as 2nd Viscount Melbourne in 1829	*Whig*	*1835 March*
Sir Robert Peel (b.1788, d.1850).	*Tory*	*1841 September*
Lord John Russell (b.1792, d.1878). Created Earl Russell in 1861	*Whig*	*1846 July*
Edward Stanley (b.1799, d.1869). Succeeded as 14th Earl of Derby in 1851	*Tory*	*1852 February*
George Hamilton Gordon (b.1784, d.1860). Succeeded as 4th Earl of Aberdeen in 1791	*Peelite*	*1852 December*
Henry John Temple (b.1784, d.1865). Succeeded as 3rd Viscount Palmerston in 1802	*Whig*	*1855 February*
Edward Stanley (see above)	*Conservative*	*1858 February*
Henry John Temple (see above)	*Liberal*	*1859 June*
Lord John Russell (see above)	*Liberal*	*1865 November*
Edward Stanley (see above)	*Conservative*	*1866 July*
Benjamin Disraeli (b.1804, d.1881). Created Earl of Beaconsfield in 1876	*Conservative*	*1868 February*
William Ewart Gladstone (b.1809, d.1898).	*Liberal*	*1868 December*
Benjamin Disraeli (see above)	*Conservative*	*1874 February*

William Ewart Gladstone (see above)	*Liberal*	*1880 April*
Lord Robert Cecil (b.1830, d.1903). Succeeded as 3rd Marquess of Salisbury in 1868	*Conservative*	*1885 June*
William Ewart Gladstone (see above)	*Liberal*	*1886 February*
Lord Robert Cecil (see above)	*Conservative*	*1886 August*
William Ewart Gladstone (see above)	*Liberal*	*1892 August*
Archibald Philip Primrose (b.1847, d.1929). Succeeded as 5th Earl of Rosebery in 1868	*Liberal*	*1894 March*
Lord Robert Cecil (see above)	*Conservative*	*1895 July*

Victoria, the daughter of the deceased Prince Edward, Duke of Kent and Strathearn, the fourth son of King George III, was 18 years of age when she succeeded her uncle, William IV, as sovereign in 1837.

A remarkable era of over sixty years built on social improvements commenced during the previous decades: the strength and generated wealth from industrialization and natural resources from the Empire, turned the United Kingdom into the dominant nation in the World. Many small countries sought the United Kingdom's protection against aggressors, to be Protectorates. The Empire was greatly expanded in every continent and some colonies were progressing with independent governments, and remaining within the Empire. It was a period for the United Kingdom of peace: it did not get involved with European problems, other than the distant Crimea in the 1850s; it had naval ships patrolling the World, protecting its own interests. Governments of differing political persuasions worked for the improvement of the country and its people. In sport, many games were invented and developed by the English; games became organized and professional; leisure activities were becoming part of the life for all, regardless of class or wealth although there were areas of poverty. The population of England and Wales was about 16 millions and Scotland's about 2.5 millions.

The Empire became important for trading and emigration. It became a source of pride for the people. From the 1840s many changes occurred during the next century and a quarter.

Upper Canada (mainly settled by the British) and Lower Canada (mainly settled by the French) were united into the Province of Canada under the 1840

Union Act, to be governed by a legislative council and assembly with equal representation of the two domains. In 1842 the boundary between Canada and the United States of America was agreed to be the 49th Parallel, where practical. The British North American Act of 1867 recognized the Dominion as a Confederation of its provinces.

New Zealand, inhabited by Maoris (meaning 'native' in their own language) was colonized in the early 1800s, and brought under British sovereignty with the signing of the (now controversial) Treaty of Waitangi of 1840. Originally administered as part of the Australian colony of New South Wales it became a colony in its own right in 1841. The New Zealand Act of 1851 established a Parliament with some degree of self-government; in the House of Representatives, four Maoris, elected by Maoris, to be members, the first colonial parliament where the indigenous people had the right of election. In 1856 New Zealand gained full responsible self-government.

During King George III's reign, those parts of India under British control were governed in accordance with the 1784 India Act. Various conflicts and wars were fought to protect those areas and, also, to annex adjacent territories, i.e. Afghanistan and Burma. India gradually came under greater control of the United Kingdom: its infrastructure and communications were being improved to further develop the already substantial commercial trading; railways were introduced in 1853. The Indian Mutiny of 1857, lasting thirteen months, resulted in the India Act of 1858 which transferred governing the country from the East India Company to the Crown, conducted by a government Secretary of State in London, with a council of fifteen members under a Viceroy based in India. The government wanted greater influence and control over Indian affairs. As a step to achieve this, the Prince of Wales (Prince Edward) made an extensive visit to India during 1875 and 1876. To cement this aim, Victoria was declared 'Empress of India' in 1877. The East India Company had extensive administrative control in Burma (now Myanmar); in 1886 it was annexed to India, transferring the authority to the Viceroy and the council.

In the early 1850s, settlers started to establish the colony of Victoria in Australia. Referenda in support of a united and independent country were held in the six states, leading to the Commonwealth of Australia Constitution Act of 1900. Australia received its independence on January 1, 1901, and remained in the Empire as a Dominion.

The Gambia, west Africa, having previously been settled by various companies of English merchants became a Crown colony. (A Crown colony had certain internal self-government but little control over the British appointed governor-general.)

In 1896, the United Kingdom proclaimed the whole of Sierra Leone (west Africa) as a protectorate.

Basutoland (now Lesotho) in southern Africa was constituted a native state under British protection from its near neighbours. In 1868 it became a protectorate and three years later it was annexed to the Cape Colony (now part of South Africa).

THE HANOVERS: QUEEN VICTORIA

Bechuanaland (now Botswana) became a protectorate in 1885 as protection from its near neighbours, the Boers of the Transvaal.

In 1853 the Cape Colony was advanced from a Crown colony to having a representative government with two elected chambers; in 1871 it was granted responsible self-government. After some years of antagonism, the Dutch settlers rebelled against the British at the end of 1880, lasting until the following March. The Boers, as they were known, were given self-government in the Transvaal territory under British authority. Natal (in southern Africa) was given responsible government in 1893, having been declared a Crown colony in 1842.

The British Empire, after the 1884 European nations 'Scramble For Africa' Conference of Berlin, extended its domain. The British South Africa Company, established by Cecil Rhodes, received its Royal Charter in 1889 to develop and govern much of south-central Africa, with similar powers to those which the East India Company had had in India.

Zanzibar (now part of Tanzania), an island off the south-east African coast, became another British protectorate in 1890, and the following year the United Kingdom annexed Nyasaland (now Malawi), and it became a protectorate.

British Honduras (now Belize), situated in Central America, had British settlers from the 17th century; the Spanish failed to dislodge them in 1798; and it became a British colony in 1862, administered by the governor of Jamaica until its own was appointed in 1884.

Jamaica, in the Caribbean, became a Crown colony in 1866 after an uprising about sugar prices and unemployment the previous year.

Barbados, settled by the English in 1627, became a Crown colony in 1885.

At the conclusion of the Opium War 1839 to 1842, when China attempted to stop Britain paying with opium for the purchase of tea and silk, which caused social and health problems, in defeat China was forced to open its ports to British shipping for trade and commerce. The islands of Hong Kong were ceded to the United Kingdom in 1841, and the adjacent New Territories were leased from China for 99 years from 1898.

Brunei, a sultanate off the north-east coast of the island of Borneo in the South China Sea, had trading arrangements with the United Kingdom, and became a British protectorate in 1888.

The Maldive Islands, a group of islands in the Indian Ocean, south-west of Sri Lanka, came under British protection to prevent them being colonized by Germany, Italy or France: they were made a dependency of the then colony of Ceylon (now Sri Lanka).

The Gilbert (now Kiribati) and Ellice (now Tuvalu) islands, a widely separated group of islands in the south-west Pacific Ocean, became protectorates of Britain in 1892. Fiji, another group of south-western Pacific islands were proclaimed a dependency of the Crown in 1874 in response from threats from other European nations for their control. The governance of the Solomon Islands, a group of islands in the south Pacific Ocean, was divided between the United Kingdom and Germany. The king of a further group of South Pacific islands, Tonga, signed a treaty of friendship and became a protectorate in 1900.

In 1897 Kuwait, situated north-east of the Arabian peninsula in the Persian Gulf, obtained British protectorate against the Turks.

The United Kingdom's business and industry were flourishing, exporting throughout the World, and in 1838 the first coal-driven steamship, the SS Great Western, built by Isambard Kingdom Brunel, crossed the Atlantic Ocean from Bristol to New York, the United States of America, in the record time of only fifteen days.

The Reform Act of 1832 had extended the vote to almost one million men: in 1838 a new movement, The Chartist, issued the 'Peoples Charter' demanding further reforms and to extend the vote to working men and the lower middle classes. Their petition of 1.25 million signatures, in support, submitted to Parliament was rejected. Rioters in Birmingham supported the cause the following year.

In 1839 an Anti-Corn Law League was formed in Manchester to campaign for the repeal of the 1815 Corn Law. This law prohibited the importation of cheaper priced foreign corn in order to protect home production, but it resulted in high costs for basic foods, e.g. bread. Also, manufacturers and merchants wanting to increase their foreign trade found the prevention of corn imports caused a problem for their export business dealings.

The charge for postage of letters was based on the distance of delivery and was paid by the receiver. In January 1840 a standard charge was introduced: the Penny Post, regardless of distance, paid by the sender, proved very popular and successful.

In 1840 Victoria married Prince Albert of Saxe-Coburg and Gotha, a cousin. Prince Albert proved to be a very supportive husband for Victoria, and took a great interest in promoting the United Kingdom's interests.

Income Tax commenced in 1841. Previously duty had been levied on practically all goods: the rich and poor had to pay the same rate of duty on all purchases. Some one thousand duties were reduced and six hundred abolished. The lower priced goods resulted in a substantial increase in trade.

The Chartists submitted a second petition to Parliament in 1842 with their demands. This time it was supported by over four million signatures. Again it was rejected.

Parliament was concerned about the employment and conditions of the young. The Mines Commission reported that children as young as 5 years of age were employed for up to sixteen hours a day. The 1842 Collieries Act prohibited the employment in the mines of boys under the age of 10 and all females. Inspectors were to be appointed to ensure the law being enforced. Further, the Factory Act of 1847 introduced a ten-hour maximum working day for all those under the age of eighteen.

THE HANOVERS: QUEEN VICTORIA

The Irish potato blight from 1842 onwards caused terrible starvation. It was estimated about 750,000 people died, and the high price of corn exacerbated the situation. In England the price of corn and the failed harvests, also, resulted in starvation. After serious problems for parliamentary support, the repeal of the 1815 Corn Law and subsequent relevant measures was enacted in 1846. The Importation Act was passed in both the Houses of Commons and Lords; this gradually made bread affordable, particularly, to the benefit of the poor.

The Chartists, continuing their campaign, held a large rally in London to support the presentation to Parliament of a third petition demanding reform and to extend the voting franchise, in 1848. It was ridiculed: the claim of six million signatures, when counted, totalled only two millions, and many of the signatures were fraudulent. Nevertheless, during the next sixty years, five of their demands became law.

During the 19th century, mechanization began to replace hand-produced manufactured goods, making the United Kingdom the leading industrial nation of the World. Victoria's husband, Prince Albert, was instrumental for the Great Exhibition of 1851, a massive glass construction, the Crystal Palace, in Hyde Park, London. It was to advertise and promote British goods, to celebrate the great advances of the British industrial age, and the expansion of the Empire, an example being the under-water cable for telegraphic communication being laid on the seabed of the English Channel between Dover (England) and Calais (France).

The United Kingdom and France became involved, as allies, in the Crimean War (southern Ukraine) in 1853 in support of the Ottoman (Turkish) Empire against the aggression of Russia. Medical conditions were appalling with more soldiers dying from disease than were killed: the British had 4,600 killed in battles, but 17,500 died from disease; altogether the allies lost more than 150,000 troops. In response to the medical problems, the Government approached Florence Nightingale to supervise the introduction of female nurses into military hospitals in Turkey. Her success made her a heroine in the annals of medical and war history. Eventually, the signing of the Treaty of Paris in 1856 brought an end to the, mainly, Black Sea war.

The Victoria Cross (VC), in the shape of a bronze Maltese Cross, was instituted in 1856. Awarded retrospectively to 1854, it is the highest military decoration awarded to armed forces personnel 'For Conspicuous Valour'. The explanation of the source of the gunmetal, from which the medals are struck, is that it derives from Russian cannon captured at the siege of Sevastopol during the Crimean War.

The Coldstream Regiment of Foot Guards, having had their name changed to the 2nd Foot Guards in 1782, were re-named the Coldsteam Guards in 1855. It remains the second-ranking regiment of Foot Guards in the country. To control and protect the United Kingdom's interests overseas, the Royal Navy had a fleet of 37 ships based in the Mediterranean Sea and about 18 ships patrolling the African coast between west Africa and the Cape (now South Africa). In 1859, the

Royal Navy Reserve was created, to supplement the navy.

From 1850 changes were made to the Entrance qualifications for both Oxford and Cambridge Universities, but Dissenters (non-conformists) continued to be debarred. The Boat Race between the two universities, first held in 1829, became an annual event from 1856 on the River Thames, London, commencing at Putney and finishing at Mortlake, where it is still contested.

In 1855, The Daily Telegraph became the first newspaper to be sold for one penny (1d).

After pressure over a period of some years by Victoria, Prince Albert was eventually created Prince Consort in 1857, seventeen years after their marriage. Senior politicians had been very reticent in this creation in order to protect Victoria's position of supremacy as monarch from her influential husband.

The Palace of Westminster was destroyed by fire in 1834. The architect Sir Charles Barry designed the new Palace of Westminster incorporating those parts of Westminster Hall that survived the fire. The new Parliament of the House of Commons and the House of Lords was completed in 1860.

1861 was a sad year for Victoria. Her mother died in the March and, to her lasting distress her husband, Prince Albert, died at Windsor Castle in December at the age of 42.

Sport was developing and increasing in popularity, both participating and watching. The Football Association (FA) was formed in 1863, and produced a set of uniform rules for the game of football, also called soccer.

With advancements in technology, in 1861 the Royal Navy commissioned its first ironclad warship, HMS Warrior, in response to the French armoured ship Gloire that was launched in 1859. Civil engineering projects included the construction of the World's first underground railway in London, connecting the mainline stations of Paddington and King's Cross. The first trains were drawn by steam engines and 40,000 passengers were carried on the four-mile line on the first day, January 10, 1863. Fourteen years after the English Channel under-water telegraphic communications cable laid between Dover and Calais, a cable was laid on the Atlantic Ocean-bed linking the United Kingdom to North America, between Valentia Island, in Kerry, south-west Ireland, and Heart's Content, in eastern Newfoundland (now part of Canada), in 1866. In 1869 the Egyptian Suez Canal was opened: it shortened the journey between Britain and the East, in particular India, by many weeks.

The number of people (men) entitled to vote increased in 1866, although initially the second Reform Bill was rejected by the House of Commons, the following year it was passed to become an Act. It extended the franchise to all men householders, and to male lodgers in towns who paid a rent of £10 per year, and £12 per year for those who lived in rural areas. Altogether, a million men gained the right to vote, many being working men. The electorate increased to about two millions.

The Irish problems continued to concern the Government. The Fenian Society in 1867 tried to release Irish prisoners from jail by attempting to blow up

Clerkenwell Prison in London. In Manchester, the Irish killed a policeman. In an effort to alleviate Irish antagonisms, the Government introduced some measures, the 1869 Disestablishment of the Irish Protestant Church Act and the Land Act of 1870.

From the end of 1868 to June 1885, the country had stable and continuous government: two Conservative and two Liberal administrations. Much beneficial legislation for social, education and military reorganization was enacted.

A comprehensive scheme for education commenced with the Elementary Education Act of 1870 that divided England into districts, each to be administered by an elected School Board. If a district needed a school the Government ensured one was built. Parents were to contribute nine pence (9d) per week for their child's education: it was intended that all children up to the age of 13 should be required to attend school. Daily scripture lessons were voluntary. Almost 3.5 million children were of school age, but there were less than 2 million places available at the start.

By this time universities in London and Durham had been founded: many others in the following years throughout the country were established. The 1673 and 1678 Test Acts were repealed in 1871 to permit non-Church of England communicants to attend Oxford and Cambridge Universities.

Parliament was forced to consider the legal position of trades unions and their members. The Trade Union Act of 1871 secured the legal status of trades unions, although the Criminal Law Amendment Act, passed the same day in Parliament that made picketing illegal, was repealed in 1875, so removing restrictions on trade union activities. To clarify the legal position of trades unions, a tidying-up measure was passed by Parliament in 1876.

Secret voting in parliamentary and municipal elections to remove corruption, coercion and disorder at elections was introduced by the Ballot Act of 1872. In the following general election of 1874, working men for the first time qualified to stand for Parliament: two were successful and elected.

Social legislation was important. The Public Health Act of 1875 gave local councils powers to tackle disease: each council had to appoint a Medical Officer of Health. In the Artisan Dwelling Act local councils were authorized to demolish slum properties and replace them with suitable housing. The same year an Act prohibited the employment of boys being used to climb the inside of chimneys, then the method of chimney cleaning.

Many ships and crews were lost at sea due to overloading. The 1876 Merchant Shipping Act gave the Board of Trade (a government department) authority to inspect all ships, and, as a safety measure the Plimsoll Line (named after the member of parliament who promoted the scheme, Samuel Plimsoll), had to be painted on the hull of every ship to show the level to which it could be loaded.

Since the Great Exhibition of 1851, overseas trading in imports and exports tripled by the 1870s to nearly £300 million a year. In 1875 the government purchased a share of the ownership of the Suez Canal that had become an important seaway to India, etc. This was the United Kingdom's first direct involvement in Egypt.

From 1876, non-hereditary peerages were conferred on eminent judges, to enable judicial procedures of the House of Lords to be implemented. They were collectively 'The Lords of Appeal in Ordinary', commonly known as the Law Lords.

Changes to the way the Empire was controlled were recommended in 1879 by the Carnarvon Commission. It stated that the Empire "should be based on command of the sea, rather than on large garrisons and fortifications" and "the strength of the Royal Navy should be increased". The United Kingdom continued to use its naval strength to control its interests in the World and protect its trade. It had developed four main naval commands: the Atlantic Fleet based at Gibraltar; the Home fleet based in the English Channel; the Mediterranean Sea fleet; and the China fleet.

[The Thirty Years' War (1618 to 1648), fought mainly in the Holy Roman Empire (Germany), had devastated that country, which collapsed into many small principalities, virtually independent of their Empire. Gradually, Prussia began to dominate northern Germany, to lay the foundation of the unification of Germany by a series of three wars, culminating in the Franco-Prussian War. At its conclusion on January 18, 1871, in the Hall of Mirrors at Versailles, Paris, King Wilhelm I of Prussia was proclaimed the German Emperor.]

In sport, the Rugby Football Union was formed in 1871 as the English governing body of Rugby. Originally twenty-one English clubs formed the organization: the game originated at Rugby School in 1823. The first FA Cup Final (Football Association Challenge Cup) was the first association football (soccer) competition in the World: in the final at Kennington Oval, London, in 1872, Wanderers beat Royal Engineers by one goal to nil (1-0). The Wimbledon Tennis Championships, the oldest championship in tennis, was first played in 1877: it is one of the four worldwide Grand Slam events of the present age. The first ever Test cricket match was held in Melbourne, Australia, where the home country beat England by 45 runs.

From 1868 many changes were introduced in the army service that improved enlistment and disciplinary matters. In 1877 the Grenadier Regiment of Foot Guards had its name changed to the Grenadier Guards, and the regiment continues to this day. The Grenadier Guards are the first-ranking regiment of Foot Guards in the United Kingdom. Further army changes were made in 1881 when single-battalion regiments were amalgamated to form several battalion strength regiments, defining them with county titles, e.g. the 28th (North Gloucestershire) Regiment of Foot and the 61st (South Gloucestershire) Regiment of Foot merged to become the Gloucestershire Regiment. The county regiments attracted most recruits from within their county boundaries.

The first public telephone exchanges opened in London and Manchester in 1879. Telephone ownership and use, naturally, increased with the opening of these exchanges and the technology.

Parliament realized the need and benefits to educate the young. From 1880 it became compulsory for children up to the age of 10 to attend school throughout the country.

After another potato failure in Ireland, the second Land Act of 1881 failed to solve any of the problems. The Irish members of parliament began to disrupt the business of the House of Commons by filibustering on all subjects: they wanted Home Rule and an independent Irish Parliament. The Coercion Act of 1881 only made matters worse, especially when their leader, Charles Stewart Parnell, was imprisoned for no actual crime.

The United Kingdom's involvement in Egypt was really unintentional. A revolt against the British and French in the Suez Canal Zone led to the Royal Navy being sent to restore peace in 1882. A consul-general was appointed in 1884 to administer the country.

Test cricket was advancing within the Empire. In 1882 the Australian test cricket team defeated England at The Oval, Surrey, being the first defeat at home for England. To lament the loss, a bail was burnt (cremated) and placed in an urn. Known as the 'Ashes', it has been contested ever since between the two countries.

Since 1880 the standard time in the United Kingdom has been Greenwich Mean Time (GMT). Greenwich, in London, was adopted as the universal meridian for the World time zones on October 13, 1884.

A united Germany wanted to be a colonial power and at the Conference of Berlin in 1884, named the 'Scramble for Africa', European countries agreed to divide the African continent into colonies. Each would have an agreed defined area, virtually by drawing straight lines on a map of the continent.

Democracy was gathering apace for fairer and wider representation. The 1884 Franchise Act, a third reform act, extended the right to vote in elections by establishing a uniform £5 voting qualification that benefited the rural population and the poorer urban man. The electorate now reached five million men. The Redistribution Act of 1885 re-organized the parliamentary constituencies, to give a greater uniformity of electorate, so giving a fairer representation in the House of Commons. Four years later an organization, The Women's Franchise League, was founded to campaign for women to have the vote in elections, a campaign to last for some decades.

To recognize bravery by military and naval personnel Victoria instituted in 1886 the Distinguished Service Order (DSO) to be awarded to officers who had performed meritorious or distinguished service in war.

The Local Government Act of 1888 set the blueprint for local government: administrative county councils, borough councils, and the London County Council were constituted. Councillors were to be directly elected by the people; the councillors would elect aldermen for the councils, and they would be jointly equal in duties and responsibilities in administering the councils.

In association football (soccer), the English Football League was formed in 1888 with twelve teams, all from Lancashire and the Midlands: Preston North End were the first champions. Two years later, in 1890, was the commencement of the English County Cricket championship competition: Surrey were the first champions.

A series of measures in relation to Ireland met obstacles. The first Home Rule Bill of 1886 was defeated in the House of Commons: also, the Queen, herself, was not in favour of losing Ireland from her kingdom. During the 1890s Parliament passed a number of Acts to improve the conditions and prosperity for the Irish. In 1892 a second Home Rule Bill was introduced, although passed by the House of Commons, it was defeated in the House of Lords.

With an enlarged electorate, the composition of the House of Commons was changing. In 1892 Keir Hardie, a Scottish miner, was elected to Parliament for a London constituency. The following year he formed the Independent Labour Party, the beginning of a socialist parliamentary party in British politics.

The District and Parish Councils Act of 1894 almost completed the new formation of local government. Each county was divided into districts, either urban or rural according to the location, and each district was divided into parishes; both district and parish councils had their responsibilities defined in the Act.

As in all aspects of this rapidly changing Victorian age, sport was developing and being organized. In 1895, twenty-two Rugby clubs formed the Northern Rugby Football League in the north of England, known as Rugby League. At the end of their first season, 1895/96, Mannington were the league champions.

The Prince of Wales (Prince Edward), in 1896 popularized the motorcar by buying a Daimler. The speed limit was 4 mph (miles per hour) and a 'flagman' was obliged to walk in front of all cars.

In Sudan, the southern neighbour of Egypt, Britain unintentionally became involved in its problems. Troops were sent to suppress disturbances in 1883 and by September 1898, after the famous Battle of Omdurman, Britain had taken responsibility for governing the country under the 'Scramble for Africa' agreement. Britain governed Sudan in conjunction with Egypt. During military action, manned balloons were used for the first time to observe the enemy movements and positions.

During this period small countries sought protection of the United Kingdom, illustrating the strength of the country during the last decades of the 19th century.

In 1899 the local government of London was further organized: around and outside but excluding the inner City of London, twenty-eight metropolitan boroughs were established.

Free education for children had been introduced at the beginning of the 1890s, and in 1899 the minimum school leaving age was raised to twelve, and a government department, the Board of Education, was established. During 1900 the school leaving age was raised again, to fourteen years of age.

In southern Africa, a Second Boer War commenced in 1899 (the limited rebellion of 1880 is referred to as the first Boer War). The United Kingdom had given the Dutch settlers independence in the Transvaal under British authority. The Boers became resentful and angered over a number of issues, including the discovery of massive gold deposits, and the subsequent influx of 'foreigners' seeking work and fortune. They declared war against the British in the October. Winston Churchill, a future Prime Minister of the United Kingdom and descendant of the famous John Churchill (Duke of Marlborough of Blenheim fame in 1704), was captured and imprisoned at Pretoria by the Boers, but he managed to escape.

Queen Victoria had a great affinity to Coburg (northern Bavaria, modern Germany), the birthplace of both her mother and Prince Albert. She made six visits, initially with Prince Albert and the last in 1896, at the age of 77, for various family occasions such as weddings. She travelled to Belgium three times, and once each to Switzerland and Italy. She was a regular visitor to France; in 1843 to northern France and in 1855 to Paris, the first royal monarch from Britain since King Henry VI in 1431. From 1882 onwards she made nine trips to the French Riviera, the last being in 1899 at the age of 79. She first went to Ireland in 1861, and in 1900 to Dublin to show her gratitude for the gallantry of the Irish soldiers in the Second Boer War.

The Queen instituted the Royal Victorian Order in 1896 as a reward for personal service to the monarchy. There are six levels of awards, and continues to be awarded by the present monarch. The 1887 Golden Jubilee and the 1897 Diamond Jubilee of Victoria's reign were celebrated in great style by representatives from every Dominion, Colony and Protectorate of the Empire, with pageants and public ceremonies throughout the United Kingdom.

Victoria, after a reign of sixty-three years died at the age of 81 on January 22, 1901 at Osborne House on the Isle of Wight. She was buried beside Prince Albert at the Frogmore Royal Mausoleum, Windsor, Berkshire.

The population during her reign for England, Wales and Scotland had increased from 18.5 million to 37 millions.

THE SAXE-COBURG

Monarchy	Reigned	Family
Edward VII	1901 to 1910	Son of Victoria

SAXE-COBURG

KING EDWARD VII

Born	**1841 November 9**
Accession	**1901 January 22**
Age at Accession	**59**
Death	**1910 May 6**
Age at Death	**68**
Reigned	**9 years**

Edward VII succeeded his mother Queen Victoria.

In 1863 he married Princess Alexandra (b.1844, d.1925), daughter of Christian IX, King of Denmark. They had 3 sons and 3 daughters.

The eldest son Prince Albert Christian Edward, Duke of Clarence and Avondale, died unmarried, January 14, 1892, at the age of 28.

Persons of note:

Elizabeth Garrett Anderson (b.1836, d.1917). One of the first English women to enter the medical profession, and the first woman to be a town mayor.

Robert Stephenson Smyth Baden-Powell (Baron Baden-Powell) (b.1857, d.1941). British army general and founder of the Boy Scouts (1908) and the Girl Guides (1910) to promote good citizenship. Chief Scout of the World from 1921 until his death.

William Booth (b.1829, d.1912). Founder and first General of the Salvation Army, in 1878.

THE SAXE–COBURG: KING EDWARD VII

Frederick Delius (b.1862, d.1934). English born composer of German parentage. Composed operas, concertos, orchestral music, and chamber music.

Sir William Schwenk Gilbert (W.S. Gilbert) (b.1836, d.1911). Humorist and librettist of the Gilbert and Sullivan light operas.

James Keir Hardie (b.1856, d.1915). Scottish Labour political leader. One of the founders of the British Labour Party. In 1892 he was the first socialist Member of Parliament.

Thomas Hardy (b.1840, d.1928). Novelist and poet. His Wessex novels, set in the south of England, include 'Far From The Madding Crowd'.

Gustav Theodore Holst (b.1874, d.1934). English born composer of part-Swedish descent, whose compositions include 'The Planets'.

Rudyard Kipling (b.1865, d.1936). Writer who portrayed contemporary British rule in India. Received the Nobel Prize for Literature 1907.

Florence Nightingale (b.1820, d.1910). Nurse and pioneer of hospital reform. Called 'The Lady of the Lamp' by British soldiers in the Crimean War. In 1907, she was the first woman to be awarded the Order of Merit (OM).

Emmeline Goulden Pankhurst (b.1858, d.1928). Suffragette, with her daughters Christobel and Sylvia, worked for women's suffrage. Founder of the Women's Social and Political Union in 1903.

Herbert George Wells (H.G. Wells) (b.1866, d.1946). Author achieved success with science-fiction works such as 'The Time Machine' in 1895.

Ralph Vaughan Williams (b.1872, d.1958). Composer. He wrote symphonies, choral and orchestral works, operas and chamber music.

Prime Ministers, First Lords of the Treasury	*Party*	*Took Office*
Lord Robert Cecil (b.1830, d.1903). Succeeded as 3rd Marquess of Salisbury in 1868	*Conservative*	*1895 July*
Arthur James Balfour (b.1848, d.1930). Created Earl of Balfour in 1922	*Conservative*	*1902 July*

THE SAXE–COBURG: KING EDWARD VII

Sir Henry Campbell-Bannerman
(b.1836, d.1908).   **Liberal   1905 December**

Herbert Henry Asquith (b.1852, d.1928).
Created Earl of Oxford and Asquith in 1925   **Liberal   1908 April**

Edward succeeded to the throne at the age of 59, as a Saxe-Coburg, his father's family name. He inherited a stable throne, government and country, but a country which had changed more in the previous sixty years than in any comparable period during the previous nine hundred years. Parliament had been very active in passing legislation to meet the demands and needs of the age. The population wanted fairness, opportunities and to be heard. They wanted employment, education, to be represented by organizations such as trade unions, and the right to vote in elections.

The Government transferred educational powers to local government by the Education Act of 1902. County and borough councils were to be responsible for the funding from local taxes, and the regulation of schools. The Church of England and the Roman Catholic schools were to be brought under the jurisdiction of the councils.

The Boer War continued through to 1902. In the war, as in the Sudan conflicts earlier, manned balloons were used to spy on the enemy movements. The British and Imperial forces lost over 21,000 troops, although 13,000 of the total died of disease. The Vereeniging Peace Treaty of May 1902 concluded the fighting: it ended the semi-independent existence of the Boer's freedom to govern themselves.

Edward instituted the Order of Merit (OM) in 1902. It is a special mark of honour conferred by the Sovereign on people of exceptional distinction. The order is limited to twenty-four members at any one time. A day to commemorate the Empire, first considered in 1897, was inaugurated on May 24, 1902 as Empire Day.

In 1903 Mrs Emmeline Pankhurst, a founder of The Women's Franchise League in 1889, formed the Women's Social and Political Union to expand the campaign for women to have the vote.

During the same year, wireless telegraphic messages were exchanged when Edward and President Theodore Roosevelt of the United States of America inaugurated the service.

Since the unification of the small principality states in 1871, Germany was developing into an important country. The threat of enlarging its navy would change the balance of European power, and the United Kingdom's efforts to negotiate an alliance with Germany were rebuffed.

THE SAXE–COBURG: KING EDWARD VII

A friendly relationship with France had been created during Queen Victoria's reign, and the French liked Edward, who was a regular visitor. The United Kingdom and France agreed to an Entente-Cordial, a series of agreements signed in 1904. Its basis was mutual agreements on colonial affairs, but also linked the United Kingdom, France and Russia together in opposing the 1882 Triple Alliance between Germany, Austria, and later Italy.

The Second Boer War revealed serious weaknesses in the forward planning of the army. In response, the reorganization included the introduction of the General Staff in 1904, to be responsible for day-to-day and long-term strategy. In addition, an army council was formed, to consist of the Secretary State for War (a Government minister), four senior officers and two senior civil servants. Three years later the Territorial Force was established to supplement the regular force for home defence.

Brunei Darussalam, part of the island of Borneo, a British protectorate in Asia since 1888, became a dependency in 1905.

The position and title of 'Prime Minister' was officially recognized in 1905; the Prime Minister still includes 'First Lord of the Treasury' in the title.

The 1906 Parliamentary general election resulted in the Labour Party having a representation of twenty-nine members in the House of Commons.

At the beginning of Edward's reign, a court case, Taff Vale, decreed that trades unions could be made liable for financial recompense to businesses for losses incurred by the effects of striking union members. The consequence of this decision made the Trade Union Act of 1871 ambiguous. The Trades Disputes Act of 1906 clarified this matter and the peaceful picketing by strikers became legal. The Workers Compensation Act of the same year, allowed employees to claim recompense for permanent injury to their health arising from their employment.

The Childrens Act of 1907 commenced the practice of medical examinations of all school children, and those in need to be provided with food.

Informal meetings of the leaders of the Dominions and others of the Empire were held at the 1887 and 1897 Golden and Diamond Jubilee celebrations commemorating Queen Victoria's reign. An Imperial Conference in London in 1907 decided that future conferences should be held every four years. New Zealand received Dominion status in 1907.

The 1907 Anglo-Russian Convention, or entente, defined the two countries spheres of interests, in particular, to prevent German expansion into those areas.

In 1908 Edward made a State visit to Tsar Nicholas II of Russia in the June, the only visit made by a British sovereign to Russia, until Queen Elizabeth II's visit in 1994. The wives of Edward and the Tsar were sisters.

The IV Olympic Games were held in London in 1908. There were 27 nations competing, 2,008 men and women athletes and 110 events. The United Kingdom won 56 gold medals, 51 silver and 39 bronze, and topped the medals table.

Amongst the many social measures that Parliament passed, the Old Age Pensions Act of 1908 provided a weekly pension to men and women over 70 years of age. This allowed many to leave or avoid the disliked workhouses that often split up families; penalties were introduced to punish those responsible for neglecting and ill-treating children; and Labour Exchanges were opened to enable people to find employment.

A serious constitutional confrontation between the elected House of Commons and the hereditary House of Lords occurred. It was customary for budgets to be accepted by the House of Lords, but in 1909 it contended that the budget bill exceeded the normal fiscal measures, so the bill was defeated. In response the government called a Parliamentary general election in January 1910 and with the support of the Labour and Irish members remained the Government.

Edward intervened and threatened to create sufficient peers for the House of Lords to pass the budget, but during the crisis the King died on May 6, 1910.

He was buried in St George's Chapel, Windsor, Berkshire.

THE WINDSORS

Monarch	Reigned	Family
George V	1910 to 1936	Son of Edward VII
Edward VIII	1936	Son of George V
George VI	1936 to 1952	Son of George V
Elizabeth II	1952 –	Daughter of George VI

WINDSOR

KING GEORGE V

Born	**1865 June 3**
Accession	**1910 May 6**
Age at Accession	**44**
Death	**1936 January 20**
Age at Death	**70**
Reigned	**25 years**

George V succeeded his father Edward VII. He was the second born son; the eldest son, Prince Albert Victor Christian Edward, Duke of Clarence and Avondale died January 14, 1892 at the age of 28, unmarried.

In 1893 he married Princess Mary (b.1867, d.1953), daughter of the Duke of Teck. They had 5 sons and 1 daughter.

Persons of note:

Sir John William Alcock (b.1892, d.1919). Aviator, with Sir Arthur Whitten Brown, flew the first non-stop flight across the Atlantic Ocean in a Vickers-Vimy bomber in 1919. (See below)

Elizabeth Garrett Anderson (b.1836, d.1917). One of the first English women to enter the medical profession, and the first woman to be a town mayor.

Nancy Astor (Viscountess Astor) (b.1879, d.1964). In 1919, the first woman to become a member of parliament in the House of Commons. Her husband was Waldorf Astor (Viscount Astor of Hever) (b.1879, d.1952). When he succeeded to his title and, therefore, debarred from the House of Commons, she was elected at the subsequent by-election and remained a member of parliament until 1945.

Herbert Austin (Baron Austin) (b.1866, d.1941). Motor manufacturer, pioneer of the small car in England, which sold from 1921 onwards.

Robert Stephenson Smyth Baden-Powell (Baron Baden-Powell) (b.1857, d.1941). British army general and founder of the Boy Scouts (1908) and the Girl Guides (1910) to promote good citizenship. Chief Scout of the World from 1921 until his death.

Sir Thomas Beecham (b.1879, d.1961). Symphony conductor who founded the London Philharmonic Orchestra in 1931 and promoted the works of Frederick Delius.

Sir Arthur Whitten Brown (b.1886, d.1948). Aviator, with Sir John William Alcock, flew the first non-stop flight across the Atlantic Ocean in a Vickers-Vimy bomber in 1919. (See above)

Sir Malcolm Campbell (b.1885, d.1948). Racing driver who held the land-speed record of 301 mph, and the water-speed record of 141 mph. He broke both speed records many times.

Howard Carter (b.1874, d.1939). Egyptologist who was associated with the Earl of Carnarvon in discovering the Tomb of Tutankhamen.

Sir Charles Spencer Chaplin (Charlie Chaplin) (b.1889, d.1977). Film star of the silent movies, director, producer, choreographer and composer. Knighted 1975.

Frederick Delius (b.1862, d.1934). English born composer of German parentage. Composed operas, concertos, orchestral music and chamber music.

Thomas Hardy (b.1840, d.1928). Novelist and poet. His Wessex novels, set in the south of England, include 'Far From The Madding Crowd'.

Gustav Theodore Holst (b.1874, d.1934). English born composer of part-Swedish descent, whose compositions include 'The Planets'.

Amy Johnson (b.1903, d.1941). The first woman aviator to fly solo from England to Australia, in 1930.

Rudyard Kipling (b.1865, d.1936). Writer who portrayed contemporary British rule in India. Received the Nobel Prize for literature 1907.

Sir Edwin Landseer Lutyens (b.1869, d.1944). Architect of country houses and public buildings; designed the Cenotaph in Whitehall, London.

Henry Moore (b.1898, d.1986). Sculptor. Carved abstract figures in many forms.

Emmeline Goulden Pankhurst (b.1858, d.1928). Suffragette, with her daughters Christobel and Sylvia, worked for women's suffrage. Founder of the Women's Social and Political Union in 1903.

Frederick John Perry (Fred Perry) (b.1909, d.1995). The greatest English player in the history of lawn tennis. Won the Wimbledon men's singles title in 1934, 1935 and 1936.

Graham Vivian Sutherland (b.1903, d.1980). Artist. He was an official war artist (1941 to 1945), and designed the tapestry for Coventry Cathedral 'Christ in Majesty'.

Sir William Turner Walton (b.1902, d.1983). Composer whose works include concertos, symphonies and two coronation marches. Awarded Order of Merit in 1967.

Herbert George Wells (H.G. Wells) (b.1866, d.1946). Author achieved success with science-fiction works such as 'The Time Machine' in 1895.

Ralph Vaughan Williams (b.1872, d.1958). Composer. He wrote symphonies, choral and orchestral works, operas and chamber music.

Prime Ministers, First Lords of the Treasury	*Party*	*Took Office*
Herbert Henry Asquith (b.1852, d.1928). *Created Earl of Oxford and Asquith in 1925*	*Liberal*	*1908 April*
Herbert Henry Asquith (see above)	*Coalition*	*1915 May*
David Lloyd George (b.1863, d.1945). *Created Earl Lloyd-George of Dyfor in 1945*	*Coalition*	*1916 December*
Andrew Bonar Law (b.1858, d.1923).	*Conservative*	*1922 October*
Stanley Baldwin (b.1867, d.1947). *Created Earl Baldwin of Bewdley in 1937*	*Conservative*	*1923 May*
James Ramsay MacDonald (b.1866, d.1937).	*Labour*	*1924 January*

Stanley Baldwin (see above)	*Conservative*	*1924 November*
James Ramsay MacDonald (see above)	*Labour*	*1929 June*
James Ramsey MacDonald (see above)	*National/ Coalition*	*1931 August*
Stanley Baldwin (see above)	*National/ Coalition*	*1935 June*

George V succeeded his father as King during a constitutional crisis. The House of Lords had rejected the 1909 Budget; a general election had been held in January 1910; the Liberal Party with the support of Labour and Irish members remained the Government. During this crisis George's father King Edward VII died in the May. The budget was presented again, and, the House of Lords rejected it again, and the Government called another general election, in the December. Again the Liberal Party was returned to power with the support of Labour and the Irish members.

When the King threatened to end the impasse by creating sufficient peers to outvote the dominant Conservatives in the House of Lords, the budget bill was accepted and passed.

The 1911 Parliament Act introduced limitations on the power of the House of Lords; it could no longer delay 'money bills', and other Bills if passed by the House of Commons could only be delayed according to the status of the Bill, before being automatically enacted. Further, the maximum period of a parliament between general elections was reduced from seven years to five years. For the first time members of the House of Commons were to receive payment, set at £400 per year.

The National Insurance Act of 1911 introduced payments to employees when ill; free medical attention for each person; maternity benefit for women; and in some instances unemployment benefits. Weekly contributions to fund the scheme were to be funded by both employers and employees.

Airplanes were introduced into the Royal Navy with naval officers being trained as pilots in 1911: in 1912 the Royal Flying Corp was formed, with a naval wing, a military wing, and a central flying school.

The RMS Titanic sailed from Southampton, Hampshire, on its maiden voyage to New York, United States of America, on April 10, 1912. It was the largest ship afloat, and stated to be the safest ever built, but four days later in mid-Atlantic Ocean it struck an iceberg and sank. Over 1,500 people drowned and 705 were rescued.

The increasing demands for women to have the right to vote campaigned by the suffragette movement and Mrs Emmeline Pankhurst became vociferous, and at times violent.

Also, the trade union movement had become militant by organizing strikes, particularly, the coal-miners and the railwaymen. In 1913 it became legal for trades unions to raise funds for political purposes. The contributions had to be paid voluntarily by their members, completely separate from the general union membership subscriptions.

The Irish were restless in demands for Home Rule for Ireland. The Protestants of Ulster (northern Ireland) did not want to be ruled by the Roman Catholics who were dominant in the rest of the island. George tried to mediate to ease the situation.

Aviation for warfare was developing: the naval wing of the Royal Flying Corp was reformed as the Royal Naval Air Service in January 1914, and soon it had a total of 217 pilots and 95 aircraft, of which 55 were seaplanes and flying boats.

During the reigns of Queen Victoria and King Edward VII, a period of seventy years, wars between European states did not involve the United Kingdom other than the Crimean War of 1853, but the general situation in Europe of 1913 had become tense, and the government was uncertain in its policy. Initially it considered the disputes to be localized and limited, but treaties and obligations eventually involved the whole of Europe and the United States of America.

It started when Austria wanted to control Serbia;
then Austria's Crown Prince, the Archduke Franz Ferdinand,
was assassinated on June 28, 1914;
the Austrians accused the Serbians of having instigated the murder and demanded outrageous conditions of compensation.
The Serbians, being Slavs, appealed to their allies, the Russians for support;
and Russia was willing to attack Austria.
Meanwhile, Germany had been increasing the size and training of its own army and building a strong naval fleet, and was bound by treaty to assist Austria.
Now Russia called on France to fulfil their treaty obligations for support;
therefore, France and Russia prepared for war against Austria and Germany.
The Germans invaded Belgium to capture coastal ports, in readiness to invade France.
The 1839 Treaty of London, signed when Belgium became an independent country, bound the United Kingdom to support Belgium.
The United Kingdom called on Germany to withdraw

their forces from Belgium, which they refused.
The United Kingdom declared war against Germany on
August 4, 1914.

The war was fought in continental Europe, the Atlantic Ocean, the Indian Ocean, the Pacific Ocean, and even the Falkland Islands in the south Atlantic Ocean: by traditional army combats, airplanes, balloons, surface naval fleets, submarines and by the new invention, the tank. The United Kingdom was supported by the Dominions and Empire providing personnel, including six million men from India.

The women's suffragette movement agreed not to campaign for the duration of the war, but a demonstration by 30,000 in London, demanded that trades unions allow them to work in industries traditionally dominated by men. The women wanted to be part of the war effort to combat the enemy.

At the outbreak of hostilities, with Turkey allying with Germany, the United Kingdom annexed the Mediterranean island of Cyprus, and Egypt became a protectorate. (Australia took control of the German part of the Solomon Islands, in the south Pacific Ocean.)

The German surface naval fleet was not too effective: after the Battle of Jutland (a peninsular of Denmark) in 1916, the Germans did not risk another surface naval fight, but their submarines almost destroyed the United Kingdom's supply of food and aid from overseas. Merchant shipping of any nation sailing to Britain was likely to be attacked and much was sunk.

The Gilbert (now Kiribati) and the Ellice (now Tuvalu) islands in the south Pacific Ocean, which had become a protectorate in 1892, were annexed in 1915/16 to become a colony. Qatar, a peninsular on the Persian Gulf, was given British protection in 1916.

In Europe, the war was virtually a stalemate. British forces remained on the 'Western Front' of Belgium and northern France for four years. There were many battles resulting in millions killed and even more wounded, many badly maimed.

The Women's Royal Navy Service (WRNS, popularly known as the Wrens) was the first of the armed forces to recruit women for shore-based duties.

Two events changed the course of the war. Firstly, the Bolshevik Revolution in 1917 resulted in the Russians withdrawing from the war, so enabling the Germans to transfer their forces to western Europe. Secondly, German submarines attacked American shipping: this brought the United States of America into the war.

The Germanic royal household name of Saxe-Coburg, Prince Albert's family name, caused disquiet in the country, so George changed the Royal House name to Windsor in 1917.

In the year, the Most Excellent Order of the British Empire, and the Order of the Companions of Honour were instituted. George wanted to recognize civilians and service personnel who had given outstanding service in war and peace to the country. There are five degrees of the first order: GBE, KBE/DBE, CBE, OBE and MBE. The Order of the Companions of Honour (CH) is awarded for recognized services of national importance, and limited to sixty-five recipients at any one time (excluding honorary members).

The Air Force (Constitution) Act passed by Parliament in November 1917, set up the Royal Air Force from April 1, 1918: in November 1918 it was the largest air force in the World, with over 22,000 aircraft, and almost 300,000 personnel. The Women's Royal Air Force and the Royal Air Force Nursing Service were founded during the year. In June 1918, four new medals were instituted for acts of gallantry in the air, being the Distinguished Flying Cross (DFC), Distinguished Flying Medal (DFM), Air Force Cross (AFC) and Air Force Medal (AFM).

By 1918 Germany began to break through the allied defences, but with the addition of over four million United States of America troops, not only were the German advances halted, but the Allies brought the Great War to an end with victory.

In 1918 the United Kingdom had overrun Palestine and Mesopotamia (modern Iraq), this being the first time since 1187 that Jerusalem, in Palestine, had been under Christian control.

The armistice for the Great War (nowadays referred to as World War I) was signed on November 11, 1918, and the peace was signed by the Treaty of Versailles, Paris, in June 1919.

The war was the most horrendous in the history of the World, to that time. The United Kingdom and the Empire had 1.1 millions killed and 2 millions wounded, mainly badly maimed. Altogether the allies had 9 millions killed and missing, 13 millions wounded; the enemy over 7 millions killed and missing, and 8 millions wounded.

The National Debt of the United Kingdom in 1914 was £708 million: by the end of the war it had risen to £7,475 million.

Before the outbreak of the war, Parliament had passed the Home Rule Act 1914 for Ireland. It was mutually agreed that the implementation of the Act should wait until war end, expected to be within a year, but those opposed to the Act being delayed revolted in 1916, the Easter Rising. A new party Sinn Fein (Ourselves Alone) was formed, demanding complete independence.

The Representation of the People Act 1918 gave the vote to women for the first time: they had to have a property qualification and to be over the age of 30; the age for men to vote was reduced to 21. In the following general election of December 1918, an Irish woman was victorious, but being a Sinn Fein member she refused to take her place in the House of Commons, along with the other seventy or so Sinn Fein victors.

The years following the end of the war were very difficult for the country and its people. Trade had been damaged; investment in businesses destroyed; troops were demobilized; work was scarce; the cost of living had doubled since 1914; but wages were lower. To compound the problems, an influenza epidemic caused 250,000 death in the United Kingdom; worldwide probably 50 millions died.

An international organization, the League of Nations, was instituted to ensure that war "never broke out again". The constitution was adopted at the Paris Peace Conference in April 1919. Based in Geneva, Switzerland, it was not representative of the then important countries, and was too weak to stop further war-like situations.

In 1919, Captain John Alcock and Lieutenant Arthur Brown made the first non-stop air flight, in a modified Vickers-Vimy bomber, crossing the Atlantic Ocean from Newfoundland (now part of Canada) to Ireland in 16 hours and 27 minutes, crash-landing in a boggy field in County Galway. Both men were knighted in recognition of their achievement. A few weeks later, the Royal Air Force airship R34, with a crew of thirty, flew from Scotland to New York, United States of America, in four days, July 2 to 6. It returned to England, July 9 to 13.

The first woman to take a seat in the House of Commons was Nancy Astor, the American born wife of Waldorf Astor. On the death of his father, Waldorf Astor inherited the Viscount title: now a peer he was debarred from the House of Commons. Although a viscountess but not the title-holder, Nancy Astor was able to stand for Parliament and contested the by-election at her husband's former constituency at Plymouth, Devon, as the Conservative candidate.

With the passing of The Government of India Act 1919, a Council of State and an elected Legislative Assembly representing all of India was formed. These measures were opposed by much of the population. Independence was demanded.

Mandates given by the League of Nations, Mesopotamia (modern Iraq), Palestine, and Tanganyika (a German colony, now part of Tanzania in east Africa), came under British jurisdiction. Kenya (east Africa) formerly a protectorate became a Crown colony in 1920.

In 1920 a Home Rule Bill for Ireland was passed by Parliament but rejected by the Irish. The country was to be divided, with part of Ulster (northern Ireland) being partitioned from the rest of the island.

The war memorial, the Cenotaph in Whitehall, London, was unveiled on November 11, 1920 to commemorate the British, Dominions and Empire service men and women who had died in war.

The Territorial Force, founded in 1908, was renamed the Territorial Army in 1921, and this new force was required to serve overseas as well as at home. There was some reorganization in the army with battalions being amalgamated, and consequently, some renaming of regiments.

The 1921 Census showed the population of England and Wales as almost 38 millions, Scotland 4.9 millions; an overall increase of 2 millions from the previous census of 1911.

The Railways Act 1921, as an economic measure, reorganized the railway system throughout the United Kingdom. The 120 companies were combined into four main groups.

In 1921, the 1911 National Health Insurance Act was amended to extend the social benefits to people who became invalided as a result of their employment.

In Mesopotamia, a provisional government was established and the following year, 1922, it became the Kingdom of Iraq. Egyptian nationalism forced the United Kingdom to declare Egypt an independent sovereign state, but with the canal being an important international sea-route, the Suez Canal Zone and the overall defence of the country remained with Britain. In 1920 Transjordan (nowadays Jordan) was separated from Palestine, became a Kingdom, and in 1923 the United Kingdom recognized its independence, subject to the provisions of the League of Nations mandate of 1918. The settlers of Southern Rhodesia (now Zimbabwe) voted to become a self-governing British colony.

The 1922 Treaty for the Limitation of Naval Armament held in Washington, United States of America, agreed the future sizes of the naval fleets for the United Kingdom, the United States of America, and Japan (then an ally).

The first Association Football (FA) Cup Final played at the new Wembley Stadium in 1923 was won by Bolton Wanderers against West Ham United by two goals to nil (2-0).

The successful Sinn Fein candidates at the 1918 general election refused to take their seats in the House of Commons, and created their own Irish Parliament. The Government in 1923 reached an agreement with them to form the Irish Free State, excluding part of Ulster (northern Ireland), as a Dominion of the United Kingdom.

An important constitutional policy was approved by Parliament on colonial matters: the interests of the 'native' population would be paramount over all issues in their country, including that over the white settlers.

At the general election of November 1922, the Labour Party won 142 seats in the House of Commons, and at the following general election of December 1923, they increased this total to 191: the combined number of members of parliament of the Labour and Liberal parties was greater than the opposition parties, and Ramsay MacDonald, became the first Labour Party Prime Minister of the United Kingdom. The 'hung' parliament failed, and the general election of October 1924 returned the Conservatives to government with a large majority.

The Fleet Arm of the Royal Air Force was formed under the joint control of the Air Ministry and the Admiralty at this time.

The administration of Northern Rhodesia (now Zambia) was transferred to the Crown from the British South Africa Company in 1923; Cyprus was declared a Crown colony in 1925.

The heir to the throne, the Prince of Wales (Prince Edward), visited every Dominion between 1920 and 1924.

The leaders of Britain, the Dominions and the Empire meeting at the Imperial Conference in 1926 resolved that each Dominion should be equal with each other and with Britain, to be linked by a common allegiance to the Crown.

The economy was declining; unemployment increasing; and discontent throughout the country. A Royal Commission was constituted to find ways of restoring employment and prosperity. Railwaymen, coal-miners, and printers were prominent in a General Strike of May 2, 1926, but generally support was weak, and it collapsed within ten days, when it was ended by the Trades Union Congress (TUC).

Women finally achieved equal voting rights with men when Parliament passed the Equal Franchise Act on June 14, 1928. Now everyone had a vote at the age of 21: the electorate totalled 15 million women and 13 million men. Of the leading campaigners, Elizabeth Garret Anderson died in 1917; Emmeline Pankhurst died in June 1928; and Millicent Fawcett, the President of the National Union of Women's Suffrage from 1897, died in December 1929.

With no party having an overall majority in the House of Commons following the May 1929 general election, and with the whole World in the grip of an economic depression, George persuaded the three main political parties (Conservative, Liberal and Labour) to unite into a coalition National Government. Britain abandoned the Gold Standard; it abandoned free trade; and introduced tariffs on imported goods.

In 1931 Ceylon (now Sri Lanka) gained a large measure of self-government, and the following year the British League of Nations mandate over Iraq was terminated.

The King made history by broadcasting to the nation for the first time on Christmas Day 1932. It was the monarch's first Christmas Day Message, which has been followed by successive monarchs every year.

The 1933 Imperial Conference agreed to increase tariffs on foreign imports (not from within the Empire), and an economic policy for the Empire.

The 1935 Anglo-German Agreement allowed Germany's surface naval fleet to total one-third of the tonnage of the Royal Navy's surface fleet, and an equal tonnage of submarines. (Germany did not keep to this agreement.)

The country celebrated George's Silver Jubilee as King in 1935, but on January 20, 1936 at the age of 70, he died at Sandringham House, Norfolk. He was buried in the Chapel of the Knights of the Garter at Windsor Castle, Berkshire.

WINDSOR

KING EDWARD VIII

Born	**1894 June 23**
Accession	**1936 January 20**
Age at Accession	**41**
Abdicated	**1936 December 10**
Reigned	**325 days**
Death	**1971 May 28**
Age at Death	**77**

Edward VIII succeeded his father George V.

He abdicated, unmarried.

In 1937, after his abdication, he married Mrs Wallis Warfield Simpson (b.1896, d.1986). They had no children.

Prime Minister, First Lord of the Treasury	*Party*	*Took Office*
Stanley Baldwin (b.1867, d.1947).	*National/*	
Created Earl Baldwin of Bewdley in 1937	*Coalition*	*1935 June*

On succeeding his father, Edward precipitated a constitutional crisis by his determination to marry Mrs Wallis Warfield Simpson, a twice-divorced United States of America citizen.

The Church of England opposed the marriage because Mrs Simpson's two previous husbands were still living, and, as such this contravened the Articles of

Faith of the Church. Edward accepted the constitutional position; as monarch he would have been Supreme Governor of the Church of England. He was determined to marry Wallis Simpson and accepted, in the circumstances, that abdication as King was likely.

The continuing effects of the worldwide economic depression continued to be a problem for the National Coalition Government. Poor quality housing and the lack of employment were recognized as a serious problem. During 1936 some 300,000 new homes were built, so creating employment throughout the industry and its ancillary businesses. Gradually the economy improved.

In March, Germany invaded the demilitarized Rhineland, in contravention of the 1919 Peace Treaty of Versailles, Paris. Italy had colonized Eritrea, north-east Africa, in 1885, and invaded the neighbouring Abyssinia (now Ethiopia) in October 1935. (Germany and Italy signed the Roma-Berlin Axis agreement for military co-operation in October 1936.)

During the year, British troops were withdrawn from most of Egypt, other than the Suez Canal Zone.

Edward abdicated on December 10; his abdication was confirmed by Parliament the following day. He left England to live abroad. Stripped of several titles, including that of Prince of Wales, he was created the Duke of Windsor on December 12.

At his death in 1972 at the age of 77, he was buried in Frogmore, in the grounds of Windsor Castle, Berkshire.

WINDSOR

KING GEORGE VI

Born	**1895 December 14**
Accession	**1936 December 10**
Age at Accession	**40**
Death	**1952 February 6**
Age at Death	**56**
Reigned	**15 years**

George VI was the second son of George V, and succeeded his brother Edward VIII.

In 1923 he married Lady Elizabeth Angela Marguerite Bowes-Lyon (b.1900, d.2002), daughter of the 14th Earl of Strathmore and Kinghorne. They had 2 daughters.

Persons of note:

Nancy Astor (Viscountess Astor) (b.1879, d.1964). In 1919, the first woman to become a member of parliament in the House of Commons. Her husband was Waldorf Astor (Viscount Astor of Hever) (b.1879, d.1952). When he succeeded to his title and, therefore, debarred from the House of Commons, she was elected at the subsequent by-election and remained a member of parliament until 1945.

Herbert Austin (Baron Austin) (b.1866, d.1941). Motor manufacturer, pioneer of the small car in England, which sold from 1921 onwards.

Sir Thomas Beecham (b.1879, d.1961). Symphony conductor who founded the London Philharmonic Orchestra in 1931 and promoted the works of Frederick Delius.

Edward Benjamin Britten (Baron Britten) (b.1913, d.1976). Composer. Reputation mainly for his vocal compositions. Awarded Order of Merit in 1965.

Sir Malcolm Campbell (b.1885, d.1948). Racing driver who held the land-speed record of 301 mph, and the water-speed record of 141 mph. He broke both speed records many times.

Sir Charles Spencer Chaplin (Charlie Chaplin) (b.1889, d.1977). Film star of the silent movies, director, producer, choreographer and composer. Knighted 1975.

Sir Winston Leonard Spencer Churchill (b.1874, d.1965). Statesman and author. Prime Minister 1940 to 1945, and 1951 to 1955. His greatest achievement was leading the United Kingdom to victory in World War II. Awarded Nobel Prize for Literature 1953. Knighted 1953.

Sir Geoffrey de Havilland (b.1882, d.1965). Pioneer of civil and military aviation. His company produced the Mosquito fighter for World War II, and the Comet that was the World's first commercial jet-airliner.

Dame Margot Fonteyn (b.1919, d.1991). Prima ballerina of the Royal Ballet, considered the greatest ballerina of her time, especially when in partnership with Rudolf Nureyev (b.1938, d.1993).

Amy Johnson (b.1903, d.1941). The first woman aviator to fly solo from England to Australia, in 1930. She drowned after bailing-out of her airplane into the River Thames estuary, whilst on war service.

Dame Vera Lynn (b.1917). Immensely popular singer, the 'Forces Sweetheart', during and after World War II. Created Dame 1976.

Sir Stanley Matthews (b.1915, d.2000). First association football player to be knighted, 1965. One of the greatest of all footballers.

Bernard Law Montgomery (Viscount Montgomery of Alamein) (b.1887, d.1976). Field-Marshal of the army; successful strategist. Commander of the 8th Army in north Africa, Sicily and Italy, to victories from 1942 to 1944; Commander-in-Chief, British Group of Armies and Allied armies in northern France in 1944.

Henry Moore (b.1898, d.1986). Sculptor. Carved abstract figures in many forms.

Lawrence Kerr Olivier (Baron Olivier of Brighton) (b.1907, d.1989). Actor and director, especially in Shakespearean roles. Awarded Order of Merit in 1981.

William George Penney (Baron Penney) (b.1909, d.1990). Physicist who was responsible for the development of British nuclear technology.

Sir Gordon Richards (b.1904, d.1986). Foremost race-jockey who rode 4,870 winners. He was champion jockey 25 times between 1925 and 1953. Knighted 1953.

Graham Vivian Sutherland (b.1903, d.1980). Artist. He was an official war artist (1941 to 1945), and designed the tapestry for Coventry Cathedral 'Christ in Majesty'.

Sir Michael Tippett (b.1905, d.1998). Composer whose works include the opera 'The Midsummer Marriage', the oratorio 'A Child of Our Time', and the cantata 'The Vision of St Augustine'.

Sir Barnes Neville Wallis (b.1887, d.1979). Aeronautical engineer. Designed and/or involved in the development of the airship R100, the Wellington bomber aircraft, the bouncing bombs used to destroy the Ruhr dams (in Germany) during World War II, and, later, the swept-wing supersonic aircraft.

Sir William Turner Walton (b.1902, d.1983). Composer whose works include concertos, symphonies and two coronation marches. Awarded Order of Merit in 1967.

Herbert George Wells (H.G. Wells) (b.1866, d.1946). Author achieved success with science-fiction works such as 'The Time Machine' in 1895.

Sir Frank Whittle (b.1907, d.1996). Named 'the father of jet flight'. He designed and developed the jet engine, in 1941. Awarded Order of Merit in 1986.

Ralph Vaughan Williams (b.1872, d.1958). Composer. He wrote symphonies, choral and orchestral works, operas and chamber music.

Prime Ministers, First Lords of the Treasury	*Party*	*Took Office*
Stanley Baldwin (b.1867, d.1947). *Created Earl Baldwin of Bewdley in 1937*	*National/* *Coalition*	*1935 June*

Arthur Neville Chamberlain (b.1869, d.1940).	*National/ Coalition*	*1937 May*
Winston Leonard Spencer Churchill (b.1874, d.1965). Knighted in 1953	*Wartime Coalition*	*1940 May*
Winston Leonard Spencer Churchill (see above)	*Conservative*	*1945 May*
Clement Richard Attlee (b.1883, d.1967). Created Earl Attlee in 1955	*Labour*	*1945 July*
Winston Leonard Spencer Churchill (see above)	*Conservative*	*1951 October*

Following the abdication of King Edward VIII, George relied on his government ministers for advice and guidance. He had not expected or been trained for kingship.

George and his consort, Queen Elizabeth, made a State visit to France in 1938. The following year in May and June they travelled to North America, firstly to the Dominion of Canada, and then became the first ever British monarch to visit the United States of America.

The United Kingdom was aware of Germany's threatening developments of its armed forces and behaviour towards its neighbours. In 1938 the national/coalition government realized the need for Britain to re-arm after twenty years of neglect.

Early in 1938, the Naval Base in Singapore, south-east Asia, was opened. The government was preparing for war, and rearming at sea as fast as it could, commissioning a complete fleet of necessary ship: the Royal Navy was fully mobilized by the September. At the start of the war, Germany had an estimated 4,000 aircraft, compared to Britain's front-line strength of 1,660. Production of new aircraft was rapidly increased, but the major problem was the shortage of trained pilots and crews.

> By 1939 Germany and Italy were intimidating and invading
> their near neighbours;
> conscription into the armed forces was introduced in the
> United Kingdom on April 27.
> Germany terminated the 1935 Anglo-German Naval Agreement;
> the following month, May 1939, the United Kingdom and
> France signed defensive agreements with Turkey;
> and the Anglo-Polish Treaty for defence was signed in London.

THE WINDSORS: KING GEORGE VI

The German-Soviet Union Pact was signed in August;
and Germany invaded Poland on September 1.
The United Kingdom declared war at 11 am on September 3
against Germany, in accordance with the Anglo-Polish Treaty;
and a week later the first British troops landed in France.
At the beginning of October, compulsory military service was
ordered for all men between the ages of 20 and 41.

The war was the biggest, most destructive conflagration ever in the history of the World.

In May 1940, Winston Churchill, grandson of a Duke of Marlborough, and ancestor of the great 1st Duke of Marlborough, famous for the 1704 Battle of Blenheim victory, became Prime Minister to lead the United Kingdom in war, with a coalition government of Conservatives, Labour (Socialists) and Liberals.

In July 1940 the Germans invaded the Channel Islands: the islands became the only part of the United Kingdom to have been occupied by the enemy during the war.

The United States of America instituted the Lend-Lease aid programme in 1941, to provide food, munitions, etc. to the strategic countries threatened by Germany and Italy.

This war was fought in Europe, Asia, north Africa, the Americas, and the oceans throughout the World, by the most numerous armies, navies and air forces ever assembled. Atrocities against military and civilians were abominable: bombing of cities and towns creating unprecedented devastation to homes and families, factories, docks and military establishments. There was no limit to the war-zone; whole countries and their peoples were the war-zones.

The three major allies, the United Kingdom, the United States of America, and the Soviet Union defeated Germany and its Axis partners officially on May 8, 1945: Japan continued to fight until the first use of Atomic Bombs in war destroyed Hiroshima and Nagasaki, forcing surrender on August 14, 1945.

The United Kingdom, the Dominions, and the Crown colonies of the Empire had over 11 million troops in the war: nearly 600,000 were killed, and over 475,000 were wounded, many badly maimed. Worldwide, including the United States of America, the Soviet Union (in particular), and the enemies, it is estimated between 50 million and 70 million civilian and military personnel were killed during the World War II.

In 1940, the King instituted the George Cross for gallantry. The George Cross is primarily awarded to civilians for acts of the greatest heroism or in the most conspicuous circumstances of extreme danger. Parliament devoted some of its time for the future of the country: in welfare, the Sir William Beveridge report on Social Insurance and Allied Services in 1942 declared 'Five Freedoms from Want, Disease, Ignorance, Squalor and Idleness'. Future educational improvements were prepared in 1944.

The ending of the World War II saw an end to 'the old order' and the beginning of a new chapter for the United Kingdom and the World as a whole. Vast areas of Europe had been destroyed and obliterated, and whole communities and peoples killed or murdered. This precipitated a mass migration of Europeans wanting to find new homes and to start new lives throughout the World. A new beginning.

In the years and decades following, international institutions would be founded resulting in the United Kingdom gradually losing its World and Empire dominance, and in later years, its independence to these new bodies and institutions.

The election of a Labour government in Britain in 1945 mirrored most of Europe's lurch to Communist and Socialist governments. The Labour government believed in "the public ownership of the means of production and distribution", but after such a long, expensive war that drained the finances and investments, the country was near to bankruptcy. German bombing had destroyed cities and towns, industries and housing. No war in the history of the United Kingdom, and England's, had left such catastrophic consequences.

The League of Nations, established in 1920 to promote peace, was dissolved, and a new organization the United Nations was founded as an international body of independent countries to promote security and co-operation, in 1945. The United Kingdom was appointed, and remains, one of the five Permanent Members of the important Security Council of the United Nations. Other United Nations bodies were formed, such as the United Nations Educational, Scientific, and Cultural Organization (UNESCO), in Paris at the end of the year.

The International Monetary Fund (IMF) was set-up to regulate the exchange values of currencies; to promote international trade; and to make loans to member nations when in difficulty. The World Bank was founded to assist the economic development of the 'Third World' by means of loans from the richer countries.

The 1941 Lend-Lease aid programme of the United States of America was wound-up on August 21, at the end of the war.

During its period in power, the Government nationalized (i.e. it owned and controlled) the Bank of England, coal-mining, railways, electricity, gas, civil aviation, road haulage, the iron and steel industry, and other concerns and companies. Those spheres that were not nationalized, controlling Boards were set up to oversee, e.g., the cotton, wool, lace, furniture, jewellery, silverware, and clothing industries.

Trades Unions were given positions of influence and power in being represented on the various governing institutions and Boards.

George, Queen Elizabeth and their two daughters made a three month tour to South Africa during the early part of 1947.

The United Kingdom was one of many European countries that were failing economically to recover from the war. The United States of America's European Recovery Programme, popularly known as the Marshall Aid Plan, named after its initiator General George Marshall, supplied aid to rescue Europe in 1947: the loan to Britain was £937 million.

The British Empire commenced to transform itself into the British

Commonwealth of Nations. In 1946 the Straits Settlement in Asia was dissolved, part of it becoming the Union of Malaya, and Singapore becoming a separate Crown colony. The British League of Nations mandate over Jordan was abolished. India, a sub-continent, was divided by religion: it was decided to form two countries, India and Pakistan, both becoming independent within the Commonwealth, as Dominions. The India Independence Act was passed by Parliament and received its Royal Assent on July 18, 1947. The monarch ceased to be Emperor of India, a title instituted for Queen Victoria in 1877. In 1948, Burma (now Myanmar) became an independent country and did not join the Commonwealth. Ceylon (now Sri Lanka) became a self-governing Dominion; and the Maldive Islands (now Maldives), no longer affiliated to Ceylon, came under British control.

The 1948 Treaty of Brussels was signed by the United Kingdom, France, Belgium, Luxembourg and the Netherlands for mutual inter-governmental self-defence, to promote economic, cultural and social collaboration. The Organization for Europe Economic Co-operation (OEEC) was founded to organize the distribution of the Marshall Aid Plan.

A series of Parliamentary Acts set-up the National Health Service in 1948, as part of the country's Welfare State system, to provide free health care for everyone.

Arranged at short-notice, the XIV Olympic Games were held in London during July and August 1948. George officially opened the Games at Wembley Stadium, London. The United Kingdom won 3 gold medals, 14 silver and 6 bronze, to finish 12th in the medals table.

The British mandate from the League of Nations for Palestine ended in May. The Government of the Irish Free State, which had declared independence in 1937, decided to leave the Commonwealth and became a republic in December 1948.

To counter the threat from the Soviet Union bloc, the North Atlantic Treaty Organization (NATO), primarily a military body, was formed in 1949, principally to defend western Europe. The United States of America, Canada, and the United Kingdom were, and continue to be, amongst its members.

The 1949 Treaty of London founded the Council of Europe with originally ten countries, with particular emphasis on legal standards, human rights, democratic development, the rule of law, and cultural co-operation. One of its components is the European Council of Human Rights that enforces the European Convention on Human Rights within its membership, to which the United Kingdom is a member.

The Government decided to reduce the period by which the Conservative dominated House of Lords could delay parliamentary bills which had been passed by the House of Commons. Similar to some of the clauses of the 1911 Act, the 1949 Parliament Act was accepted and passed without any serious problems.

The country continued to struggle economically. Trade union activity by communist influences disrupted factory production, and the pound currency (£) was devalued by a third against the value of the American dollar ($). At this time, the rates between the currencies were at a fixed price.

At the beginning of the year, the Women's services for the army, navy and air force were incorporated with the regular forces of their respective service.

At the Commonwealth of Nations Conference in London it recognized George as Head of the Commonwealth. Newfoundland, an island colony, became part of the Dominion of Canada in the April. The following year, 1950, Italy replaced the United Kingdom as administrator for Somaliland, in north-east Africa.

The new chamber of the House of Commons (the old chamber having been destroyed by enemy bombing in World War II) opened at Westminster on October 26, 1950.

Fighting between communist forces of the north and non-communist forces of the south started a serious war in Korea, south-east Asia, in 1950. British troops were sent to support the United States of America in the war.

Nationalism was developing in Arabia, threatening the United Kingdom's interests in the middle-east, particularly oil from Persia (now known as Iran), and the usage of the Suez Canal in Egypt. Egypt abrogated the Anglo-Egyptian Treaty of 1936 and the 1883 Sudan Condominium agreement.

Slowly, the United Kingdom's economy was recovering, sufficiently for the Marshall Aid to be suspended.

In July 1951, the State of War between the United Kingdom and Germany was officially ended, six years after Germany's surrender. Two months previously, Germany had been admitted to the Council of Europe as a member. Germany was being accepted into international organizations, as opposed to the international policy on Germany after World War I of restricting its development, which partly resulted in the rise of the Nazi party and the following World War II.

As a celebration of the 1851 Great Exhibition, the 1951 Festival of Britain in London was an attempt to give the people a feeling of recovery and progress since 1945. It was a great success.

Although ill, George died unexpectedly at Sandringham House, Norfolk, on February 6, 1952 at the age of 56. He was interred at Windsor Castle, Berkshire.

The population of England and Wales had risen to 44 millions, for the United Kingdom as a whole to 49 millions. Trade Union membership was just under 9.5 millions.

WINDSOR

QUEEN ELIZABETH II

Born	**1926 April 21**
Accession	**1952 February 6**
Age at Accession	**25**

Elizabeth II, heir presumptive, succeeded her father George VI.

In 1947 she married Prince Philip, son of Prince Andrew of Greece and Denmark. He became a naturalized British subject, created Duke of Edinburgh, Earl of Merioneth, and Baron Greenwich in 1947; granted the title of Prince of the United Kingdom in 1957. They have 3 sons and 1 daughter.

Persons of note:

Sir Roger Gilbert Bannister (b.1929). A medical student at Oxford University, he became the first man to run the mile distance in less than four minutes, in 3 minutes 59.4 seconds, on May 6, 1954. He was British Mile Champion in 1951, 1953 and 1954. Knighted 1975.

The Beatles: a Liverpool pop group whose music has worldwide appeal and continues to be popular. The group were: Sir Paul McCartney (b.1942, knighted 1997), John Lennon (b.1940, d.1980), George Harrison (b.1943, d.2001), and Ringo Starr (b.1940).

Sir Thomas Beecham (b.1879, d.1961). Symphony conductor who founded the London Philharmonic Orchestra in 1931 and promoted the works of Frederick Delius.

Sir John Betjeman (b.1906, d.1984). Poet, author and broadcaster; Poet Laureate 1972 until his death.

THE WINDSORS: QUEEN ELIZABETH II

Edward Benjamin Britten (Baron Britten) (b.1913, d.1976). Composer. Reputation mainly for vocal compositions. Awarded Order of Merit in 1965.

Sir Charles Spencer Chaplin (Charlie Chaplin) (b.1889, d.1977). Film star of the silent movies, director, producer, choreographer and composer. Knighted 1975.

Sir Francis Chichester (b.1902, d.1972). He made the first long-distance seaplane flight in 1931; won the first solo Transatlantic yacht race in 1960; circumnavigated the World, single-handedly in Gypsy Moth IV in 107 days in 1966/67. Queen Elizabeth knighted him on the quayside at Greenwich, London.

Sir Winston Leonard Spencer Churchill (b.1874, d.1965). Statesman and author. Prime Minister 1940 to 1945, and 1951 to 1955. His greatest achievement was leading the United Kingdom to victory in World War II. Awarded Nobel Prize for Literature 1953. Knighted 1953. He was accorded a State Funeral, the most recent for a non-royal person.

Francis Harry Compton Crick (b.1916, d.2004). Biophysicist who, with James Dewey Watson (b.1928), pioneered the study of DNA, proposing a spiral model for the molecular structure. Nobel Prize Winner in 1962.

Sir Geoffrey de Havilland (b.1882, d.1965). Pioneer of civil and military aviation. His company produced the Mosquito fighter of World War II, and the Comet that was the World's first commercial jet-airliner.

Dorothy Mary Donaldson (Lady Donaldson) (b.1921, d.2003). First woman admitted to the Court of Aldermen of the City of London; first woman to be City of London Sheriff, in 1981 and 1982; first woman to be Lord Mayor of the City of London in its 800 year history, in 1983.

Michael Foale (b.1957). Second British astronaut (see below, Helen Sharman), in 1992 with the United States of America NASA; first Briton to walk in space 1995. (Piers Sellers and Nicholas Patrick, other British astronauts.)

Dame Margot Fonteyn (b.1919, d.1991). Prima ballerina of the Royal Ballet, considered the greatest ballerina of her time, especially when in partnership with Rudolf Nureyev (b.1938, d.1993).

THE WINDSORS: QUEEN ELIZABETH II

Sir Vivian Ernest Fuchs (b.1908, d.1999). Geologist and explorer. Leader of the British Commonwealth Trans-Antarctic expedition 1957/8; the first to cross the Antarctic continent.

Henry Graham Greene (b.1904, d.1991). Novelist and playwright. Widely regarded as one of the greatest English novelists. Awarded Order of Merit in 1986.

Henry Cecil John Hunt (Baron Hunt) (b.1910, d.1998). Leader of the 1952/3 British Everest expedition in which Sir Edmund Percival Hillary (b.1919, d.2008) and Sherpa Tenzing Norgay became the first men to reach the summit of Mount Everest, the highest mountain in the World, in the Himalayas, Nepal, in 1953.

Sir Leonard Hutton (b.1916, d.1990). One of the greatest cricket players and captain of England. He made a record Test score of 364 in 1938, which was not bettered until 1958.

Dame Elizabeth Lane (b.1905, d.1988). First woman judge to sit in the County Court, in 1962; first woman judge to sit in the High Court, in 1965.

Sir Andrew Lloyd-Webber (Baron Lloyd-Webber) (b.1948). Composer of many popular musical shows, including 'Jesus Christ Superstar', 'Cats', and 'Phantom of the Opera'.

Dame Vera Lynn (b.1917). Immensely popular singer, the 'Forces Sweetheart' during and after World War II. Created Dame 1976.

Dame Ellen MacArthur (b.1976). English sailor who broke the record for the fastest solo circumnavigation of the World in 2005; created Dame 2005.

Sir Stanley Matthews (b.1915, d.2000). First association footballer to be knighted, 1965. One of the greatest of all footballers.

Bernard Law Montgomery (Viscount Montgomery of Alamein) (b.1887, d.1976). Field-Marshal of the army; successful strategists. Commander of the 8th Army in north Africa, Sicily and Italy, to victories in 1942 to 1944; Commander-in-Chief, British Group of Armies and Allied armies in northern France in 1944.

Henry Moore (b.1898, d.1986). Carved abstract figures in many forms.

Lawrence Kerr Olivier (Baron Olivier of Brighton) (b.1907, d.1989). Actor and director, especially in Shakespearean roles. Awarded Order of Merit in 1981.

William George Penney (Baron Penny) (b.1909, d.1990). Physicist who was responsible for the development of British nuclear technology.

Lester Keith Piggott (b.1935). Outstanding race-jockey who won the Epsom Derby race 9 times; champion jockey 11 times; won his 4,000[th] British winner in 1982.

Sir Gordon Richards (b.1904, d.1986). Foremost race-jockey who rode 4,870 winners. Knighted in 1953 after he won the Epsom Derby race on 'Pinza'. He was champion jockey 25 times between 1925 and 1953.

Sir Richard George Rogers (Baron Rogers) (b.1931). Architect of international repute. Designs include the Lloyd's building in London; the Pompidou Centre in Paris; and the European Court of Human Rights building in Strasbourg, France.

The Rolling Stones: Rock group of the 1960's revolution of pop music. The group: Sir Mick Jagger (b.1943, knighted 2002), Brian Jones (b.1942, d.1969), Keith Richard (b.1943), Charlie Watts (b.1941), and Bill Wyman (b.1936).

Helen Sharman (b.1963). The United Kingdom's first astronaut/cosmonaut, in 1991 with the Soviet Union. Spent 8 days in the Mir space station.

Graham Vivian Sutherland (b.1903, d.1980). Artist. He was an official war artist (1941 to 1945), and designed the tapestry for Coventry Cathedral 'Christ in Majesty'. He painted the 80th birthday portrait of Sir Winston Leonard Spencer Churchill for Parliament. Awarded Order of Merit in 1960.

Margaret Hilda Thatcher (Baroness Thatcher) (b.1925). First woman leader of a major political party (Conservative Party) in the United Kingdom; first woman Prime Minister of the United Kingdom, 1979 to 1990; the longest serving Prime Minister since Herbert Henry Asquith in 1916.

Sir Michael Tippett (b.1905, d.1998). Composer whose works include the opera 'The Midsummer Marriage', the oratorio 'A Child of Our Time', and the cantata 'The Vision of St Augustine'.

Sir Barnes Neville Wallis (b.1887, d.1979). Aeronautical engineer. Designed and/or involved in the development of the airship R100, the Wellington bomber aircraft, the bouncing bombs used to destroy the Ruhr dams (in Germany) in World War II, and the swept-wing supersonic aircraft.

Sir William Turner Walton (b.1902, d.1983). Composer whose works include concertos, symphonies and two coronation marches. Awarded Order of Merit in 1967.

Sir Frank Whittle (b.1907, d.1996). Named 'the father of jet flight'. He designed and developed the jet engine for aircraft, in 1941. Awarded Order of Merit in 1986.

Ralph Vaughan Williams (b.1872, d.1958). Composer. He wrote symphonies, choral and orchestral works, operas and chamber music.

Prime Ministers, First Lords of the Treasury	Party	Took Office
Winston Leonard Spencer Churchill (b.1874, d.1965). Knighted 1953	Conservative	1951 October
Robert Anthony Eden (b.1897, d.1977). Knighted 1954. Created Earl of Avon in 1961	Conservative	1955 April
Maurice Harold Macmillan (b.1894, d.1986). Created Earl of Stockton in 1984	Conservative	1957 January
Alexander (Alec) Frederick Douglas-Home (b.1903, d.1995). 14th Earl of Home who renounced his peerage in 1963. Created Baron Home in 1974	Conservative	1963 October
James Harold Wilson (b.1916, d.1995). Knighted 1976. Created Baron Wilson in 1983	Labour	1964 October
Edward Richard George Heath (b.1916, d.2005). Knighted 1992	Conservative	1970 June
James Harold Wilson (see above)	Labour	1974 March
Leonard James Callaghan (b.1912, d.2005). Created Baron Callaghan in 1987	Labour	1976 April
Margaret Hilda Thatcher (b.1925). Created Baroness Thatcher in 1992	Conservative	1979 May
John Major (b.1943). Knighted 2005	Conservative	1990 November

THE WINDSORS: QUEEN ELIZABETH II

Anthony Charles Lynton Blair (b.1953).   **Labour**   *1997 May*

James Gordon Brown (b.1951).   **Labour**   *2007 June*

David William Donald Cameron (b.1966).   **Coalition**   *2010 May*

The heir presumptive, the eldest daughter and child of King George VI, succeeded to the throne as Elizabeth II, at the age of 25.

Increasingly easy worldwide communications and transportation; the desire for conventions, meetings and organizations, e.g. the United Nations Organization; the moves for closer European integration; colonies, protectorates and dependencies of the Empire evolving into independent states, with most choosing to become members of the Commonwealth of Nations; the United Kingdom's role in the World, Europe and Empire changed.

Elizabeth declared that Windsor would be the family name of her children and their descendents, instead of her husband's Germanic family name of Mountbatten (which had been changed from Battenburg earlier in the century).

During the 1950s, Elizabeth and her husband, the Duke of Edinburgh (he was granted the title of Prince of the United Kingdom in 1957), made visits to many Empire and Commonwealth countries. With the advent of television, people witnessed the royal family regularly, including Elizabeth's Coronation as monarch at Westminster Abbey on June 2, 1953.

The Queen's annual Christmas Message to the United Kingdom and Commonwealth; the annual State Opening of Parliament when Elizabeth outlines the Government's legislative programme for the following year; and the annual Trooping the Colour, are all televised.

Regardless of the political party in government, much social legislation was enacted, mainly based on, amending and improving the Acts passed during the previous hundred years. Education; help for the needy; and health care, were essential aspects. The school leaving age was raised to 16, in 1959; the Criminal Justices Act of 1961 raised the minimum age an offender could be sent to a prison for adults to 17; in 1969 Parliament voted for the permanent abolition of the death penalty; the 1971 Divorce Reform Act permitted married couples to divorce on a no-fault basis; and in 1975, the Sex Discrimination and Equal Pay Act helped to lay the foundations for a more compassionate, understanding and equal society.

As in past centuries, Parliament and governing the country continued to evolve. The Life Peerages Act of 1958 conferred lifetime peerages upon distinguished men and women for membership of the House of Lords, which needed more full-time and knowledgeable members. The Peerage Act of 1963 enabled a peer to disclaim his peerage for the duration of his life: the title remained in abeyance until his heir inherited it. Later in the century, the composition of the House of Lords was altered to deprive most of the hereditary peers of membership; and in 2004 the Lord Chancellor, a post dating back to Norman times, and possibly earlier, was transformed.

The Labour governments from 1945 to 1979 nationalized (i.e. government owned and controlled) certain categories of businesses: the Conservative government from 1979 onwards, privatized (denationalized) most of these concerns.

Radio broadcasting and television commenced to cover parliamentary proceedings in both the House of Commons and House of Lords: radio from 1978, television from 1989.

The 1950s was a troubled period, with a power battle for supremacy by the two new super powers: the United States of America and the Soviet Union, the former having to defend and finance the 'free' World, the latter wanting to bring the World under its totalitarian communistic control, as it had for many eastern and central European countries in the late 1940s.

Threatening Asia, including the Asian countries of the Commonwealth and Empire, was the People's Republic of China, ruled by the communists since 1949. The war in Korea between the communists and its opponents, in which British troops were heavily engaged, ended with the armistice in 1953.

After the Egyptian government nationalized the Suez Canal Company, the United Kingdom and France launched an abortive invasion of Egypt in 1955.

The Empire began rapidly to disintegrate from 1956, sometimes with violence against British rule, but most of the newly independent countries, even those where fighting occurred, wished to retain a link with the United Kingdom, by joining the Commonwealth of Nations. Many became republics, either at or within a few years of gaining independence. (Full details are available in Appendices A and B of all the relevant countries, etc.) Empire Day, celebrated on May 24, constituted after Queen Victoria's death, was changed several times and is now Commonwealth Day, celebrated on the second Monday of March.

The ratification of numerous agreements granted full sovereignty to West Germany (Germany then being divided between West and East, the communists governing the East), and together with Italy, was admitted to the Western European Union in 1955, a body founded in 1948 for mutual intergovernmental self-defence, cultural and social collaboration of the United Kingdom, France, Belgium, Luxembourg and the Netherlands. The mistakes of isolating Germany after World War I were being avoided.

[In 1957, the Treaty of Rome was signed. Although not involving the United Kingdom, at the time, it was the commencement of European co-operation leading to the development of the European Union. The original member countries being France, Italy, West Germany, Belgium, Luxembourg, and the Netherlands.]

With the ending of compulsory National Service in the armed forces, the lesser requirements to station troops in the declining empire, the general peace throughout the World, and particularly Europe, the United Kingdom was able to reduce its military structure. In 1962, the new Ministry of Defence combined the previously separate government departments for each of the armed services; regiments were amalgamated, the Royal Air Force re-organized; and the Royal Navy Fleet reduced in numbers. Nevertheless, the Soviet Union threat required sophisticated defending from possible nuclear attacks, so that the Ballistic Missile Early Warning Station at Fylingdales, on the North Yorkshire Moors, became operational in 1964.

In technology, the United Kingdom's first atomic bomb was test exploded at Monte Bello Island, off the north-west coast of Australia, in 1952; its first hydrogen bomb was tested on Christmas Island, a coral atoll in the Pacific Ocean, in 1957; the first satellite 'Ariel', for atmospheric scientific research, was launched from Cape Canaveral, Florida, United States of America, in 1962; the nuclear submarine 'Dreadnought' was commissioned the following year; the ballistic rocket 'Blue Streak' was successfully fired from Woomera, Australia, in 1964; the first, and only successful supersonic passenger aircraft, 'Concorde', was developed jointly by the United Kingdom and France, the British 'Concorde' making its maiden flight in 1969 from Filton, Bristol, where it was constructed.

The first 'breeder reactor' commenced operation in the nuclear energy field in 1954, to produce electrical power generation at Harwell, Essex; the first atomic power station at Calder Hall, Cumberland, started generating electricity in 1956. In 1961, a submarine cable was laid on the seabed of the English Channel, linking the electricity systems of England and France.

The largest radio telescope in the World, at the time, was constructed in 1957 at Jodrell Bank, Cheshire, for Manchester University.

To recognize export and technological achievements, the 'Queen's Award to Industry' was inaugurated in 1965.

In sport, the four-yearly Association Football World Cup, competed by qualifying nations, was held in England in 1966. England won the competition for the first and only time, beating West Germany in the final by 4 goals to 2 goals (4-2) at Wembley Stadium, London.

Civil disturbances in Northern Ireland occurred in October 1968 between the police and protesters in Londonderry (also known as Derry), leading to serious strife that affected Northern Ireland and England until the late 1990s. The problems were caused by sectarian strife between the Roman Catholic supported pro-Irish Republican Army (IRA) wanting equality in society and unification with the Republic of Ireland, and the militant Protestants who were determined for Northern Ireland to remain in the United Kingdom. A State of Emergency was declared in 1974.

Local government of the county, district, parish and new metropolitan councils were reorganized several times during this reign. The qualification for voting in all elections was lowered to 18 years of age from 1969, and from 2005 people of that age became eligible to stand for election to local government and parliament.

To defend the individual against the might of government and official organizations was the introduction of a Parliamentary Commission, known as the Ombudsman, a Swedish term, in 1966.

Religious and moral attitudes were gradually changing: people were prepared, even wanted, a relaxing of once accepted laws. The Lord Chamberlain, since 1737, was the arbiter of moral taste and decency in stage productions and in the entertainment world: the Theatre Act of 1968 abolished this censorship.

[The United States of America's space programme (NASA) sent astronauts to the Moon in 1969. Neil Armstrong became the first person from Earth ever to walk on the surface of another celestial body; Buzz Aldren the second; Mike Collins, as commander, remained in the orbiting spacecraft Columbia, named after the 15th century explorer, Christopher Columbus.]

During her reign, Elizabeth with Prince Philip has visited many countries throughout the World. As Supreme Governor of the Church of England, Elizabeth met the Roman Catholic Pope John XXIII at the Vatican in 1961, the first time a monarch of England (and of the United Kingdom) and a Pope had met in modern times. Five years later, the Archbishop of Canterbury (Michael Ramsay) visited Pope Paul VI at the Vatican.

New forms of religious services to be used in the Church of England were issued in 1965. In 1970, a modern translation of the Holy Bible and Apocrypha, prepared by an interdenominational panel was published. The non-conformist Presbyterian and Congregational Churches of England and Wales combined to form the United Reformed Church, in 1972.

Parliament decided the United Kingdom should become part of the integration of European states by joining the European Economic Community (EEC). On January 1, 1973, the United Kingdom with Ireland and Denmark combined with the original six countries, France, West Germany, Italy, Belgium, Luxembourg and the Netherlands, to form the enlarged organization.

The government introduced a new form of taxation, named Value Added Tax (VAT), a tax on most goods purchased and services obtained.

In 1975, a plebiscite was held to determine the United Kingdom's membership of the EEC. The vote for continued membership had a 2 to 1 majority: 17.4 millions in favour, 8.5 millions against. The electorate turn-out was 64.5 per cent.

The European Council (comprising the heads of each state or government, and the president of the European Commission) adopted the European Monetary System (EMS), which used the Exchange Rate Mechanism (ERM) to encourage participating countries to control their currencies, in 1979. The United Kingdom did not join. Initially, members of the European Parliament had been appointed by their countries' parliaments, but at the 1979 European election, and thereafter, the electorate of all countries voted directly for their own members.

At the United Kingdom's general election of 1979, the leader of the

Conservative Party, Margaret Hilda Thatcher, became the first ever woman Prime Minister of the country.

Two events in 1981 were the result of changing the Sunday sporting laws. Professional Association Football games were played on a Sunday for the first time; and the 26-mile Marathon run was held in central London, attracting 6,700 runners. This annual event has proved so popular, now many tens of thousands compete, including many international runners. Sunday is now accepted as a sports-playing day.

The Falkland Islands, a British dependency in the south Atlantic Ocean, were invaded by Argentina, claiming sovereignty, on April 2, 1982. A large fleet sailed from England to the islands; fierce fighting ensued: 7 British ships were sunk; 33 harrier jets and helicopters destroyed; the biggest naval action since World War II took place on May 1. Altogether, 255 British and 635 Argentinian troops were killed, and many more injured, before the British victory was completed on June 14.

During this campaign, on May 28 the much-travelled Roman Catholic Pope John Paul II made an historic visit to England, the first by a Pope. His tour included London, Coventry, Manchester, Cardiff, Liverpool, and York. In the Church of England, Wilfred Denniston Wood (b.1936, d.2003) was installed as the Bishop of Croydon in 1985: born in Barbados, he was the first United Kingdom bishop of African descent.

[During 1989, the Soviet Union's 'satellite' states began to disintegrate; by the end of 1991 the Soviet Union communist bloc had completely collapsed. East Germany united with West Germany in October 1990; the Soviet Union separated into fifteen independent states.]

The United Kingdom's membership of the European Economic Community (EEC) resulted in losing some of its independence. The Single European Act (SEA) of 1987 revised the Treaty of Rome in order to add new momentum to closer European integration, one of its original aims, and to complete an open customs-free trading community. The Act amended the rules governing the workings of the European institutions and expanded Community powers, mainly in research and development, the environment and a common foreign policy. The implementation of this Act was completed by 1992.

The next stage of European integration was the Treaty of the European Union, the Maastricht Treaty of 1992. It created a European Union of three strata: European Communities Community; Foreign and Security Policy; police and judicial co-operation in criminal matters. The Treaty introduced the concept of European citizenship; reinforced the powers of the European Parliament; and launched economic and monetary union (EMU).

Betty Boothroyd (b.1929), the Member of Parliament for West Bromwich (a Midland's constituency), became the first woman Speaker of the House of Commons, in 1992. In 2000 she retired and, subsequently, was created a life peer. In the Church of England, women were ordained deacons from 1987; the General Synod voted to permit women into the priesthood, in 1992; Parliament ratified the

THE WINDSORS: QUEEN ELIZABETH II

Women Priests Measures in 1994; and the first ordinations were held on March 12, 1994 at Bristol Cathedral.

The Anglo-French project to construct a twin-tunnel rail link between the two countries under the English Channel was completed in 1994. Elizabeth and the President of France officially opened the tunnel.

The Stone of Scone, referred to as the Coronation Stone, in 1296 was removed by King Edward I from Edinburgh to Westminster Abbey. Seven hundred years later in 1996 it was ceremonially returned to Scotland to Edinburgh Castle.

The electorates of Scotland, Wales, and Northern Ireland approved devolved governments in referenda. The Scotland Act, and the Government of Wales Act were passed by Parliament in 1998, and elections were held in May 1999. The Scottish Parliament and the National Assembly of Wales both have devolved powers from the central parliament at Westminster. Elizabeth formally opened both legislative buildings and parliamentary sessions in Edinburgh and Cardiff, respectively.

During 1998, the Belfast Agreement of Northern Ireland was approved by both the nationalists and unionists, bringing an end to some decades of civil strife. It was agreed to establish an elected Assembly, with the Roman Catholics and Protestants sharing the duties and responsibilities of rule and power: it would be some years before the Assembly was effective. During the conflict over 3,000 people had been murdered.

In European matters, the Treaty of Amsterdam, effective from 1999, created the political and institutional conditions to enable the European Union to react quickly to international matters; the globalization of the economy; the fight against terrorism; international crime and drug trafficking; ecological problems; and the care of public health.

The next stage of the development of the European Union was the introduction of a new single currency for most of its members. The Euro currency (notes and coins) commenced on January 1, 2002. (The United Kingdom does not participate.)

The Treaty of Nice, effective from 2003, made significant changes to the future direction of the European Union: the procedure of Qualified Majority Voting (QMV) in the European Council was extended to include more categories; national vetoes on many categories were abolished; it increased the powers of the Commission; and it strengthened the Common Foreign and Security Policy. It is estimated that about 70 percent of the laws enacted by the United Kingdom Parliament are required to comply with the European Union's directives.

Twenty-seven western, central, southern, and some eastern European countries are members of the European Union. Each national country is divided into regions for European administrative purposes. The United Kingdom has twelve regions: Scotland, Wales, Northern Ireland, and nine in England (North East, North West, Yorkshire and The Humber, West Midlands, East Midlands, Eastern, London, South East, and South West).

THE WINDSORS: QUEEN ELIZABETH II

Elizabeth, with Prince Philip, has been the most travelled monarch in the history of England and the United Kingdom. The Royal Family is continuously involved in many aspects of life in the country and Commonwealth of Nations, attending functions, businesses, international conferences, etc. Elizabeth's mother, Queen Elizabeth the Queen Mother, became the first royal to attain the age of 100 in 2000 (she died in 2002 at the age of 101; her sister-in-law, the Dowager Duchess of Gloucester, also a royal, died in 2004 at the age of 102).

In 2009, Elizabeth instituted the Elizabeth Cross, to be presented to the recognized next-of-kin of members of the British armed forces killed in action or terrorist attack. It is awarded retrospectively to those killed since the ending of World War II.

The nearly sixty years of Elizabeth's reign (to date) has witnessed extraordinary changes in the United Kingdom. Comparatively poor at the end of World War II, it is now a prosperous country, despite the occasional downturns in the economy; it has the fifth or sixth largest economy in the World; holds a permanent seat at the United Nations Security Council; is a nuclear power; and is influential in most matters throughout the World. The population has increased very considerably to about 61 millions, mainly because of an increase in immigration from Commonwealth and European Union countries: a once a wholly Christian believing white population, it is now a multi-cultural, multi-faith country. The current Archbishop of York is John Sentamu; a Cambridge University educated African from Uganda.

The age of the new millennium has been adversely affected by an international terrorist organization, Al-Qaeda, purporting to be Islamist, and wanting to spread narrow beliefs and dogma throughout the World and in the United Kingdom by any violent means.

APPENDIX A

COUNTRIES GAINING INDEPENDENCE OF THE UNITED KINGDOM

DATE OF INDEPENDENCE	FORMER NAME	CURRENT NAME	(*DENOTES A MEMBER of the COMMONWEALTH of NATIONS)
1783	13 North America Colonies	United States of America	Independence
1867		Canada *	Independence
1922		Iraq	Independent kingdom
1931		Australia *	Independence
1931		South Africa *	Independence
1936		Egypt	Independent kingdom
1946		Jordan	Independent kingdom
1947		New Zealand *	Independence
1947		India *	Independence
1947	India (part of)	Pakistan *	Independence
1948	Burma	Myanmar	Independent republic
1948	Ceylon	Sri Lanka *	Independence
1951		Oman	Independent sultanate
1952		Eritrea	Administration as a U.N. Territory ended
1956		Sudan	Independent republic

Year	Former Name	New Name	Status
1957	Gold Coast	Ghana *	Independence
1957		Federation of Malaya*	Independence
1960		Nigeria *	Independence
1960		Somalia	Independent republic
1960		Cyprus *	Independence
1961		Sierra Leone *	Independence
1961	Tanganyika	Tanzania *	Independence
1961		Kuwait	Independent Emirate
1962		Uganda *	Independence
1962		Jamaica *	Independence
1962		Trinidad and Tobago *	Independence
1963		Kenya *	Independent republic
1963	Zanzibar	Tanzania*	Independent monarchy
1964	Northern Rhodesia	Zambia *	Independent republic
1964	Nyasaland	Malawi*	Independence
1964		Malta *	Independence
1965		Gambia *	Independent republic
1965	Maldive Islands	Maldives *	Independence
1965		Singapore *	Independent republic
1966	Bechuanaland	Botswana *	Independent republic
1966	Basutoland	Lesotho *	Independent kingdom

1966		Barbados *	Independence
1966	British Guiana	Guyana *	Independence
1967	Aden	Yemen (part of)	British troops withdrew
1968		Swaziland *	Independent kingdom
1968		Mauritius *	Independence
1970		Fiji *	Independent monarchy
1970		Tonga *	Independent kingdom
1971		Qatar	Independent monarchy
1973		Bahamas *	Independence
1974		Grenada *	Independence
1975		Papua New Guinea *	Independence
1976		Seychelles *	Independent republic
1978		Dominica *	Independent republic
1978		Solomon Islands *	Independence
1978	Ellice Islands	Tuvalu *	Independence
1979	Gilbert Islands	Kiribati *	Independent republic
1979		St Lucia *	Independence
1979		St Vincent and The Grenadines *	Independence
1980	Southern Rhodesia	Zimbabwe *	Independent republic

1981		Antigua and Barbuda *	Independence
1981	British Honduras	Belize *	Independence
1983		St Kitts and Nevis *	Independence
1984		Brunei Darussalam	Independent Sultanate
1997		Hong Kong	Transferred to the People's Republic of China

APPENDIX B

COUNTRIES/TERRITORIES ONCE UNDER THE RULE OF THE UNITED KINGDOM AND DEPENDENCIES

(* Denotes a member of the BRITISH COMMONWEALTH OF NATIONS
Definitions where used: England/English until 1707
Great Britain/British 1707 to 1801
United Kingdom/British 1801 onwards)

AFRICA

BOTSWANA * (formerly Bechuanaland)
Became a protectorate 1885; granted a constitution 1961; self-government 1965; independent republic 1966.

EGYPT
After the completion of the Suez Canal construction the British were drawn into the country in 1869, occupying and ruling it from 1882, Egypt having sold its share of the Suez Canal to the United Kingdom 1875. Egypt became a protectorate 1914; nominal independence 1922, independence as a kingdom 1936; a republic 1953; Britain expelled from the Suez Canal Zone 1956.

ERITREA
After the defeat of the Italians in north Africa in World War II, Eritrea became a British protectorate in 1941; later administered as a United Nations territory until 1952, when a federation with Ethiopia was created.

GAMBIA *
During the 16th century, various European merchants settled in Gambia. The Crown colony was established in 1843; by 1902 all of modern-day Gambia was under British rule; partial self-government from 1945; independence 1965; republic 1970.

GHANA * (formerly Gold Coast)
British rule commenced in 1820 following several centuries and several countries' merchants trading along the coast. In 1874 Britain colonized the coastal regions and the interior Ashanti Empire, although rule was not firmly established until 1901. Togoland, formerly a German colony, was incorporated into the Gold Coast 1956; independence 1957, renamed Ghana; republic 1960.

KENYA *
European exploration began in the 19th century and in 1895 it became part of Britain's East African Protectorate; a Crown colony 1920; internal self-government, quickly followed by independence as a republic 1963.

LESOTHO * (formerly Basutoland)
Became a Native state under British protection 1843; annexed to British Cape Colony (now part of South Africa) 1871; restored to Crown colony status 1884; an independent kingdom 1966, and renamed Lesotho. Completely surrounded in its borders by South Africa.

MALAWI * (formerly Nyasaland)
The British missionary David Livingstone reached the area in the 1850s; in 1889 Cecil Rhodes's British South Africa Company had a charter to develop the area; became the Nyasaland and District Protectorate 1891; reorganized as the British Central Africa Protectorate 1893; Crown colony 1907; it became part of the Central African Federation with Northern Rhodesia and Southern Rhodesia (now Zambia and Zimbabwe, respectively) in 1953; became a separate country and independence as Malawi 1964, republic 1966.

MOZAMBIQUE *
Mozambique was a Portuguese colony which gained independence as a republic 1975; joined the Commonwealth of Nations 1995, the first country of the Commonwealth not to have been associated with the United Kingdom as a colony or protectorate.

NIGERIA *
The United Kingdom annexed Lagos 1851 and occupied the rest of Nigeria, in stages during the following decades, uniting the whole by 1914, first as a protectorate and then a Crown colony. It became a federation 1954; independence 1960; republic 1963.

RWANDA*
Was part of German East Africa until occupied by Belgium forces in 1916. After WW1 Belgium governed under a League of Nations mandate, and from 1946 as a United Nations trust territory; became an independent republic in 1962. It Joined the Commonwealth of Nations in November 2009, the second country of the Commonwealth not to have been associated with the United Kingdom as a colony or protectorate.

SIERRA LEONE *
The coastal area of Sierra Leone was ceded to Great Britain as a free state for former African slaves in 1788. A Crown colony 1808; protectorate over the adjacent areas 1896, the whole being united 1951; independence 1961; republic 1971.

SOMALIA
The United Kingdom and Italy conducted protectorates over the divided area from 1920; the United Kingdom ruled the entire area after 1941, until Italy returned to rule from 1950; independence as a republic 1960. Most of Somalia had come under colonial control in the 1800s; northern Somalia became British Somaliland.

SOUTH AFRICA *
The Dutch founded the colony of the Cape of Good Hope in 1652; Britain took permanent possession at the end of the Napoleonic Wars 1814; after two Boer (Dutch settlers' descendants) Wars, Britain united the four self-governing colonies to form the Union of South Africa with dominion status 1910; independence 1931; republic 1961.

SUDAN
Sudan was conquered by an Anglo-Egyptian force 1898; became an Anglo-Egyptian condominium 1899; re-affirmed by treaty 1936; self-government 1953; independent republic 1956.

SWAZILAND *
The Kingdom of Swaziland became a protectorate of the Transvaal in 1884 and jointly with Britain in 1894, and solely of the United Kingdom 1903; independent kingdom 1968.

TANZANIA * (formerly two countries of Tanganyika and Zanzibar)
Tanganyika: a German colony until World War I, after which it was administered by Britain under a League of Nations mandate, and later as a United Nations trust territory. It became independent 1961; republic 1962.
Zanzibar, including the Pembia islands became a British protectorate in 1890; independent as a constitutional monarchy 1963.
Tanganyika and Zanzibar united in 1964 to form a republic, and renamed Tanzania.

UGANDA *
A British protectorate was established over the kingdom of Buganda 1893, which was gradually extended to adjacent territories by 1903; independence 1962; republic 1963.

ZAMBIA * (formerly Northern Rhodesia)
Cecil Rhodes's British South Africa Company administered the area from 1889 until it became a protectorate in 1924; it became part of the Central African Federation with Nyasaland and Southern Rhodesia (now Malawi and Zimbabwe, respectively) in 1953; separated in 1963 for internal self-government; independent republic 1964, renamed Zambia.

ZIMBABWE * (formerly Southern Rhodesia)
Cecil Rhodes's British South Africa Company administered the area from the 1880s until it became a self-governing colony in 1923; it became part of the Central African Federation with Nyasaland and Northern Rhodesia (now Malawi and Zambia, respectively) in 1953; remained a separate Crown colony when Nyasaland and Northern Rhodesia became independent states 1964; the white minority, ruling population, unilaterally declared its independence from the United Kingdom 1965; proclaimed itself a republic 1970; renegade regime collapsed and the country became an independent republic 1980 and renamed Zimbabwe.

ASIA

ADEN
Aden, capital and chief port of South Yemen. Annexed by the United Kingdom in 1839, and a protectorate in the second-half of the 19th century. Britain withdrew in 1967.

BANGLADESH *
The East India Company ruled Bengal, *de facto*, from mid-1700 until 1858 when the region, together with the Sylhet district of Assam was incorporated into British India. On independence in 1947 it became East Pakistan, part of the new country of Pakistan, but was separated from West Pakistan by 1,000 miles. It became independent and a republic 1971.

BRUNEI DARUSSALAM
Became a protectorate in 1888; a dependency 1905; granted internal affairs control 1959; fully independent under a sultanate 1984.

HONG KONG
The islands of Hong Kong were ceded to the United Kingdom in 1841; Stonecutters Island and the Kowloon peninsula were annexed in 1860; the New Territories leased from China for 99 years from 1898. The whole was transferred to the People's Republic of China 1997.

INDIA *
The English East India Company opened its first factory at Surat (now Gujarat, north-east India) in 1612. Mumbai (formerly Bombay) became the seat of English rule in 1687. The rule of India was transferred from the East India Company to the British Crown in 1858. In 1919, the British transferred some internal responsibilities to India, and in 1935 a federal government with some self-rule was introduced. India became independent (India, Pakistan and Burma became separate countries) 1947; a republic 1950.

IRAQ
In World War I, an Anglo-Indian force occupied most of the country; Britain was given a mandate over the area in 1920 by the League of Nations; recognized Iraq as a kingdom in 1922; terminated the mandate in 1932.

JORDAN (once known as Transjordan)
With the collapse of the Ottoman Empire in 1918, the state of Transjordan was created and administered by the British under a League of Nations mandate. The United Kingdom recognized Transjordan's independence, subject to the mandate in 1923; abolishing the mandate it allowed self-rule as a kingdom in 1946; the country was renamed in 1949.

KUWAIT
Kuwait entered into a 'Special Treaty of Friendship' with the United Kingdom in 1899 for protection; becoming a protectorate in 1914; independent emirate 1961, although the United Kingdom retained a military presence until 1971.

MALAYSIA * (A federation of Malaya, Sabah (northern Borneo) and Sarawak)
The first possessions of Singapore, Penang and Malacca were formed into the Straits Settlement in 1826, becoming a Crown colony in 1867. British protectorate extended to four states, which federated in 1896, and protection treaties covered several other areas, between 1885 and 1930. The nine peninsular states formed into the Federation of Malaya 1948, becoming independent in 1957. In 1963 it combined with Singapore, Sarawak and Sabah to form the Federation of Malaysia; Singapore withdrew in 1965.

MALDIVES * (formerly Maldive Islands)
The islands were under Portuguese rule in the 16th century until 1887, when they became a dependency of Ceylon (now Sri Lanka) until the latter's independence; a British protectorate 1948; independence 1965: republic 1968.

MYANMAR (formerly Burma)
The English East India Company traded in the Bay of Bengal from 1612. Following border clashes, after the third Anglo-Burma war, Burma was annexed to become a province of British India in 1885; became a separate Crown colony with partial self-government in 1937. At independence of India, Burma became an independent republic in 1948.

OMAN
The kingdom came under British influence in the 19th century as a protectorate; independent sultanate 1951.

PAKISTAN *
The English East India Company ruled the area of Pakistan, *de facto*, for almost one hundred years until 1858 when it was incorporated into British India. In 1947 Pakistan was separated from India to become an independent country, consisting of two regions, separated by 1000 miles. It became a republic in 1956. The country divided, East Pakistan became independent in 1971, renamed Bangladesh.

PAPUA NEW GUINEA *
In 1884 a British protectorate was proclaimed over the southern coast of New Guinea (Papua) and the adjacent islands. The protectorate, British New Guinea was annexed in 1888; placed under the administration of Australia in 1906; independence 1975.

QATAR
Qatar, a peninsular on the Persian Gulf, was nominally under the rule of the Ottoman Empire from 1871 until World War I; became a British protectorate 1916; independent monarchy 1971.

SINGAPORE *
A trading location since the 12th century: as a state founded by Sir Stamford Raffles, an agent of the English East India Company, in 1819. Incorporated with Penang and Malacca to form the Straits Settlement 1826; Crown colony 1867; after the Straits Settlement was dissolved it reverted to being a Crown colony in 1946; full internal self-government 1959; part of the Federation of Malaysia 1963; withdrew in 1965 to become an independent republic.

SRI LANKA * (formerly Ceylon)
Ceylon was ceded by the Dutch in 1798 and became a Crown colony in 1802. With the annexation of Kandy in 1815, the whole of Ceylon came under British rule. In 1931 some self-governance; dominion 1948; republic 1972 when it was renamed Sri Lanka.

THE AMERICAS

ANTIGUA AND BARBUDA *
Antigua was discovered by Christopher Columbus in 1493; colonized by England in 1632. Barbuda was colonized in 1661. Leeward Island Colony 1871 to 1956; West Indies Federation 1958 to 1962; West Indies Associated States 1967 with self-governing internal affairs; independence 1981.

BAHAMAS *
The Bahamas were discovered by Christopher Columbus in 1492; settled by the English in the 17th century and became a Crown colony in 1717; internal self-governing in 1964; independence 1973.

BARBADOS *
Settled by the English 1627; a Crown colony from 1652; self-government 1961; West Indies Federation 1958 to 1962; independence 1966.

BELIZE * (formerly British Honduras)
The first English settlement was established in 1638; a Crown colony from 1862 and administered by the Governor of Jamaica until 1884; self-governing 1964. The colony was renamed in 1973; independence 1981.

CANADA *
John Cabot (an Italian, Giovanni Caboto, in the service of King Henry VII of England) reached either Newfoundland or Nova Scotia in 1497. Disputed between England and France until the Treaty of Paris in 1763 that gave control to Great Britain. It gained limited self-government in 1849; dominion status within the British Empire 1867. It severed its last formal legislative links with the United Kingdom 1982.

DOMINICA *
Dominica was discovered by Christopher Columbus in 1493; claimed by England and France until the United Kingdom asserted sovereignty in 1815. Leeward Islands Colony 1871 to 1939; Windward Islands Colony 1940 to 1958; West Indies Federation 1958 to 1962; West Indies Associated States 1967, with self-governing internal affairs until independence in 1978.

GRENADA *
Grenada was discovered by Christopher Columbus in 1498; ceded by France to Great Britain 1763; a Crown colony 1877; Windward Islands Colony 1885 to 1958; West Indies Federation 1958 to 1962; West Indies Associated States 1967 until independence 1974.

GUYANA * (formerly British Guiana)
Several areas of Guyana were ceded to the United Kingdom in 1815; a Crown colony 1831; internal self-government 1952; independence 1966, when it assumed its old name; republic 1970.

JAMAICA *
Jamaica was discovered by Christopher Columbus in 1494. England invaded in 1655, and formally took possession from the Spanish in 1670; a Crown colony 1866; received limited self-government 1944 and internal authority 1953. In 1958 it led in organizing the West Indies Federation that ended in 1962, the year Jamaica became independent.

ST KITTS (one-time St Christopher) AND NEVIS *
The islands were discovered by Christopher Columbus in 1493. St Kitts was settled by the English in 1623, becoming the first English colony in the West Indies. Nevis was settled in 1628. The islands, together with Anguilla, were amalgamated in the late 19th century; Leeward Islands Colony 1871 to 1956; West Indies Federation 1958 to 1962: West Indies Associated States 1967 (Anguilla separated in 1980) until independence 1983.

ST LUCIA *
St Lucia was sighted by Christopher Columbus in 1502. France ceded the island to the United Kingdom 1814; Windward Islands Colony 1875 to 1958; West Indies Federation 1958 to 1962: West Indies Associated States 1967 until independence 1979.

ST VINCENT AND THE GRENADINES *
St Vincent was discovered by Christopher Columbus in 1498. British settlement commenced in 1762; recognized by the French as British 1783; Windward Islands Colony 1875 to 1958; West Indies Federation 1958 to 1962; West Indies Associated States 1967; internal self-government 1969; independence 1979.

TRINIDAD AND TOBAGO *
Trinidad and Tobago were discovered by Christopher Columbus in 1498. Trinidad was ceded to the United Kingdom by Spain in 1802; Tobago ceded by France to the United Kingdom in 1814. The two islands were amalgamated as a Crown colony 1889; West Indies Federation 1958 to 1962; independence 1962, republic 1976.

UNITED STATES OF AMERICA
Representatives of thirteen colonies of North America signed the Declaration of Independence in Philadelphia on July 4, 1776. Connecticut, Delaware, Georgia, Maryland, Massachusetts, New Hampshire, New Jersey, New York, North Carolina, Pennsylvania, Rhode Island, South Carolina and Virginia gained independence with the signing of the Treaty of Versailles, Paris, on September 3, 1783; ratified by Congress on January 14, 1784.

NOTE:
LEEWARD ISLANDS COLONY, 1871 to 1956 consisted of Antigua with Barbuda, British Virgin Islands, Dominica (which left in 1940), Montserrat, and St Kitts-Nevis-Anguilla.

WINDWARD ISLANDS COLONY, 1885 to 1958 consisted of Dominica (which joined in 1940), Grenada, Tobago (which left in 1889 when it formed a union with Trinidad), St Lucia, St Vincent with The Grenadines.

WEST INDIES FEDERATION, 1958 to 1962 consisted of Antigua with Barbuda, Barbados, Dominica, Grenada, Jamaica (and its dependencies Cayman Islands, Turks and Caicos Islands), Montserrat, St Kitts-Nevis-Anguilla, St Lucia, St, Vincent, Trinidad and Tobago.

WEST INDIES ASSOCIATED STATES of eastern Caribbean islands whose status was changed from 'colony' to 'free association' with the United Kingdom in 1967. Eventually, each island became an independent state. The association consisted of Antigua (independence 1981), Dominica (1978), Grenada (1974), St Kitts-Nevis-Anguilla (Anguilla separated from St Kitts-Nevis when the others became independent 1983), St Lucia (1979), and St Vincent (1979).

AUSTRALASIA AND PACIFIC OCEAN

AUSTRALIA *
Captain James Cook in 1770 claimed possession of Australia for Great Britain, the Dutch having landed there in the previous century. From 1788 onwards, six colonies were established, which from the 1850s were self-governing; federated as the Commonwealth of Australia as a dominion in 1901. Australia became independent 1931; severed its last formal legislative and judicial links in 1986.

FIJI *
Captain James Cook visited the islands in 1774. It became a Crown colony 1874; independent monarchy 1970; a republic 1987.

KIRIBATI * (formerly part of the Gilbert and Ellice Islands)
The British first visited the Gilbert Islands in the 18th century. The Gilbert and Ellice Islands became a British protectorate in 1892; a Crown colony 1916. In 1975 administration of the islands separated and the Gilbert Islands became an independent republic in 1979, renamed Kiribati. (See Tuvalu)

NEW ZEALAND *
Captain James Cook surveyed the coastline in 1769 when the islands were claimed for Great Britain. In 1840 the United Kingdom, by the Treaty of Waitangi, annexed the islands to become a Crown colony; dominion status in 1907. (New Zealand became the first nation to grant women the right to vote, in 1893.) Independence 1947.

SOLOMON ISLANDS *
In 1886 the United Kingdom and Germany divided the administration of the islands: southern Solomon Islands became a British protectorate in 1893, adding the Santa Cruz group in 1898 and 1899. The Shortland Islands were transferred from Germany in 1900. In 1914, Australia took over the German controlled islands; the Solomon Islands became an Australian mandate in 1920. Self-government 1976, independence 1978.

TONGA *
Tonga was visited by Captain James Cook in 1773; it became a British protectorate in 1900; an independent kingdom 1970.

TUVALU * (formerly part of the Gilbert and Ellice Islands)
Ellice Islands came under British control in 1877; the Gilbert and Ellice Islands became a British protectorate in 1892; a Crown colony 1916. In 1975 administration of the islands separated and the Ellice Islands became independent in 1978 and renamed Tuvalu. (See Kiribati)

INDIAN OCEAN

MAURITIUS *
In 1810 the British occupied Mauritius and by the Treaty of Paris of 1814, France ceded the island together with its dependencies to the United Kingdom when it was deemed a Crown colony; independent 1968; republic 1992.

SEYCHELLES *
Captured from the French in 1794, formally ceded to the United Kingdom in 1814; a crown colony 1903; independence as a republic in 1976.

MEDITERRANEAN SEA

CYPRUS *
Cyprus was ceded by Turkey to the United Kingdom in 1878; formerly annexed in 1914; a Crown colony in 1925; independence as a republic 1960.

MALTA *
After a succession of occupiers, Great Britain gained control of Malta in 1799, confirmed by the Treaty of Paris of 1814; independence 1964, republic 1974. (It was awarded the George Cross for its people's resistance to Germany and Italy in World War II.)

DEPENDENCIES OF THE UNITED KINGDOM

ANGUILLA
Became a Crown colony in 1650; Leeward Islands Colony 1871 to 1956; amalgamated with St Kitts and Nevis for administration 1883; West Indies Federation 1958 to 1962; West Indies Associated States 1967 when it withdrew from the amalgamation; became an associated state of the United Kingdom; dependency 1971.

BERMUDA
Bermuda, a group of islands in the north Atlantic Ocean, off the south-east coast of the United States of America; became a Crown colony 1684; granted limited internal self-government 1968.

BRITISH ANTARCTIC TERRITORY
The territory consists of the South Shetland Islands, South Orkney Islands and nearby Graham Land on the Antarctic continent. Until 1962 administered as a dependency of the Falkland Islands; thereafter as an Overseas Territory of the United Kingdom.

BRITISH INDIAN OCEAN TERRITORY
Consisting of the Chagos Archipelago and other small island groups, were founded in 1965 by agreement with Mauritius and the Seychelles. There is no permanent civilian population.

BRITISH VIRGIN ISLES
Some 36 islands in the Caribbean Sea are economically interdependent with the United States of America's Virgin Islands; Leeward Islands Colony 1871 to 1956; a Crown colony 1956; dependency 1967.

CAYMAN ISLANDS

First settlers in 1734; islands under direct control of Jamaica 1863; West Indies Federation 1959 to 1962. When Jamaica became independent in 1962, the islands opted to remain under the Crown.

CHANNEL ISLANDS

A group of islands in the English Channel, off the north-west coast of France; the islands have remained as a part of England since the Norman Conquest in 1066. The islands are self-governing dependencies.

FALKLAND ISLANDS AND DEPENDENCIES

Great Britain established its first settlement in 1766; a British dependency by the British Antarctic Treaty of 1962; ruled by a governor as advised by the Executive Council since 1985.

GIBRALTAR

Gibraltar was captured by the Anglo-Dutch force 1704 during the War of the Spanish Succession; ceded to Great Britain by the Treaty of Utrecht 1713; constitution devolved certain internal matters 1969.

ISLE OF MAN

Situated in the North Sea, equidistant from England, Scotland and Ireland, the Isle of Man has one of the oldest established legislative assemblies in the World. It is a self-governing dependency.

MONTSERRAT

Montserrat was discovered by Christopher Columbus in 1493; a Crown colony in 1632; Leeward Island Colony 1871 to 1956; West Indies Federation 1958 to 1962; dependency 1962.

PITCAIRN ISLANDS

Situated almost midway between New Zealand and Panama in the Pacific Ocean, it was settled by British mutineers from the ship *Bounty* in 1790. Became a settlement under the British Settlement Act 1887; administered by the governor of Fiji, 1952 to 1970. Now a dependency.

ST HELENA AND DEPENDENCIES

Situated in the south Atlantic Ocean, it is believed to have been discovered by the Portuguese in 1502; annexed by the Dutch 1633; seized by the English East India Company 1659; annexed to the Crown 1834; the government is administered by a governor. (Napoleon Bonaparte of France was exiled to St Helena from 1815 until his death in 1821.)

TURKS AND CAICOS ISLANDS

The islands were part of Jamaica (as dependencies); West Indies Federation 1959 to 1962. When Jamaica became independent, the Turks and Caicos Islands became a Crown colony administered by the Bahamas 1965 to 1973: since by its own governor.

APPENDIX C

ORDER OF SUCCESSION TO QUEEN ELIZABETH II

1	HRH The Prince of Wales
2	HRH Prince William of Wales
3	HRH Prince Henry of Wales
4	HRH The Duke of York
5	HRH Princess Beatrice of York
6	HRH Princess Eugenie of York
7	HRH The Earl of Wessex
8	Viscount Severn
9	Lady Louise Windsor
10	HRH The Princess Royal
11	Peter Philips
12	Zara Philips
13	Viscount Linley
14	Hon. Charles Armstrong-Jones
15	Hon. Margarita Armstrong-Jones
16	Lady Sarah Chatto
17	Samuel Chatto
18	Arthur Chatto
19	HRH The Duke of Gloucester
20	The Earl of Ulster
21	Lady Davina Lewis
22	Lady Rose Windsor
23	HRH The Duke of Kent
24	Lady Marina-Charlotte Windsor
25	Lady Amelia Windsor
26	Lady Helen Taylor
27	Columbus Taylor
28	Cassius Taylor
29	Eloise Taylor
30	Estella Taylor
31	Lord Frederick Windsor
32	Lady Gabriella Windsor
33	HRH Princess Alexandra, the Hon. Lady Ogilvy
34	James Ogilvy
35	Alexander Ogilvy

36	Flora Ogilvy
37	Marina, Mrs Paul Mowatt
38	Christian Mowatt
39	Zenouska Mowatt

HRH Prince Michael of Kent and the Earl of St Andrews both forfeited the right of succession to the throne through marriages to Roman Catholics. Lord Nicholas Windsor and Baron Downpatrick renounced their rights to the throne on converting to Roman Catholicism in 2001 and 2003 respectively. Their children remain in succession provided that they are in communion with the Church of England.

APPENDIX D

ORDERS OF CHIVALRY

THE MOST NOBLE ORDER OF THE GARTER (1348)
Motto: Honi soit mal y pense (Shame on him who thinks evil of it)
The number of Knights and Lady Companions is limited to 24.

THE MOST ANCIENT AND MOST NOBLE ORDER OF THE THISTLE
(REVIVED 1687)
Motto: Nemo me impune lacessit (No one provokes me with impunity)
The number of Knights and Ladies of the Thistle is limited to 16.

THE MOST HONOURABLE ORDER OF THE BATH (1725)
Motto: Tria juncta in uno (Three joined in one)
Remodelled 1815, and enlarged many times. The order is divided into civil and
military divisions.
Women became eligible for the Order from January 1, 1971.
GCB Knight (or Dame) Grand Cross
KCB Knight Commander
DCB Dame Commander
CB Companion

THE ORDER OF MERIT (1902)
This order is designed as a special distinction for eminent people without
conferring a knighthood upon them. The Order is limited to 24, with the addition
of foreign honorary members.

THE MOST DISTINGUISHED ORDER OF St MICHAEL AND ST GEORGE
(1818)
Motto: Auspicium melioris aevi (Token of a better age)
GCMG Knight (or Dame) Grand Cross
KCMG Knight Commander
DCMG Dame Commander
CMG Companion

THE ROYAL VICTORIAN ORDER (1896)
Motto: Victoria
GCVO Knight (or Dame) Grand Cross
KCVO Knight Commander
DCVO Dame Commander
CVO Commander
LVO Lieutenant
MVO Member

THE MOST EXCELLENT ORDER OF THE BRITISH EMPIRE (1917)
Motto: For God and the Empire
The order was divided into military and civil divisions in December 1918.
GBE Knight (or Dame) Grand Cross
KBE Knight Commander
DBE Dame Commander
CBE Commander
OBE Officer
MBE Member

ORDER OF THE COMPANIONS OF HONOUR (1917)
The order consists of one class only and carries with it no title. The number of awards is limited to 65 (excluding honorary members).

THE DISTINGUISHED SERVICE ORDER (1886)
Bestowed in recognition of especial services in action of commissioned officers in the Army, Royal Navy and Royal Air Force and, since 1942, Mercantile Marine. The members are Companions. A Bar may be awarded for any additional act of service.

THE IMPERIAL SERVICE ORDER (1902)
Appointment as Companions is open to members of the Civil Service.

THE ROYAL VICTORIAN CHAIN (1902)
It confers no precedence on its holders.

APPENDIX E

DECORATIONS AND MEDALS (in order of importance)

Victoria Cross (VC), instituted 1856
George Cross (GC), 1940
Elizabeth Cross, 2009

British Orders of Knighthood
Baronet's Blade
Knight Bachelor's Badge

Conspicuous Gallantry Cross (CGC), 1995
Royal Red Cross Class 1 (RCC), 1883
Distinguished Service Cross (DSC), 1914
Military Cross (MC), December 1914
Distinguished Flying Cross (DFC), 1918
Air Force Cross (AFC), 1918
Order of St John

Distinguished Conduct Medal (DCM), 1854
Conspicuous Gallantry Medal ((CGM). 1874
George Medal (GM), 1940
Distinguished Service Medal (DSM), 1914
Military Medal (MM), 1916
Distinguished Flying Medal (DFM), 1918
Air Force Medal (AFM)
Queen's Gallantry Medal (QGM), 1974
Royal Victorian Medal (RVM), Gold, Silver, Bronze
British Empire Medal (BEM)
Queen's Police Medal for Distinguished Service (QPM)
Queen's Fire Service Medal for Distinguished Service (QFSM)

APPENDIX F

POET LAUREATES

The Poet Laureate is the person attached to the royal household, an office officially established in 1668, though it dates to the early Middle Ages, when minstrels were employed at the courts of English monarchs.

Geoffrey Chaucer (b.c.1340, d.1400), John Skelton (b.c.1460, d.1529) and Edmund Spenser (b.1552, d.1599), were considered unofficial poet laureates. It is customary for the poet laureate to write verse in celebration of State occasions and events of national importance.

Unofficial holders and date of appointment, if known:

	Geoffrey Chaucer
	John Skelton
	Edmund Spenser
1599	Samuel Daniel
1619	Ben Jonson
1637	Sir William d'Avenant

Official holders and date of appointment:

1668	John Dryden
1688	Thomas Shadwell
1692	Hahun Tate
1715	Nicholas Rowe
1718	Lawrence Eusden
1730	Colley Cibber
1757	William Whitehead
1785	Thomas Warton
1790	Henry James Pye
1813	Robert Southey
1843	William Wordsworth
1850	Alfred, Lord Tennyson
1896	Alfred Austin
1913	Robert Bridges
1930	John Masefield
1960	Cecil Day-Lewis
1972	Sir John Betjamin
1984	Ted Hughes
1999	Andrew Motion
2009	Carol Ann Duffy (the first woman poet laureate)

APPENDIX G

THE ALFRED B. NOBEL PRIZE (UNITED KINGDOM WINNERS)

Alfred B Nobel, (b.1833, d.1896), a Swedish chemist, entrepreneur and philanthropist, bequeathed an investment for which the interest was to be distributed yearly to those judged to have most benefited humankind in physics, chemistry, medicine-physiology, literature, and the promotion of peace. Prizes were first awarded in 1901. The first prize in economics was awarded in 1969, funded by Sweden's central bank.

(Joint recipient(s) *   Dual nationality ^)

Physics

1904 Lord Rayleigh (John W. Strutt)
1906 Sir Joseph J. Thomson
1915 Sir William H. Bragg and Sir William L. Bragg
1917 Charles G. Barka
1927 Charles T. R. Wilson *
1928 Owen W. Richardson
1933 Paul A. M. Dirac *
1935 Sir James Chadwick
1937 Sir George P. Thomson *
1947 Sir Edward V. Appleton
1948 Patrick M. S. Blackett
1950 Cecil F. Powell
1951 Sir John D. Cockcroft *
1954 Max Born *
1971 Dennis Gabor
1973 Brian D. Josephson *
1974 Sir Martin Ryle and Antony Hewish
1977 Sir Neville F. Mott *
2003 Anthony J. Leggett *
2009 Charles K. Kao ^
2010 Konstantin Novoselov ^*

Chemistry

1904 Sir William Ramsay
1908 Ernest Rutherford
1921 Frederick Soddy
1922 Francis W. Ashton
1929 Sir Arthur Harden *
1937 Walter N. Haworth *
1947 Sir Robert Robinson
1952 Archer J. P. Martin and Richard L. M. Synge
1956 Sir Cyril N. Hinshelwood *
1957 Lord (Alexander R.) Todd
1958 Frederick Sanger
1962 John C. Kendrew and Max F. Perutz
1964 Dorothy C. Hodgkin
1967 Ronald G. W. Norrish and George Porter *
1969 Derek H. R. Barton *
1973 Geoffrey Wilkinson *
1975 John Cornforth ^*
1978 Peter Mitchell
1980 Frederick Sanger *
1982 Aaron Klug ^
1993 Michael Smith ^*
1996 Sir Harold W. Kroto *
1997 John E. Walker *
1998 John A. Pople *
2009 Venkatraman Ramakrishnan *

Medicine – Physiology

1902 Sir Ronald Ross
1922 Archibald V. Hill *
1929 Sir Frederick G. Hopkins *
1932 Edgar D. Adrian and Sir Charles S. Sherrington
1936 Sir Henry H. Dale *
1945 Ernest B. Chain, Sir Alexander Fleming and Sir Howard W. Florey
1953 Hans A Krebs *
1960 Peter B. Medawar *
1962 Francis H. C. Crick and Maurice H. F. Wilkins *
1963 Alan L. Hodgkin and Andrew F. Huxley *
1970 Sir Bernard Katz *
1972 Rodney R. Porter *

1973 Nikolaas Tinbergen *
1979 Godfrey N. Hounsfield *
1982 John R. Vane *
1984 Cesar Milstein ^ and Niels K. Jerne ^*
1988 Sir James Black *
1993 Richard J. Roberts *
2001 R. Timothy Hunt and Sir Paul M. Nurse *
2002 Sidney Brenner and John E. Sulston *
2003 Sir Peter Mansfield *
2007 Sir Martin J. Evans *
2010 Robert G. Edwards

Literature

1907 Rudyard Kipling
1925 George Bernard Shaw ^
1932 John Galsworthy
1948 T. S. Eliot
1950 Bertrand Russell
1953 Sir Winston Churchill
1981 Elias Canetti ^
1983 William Golding
2001 Sir V. S. Naipaul
2005 Harold Pinter
2007 Doris Lessing

Peace

1903 Sir William R Cremer
1925 Sir J. Austen Chamberlain *
1933 Sir Norman Angell
1934 Arthur Henderson
1937 Viscount Cecil of Chelwood
1947 Friends Service Council *
1949 Lord John Boyd Orr of Brechin
1959 Philip J. Noel Baker
1976 Mairhead Corrigan and Betty Williams
1995 Joseph Rotblat ^
1999 John Hume and David Trimble

Economic Science

1972 John R. Hicks *
1977 James E. Meade *
1979 Sir Arthur Lewis *
1984 Richard Stone

1991 Ronald H. Coase ^
1996 James A. Mirrlees *
2003 Clive W. J. Granger *
2010 Christopher A. Pissarides ^*

APPENDIX H

THE EUROPEAN UNION

<u>MEMBERS</u>

From 1958:	Belgium, France, Italy, Luxembourg, The Netherlands, West Germany (after unification of the country, Germany)
From 1973:	Denmark, Ireland, and United Kingdom
From 1981:	Greece
From 1986	Portugal, Spain
From 1995	Austria, Finland, Sweden
From 2004	Cyprus, Czech Republic, Estonia, Hungary, Latvia, Lithuania, Malta, Poland, Slovakia, Slovenia
From 2007	Bulgaria, Romania

<u>COUNCIL OF THE EUROPEAN UNION (Council of Members)</u> is the main decision making body within the European Union, consisting of representatives of the twenty-seven member states; each government being represented by the minister responsible for the business, e.g. foreign affairs, environmental matters.

The presidency of the Council is held for a six-month period, by each member state on a rotational basis.

Decisions by the Council are taken by votes depending on certain criteria, i.e. simple majority, unanimous, or qualified majority. With qualified majority voting (QMV), member states receive a 'weighted' vote, based on the formula:

France, Germany, Italy, United Kingdom	29 votes each
Poland, Spain	27 votes each
Romania	14 votes each
The Netherlands	13 votes
Belgium, Czech Republic, Greece	12 votes each
Hungary, Portugal	12 votes each
Austria, Bulgaria, Sweden	10 votes each
Denmark, Finland, Ireland	7 votes each
Lithuania, Slovakia	7 votes each
Cyprus, Estonia, Latvia, Luxembourg, Slovenia	4 votes each
Malta	3 votes

THE EUROPEAN COUNCIL is the meeting of presidents and prime ministers of member states every six months, which determines the future direction of the European Union.

EUROPEAN COMMISSION is the executive branch of the European Union. It is responsible for proposing legislation, implementing decisions, upholding the European Union treaties, and the day-to-day running of the Union. There is one commissioner from each of the twenty-seven member states.

EUROPEAN PARLIAMENT was established in 1962, with direct elections from 1979, which are held at five-year intervals. British members are elected by a 'regional list' system of proportional representation. The Parliament has limited powers. It scrutinizes and votes on draft legislation, has some control over the budget, and can dismiss the Commission, which it has done on one occasion.

COMMITTEE OF REGIONS established in 1994, represents sub-national regions of the European Union. It is the political assembly that provides local and regional authorities with a representation in the Union. It is composed of representatives of regional and local government. (The United Kingdom has twelve regions: Scotland, Wales, Northern Ireland, and nine in England, being North East, North West, Yorkshire and The Humber, West Midlands, East Midlands, Eastern, London, South East, and South West.)

COURT OF JUSTICE OF THE EUROPEAN COMMUNITIES, known as the European Court of Justice, it reviews the legality of the decisions of the Commission and Council of Ministers of the European Union. The court has the power to invalidate the laws of European Union member states, when those laws conflict with Union laws.

THE LISBON TREATY, became effective from December 1, 2009. It strengthened the role of the European Parliament by increasing the co-decision procedure in policy-making, so that the Parliament has an equal standing with the Council of the European Union; it recognizes the right of a member state to withdraw from the European Union; it created the position of a President of the European Council; and a High Representative in Foreign Affairs and Security, who would also be vice-president of the European Commission. From 2014, the calculation of qualified majority voting (QVM) would be added to include a double majority when a decision is taken by 55% of the member states representing at least 65% of the European Union's population.

IMPORTANTLY:

<u>EUROPEAN COURT OF HUMAN RIGHTS</u> was established in 1959, and has forty-seven countries as members. The purpose is to protect the civil and political rights of individuals and organizations against a member state, which is bound by the convention.

The Court was established by the Council of Europe, a distinct entity from the European Union, and is not connected with the European Court of Justice.

Index

Battles

Parliament